D1572288

COMMUNITAS

Cultural Memory
in
the
Present

Mieke Bal and Hent de Vries, Editors

COMMUNITAS

The Origin and Destiny of Community

Roberto Esposito

Translated by Timothy Campbell

STANFORD UNIVERSITY PRESS

STANFORD, CALIFORNIA

Stanford University Press
Stanford, California

Communitas was originally published in Italian in 1998 under the title *Communitas: Origine e destino della comunità* © 1998, 2006, Giulio Einaudi Editore.

This book has been published with the assistance of the International Center for Writing and Translation at the University of California, Irvine.

Printed in the United States of America on acid-free, archival-quality paper

Library of Congress Cataloging-in-Publication Data

Esposito, Roberto, 1950–
    Communitas : the origin and destiny of community / Roberto Esposito ; translated by Timothy Campbell.
        p.   cm. — (Cultural memory in the present)
"Communitas was originally published in Italian in 1998 under the title Communitas: origine e destino della comunite."
    Includes bibliographical references.
    ISBN 978-0-8047-4646-5 (cloth : alk. paper)
    ISBN 978-0-8047-4647-2 (pbk. : alk. paper)
    1. Communities—Philosophy.   I. Title.   II. Series: Cultural memory in the present.
B105.C46E86 2010
307.01—dc22
                                                            2009013193

Contents

COMMUNITAS

Introduction: Nothing in Common

Nothing seems more appropriate today than thinking community; nothing more necessary, demanded, and heralded by a situation that joins in a unique epochal knot the failure of all communisms with the misery of new individualisms.[1] Nevertheless, nothing is further from view; nothing so remote, repressed, and put off until later, to a distant and indecipherable horizon. It isn't that the philosophies expressly addressed to thinking community were or are lacking. On the contrary, they tend to constitute one of the most dominant themes debated internationally.[2] Yet not only do they remain well within this unthinkability of community but they constitute its most symptomatic expression. There is something else as well that goes beyond the specific modalities in question (communal, communitarian, communicative) that contemporary political philosophy adopts now and again and that concerns instead community's very form: the community isn't translatable into a political-philosophical lexicon except by completely distorting (or indeed perverting) it, as we saw occur so tragically in the last century. This appears to contradict the tendency of a certain kind of political philosophy to see in the question of community its very same object. It is this reduction to "object" of a political-philosophical discourse that forces community into a conceptual language that radically alters it, while at the same time attempts to name it: that of the individual *and* totality; of identity *and* the particular; of the origin *and* the end; or more simply of the *subject* with its most unassailable metaphysical connotations of unity, absoluteness, and interiority.[3] It isn't by chance that beginning from similar assumptions, political philosophy tends to think community as a "wider subjectivity"; as, and this in spite of the presupposed opposition to the individualist paradigm, such a large part of neo-communitarian philosophy ends up doing, when it swells the self in the hypertrophic figure of "the unity of unities."[4] This also occurs in those cultures of intersubjectivity always intent on finding otherness in an alter ego similar in everything to the *ipse* that they would like to challenge and that instead they reproduce.

The truth is that these conceptions are united by the ignored assumption that community is a "property" belonging to subjects that join them together [*accomuna*]: an attribute, a definition, a predicate that qualifies them as belonging to the same totality [*insieme*], or as a "substance" that is produced by their union. In each case community is conceived of as a quality that is added to their nature as subjects, making them *also* subjects of community. *More* subjects, subjects of a larger entity, one that is senior or even better than simple individual identity, but from which it originates and in the end reflects. Despite the obvious historical, conceptual, and lexical differences, from this perspective the organicistic sociology of *Gemeinschaft*, American neo-communitarianism, and the various ethics of communication (and the communist tradition as well, despite quite a different categorical profile) lie beyond the same line that keeps them within the unthinkability of community. For all these philosophies, in fact, it is a "fullness" or a "whole" (the originary meaning of the lemma *teuta* is fitting then, which in different Indo-European dialects means "swollen," "potent," and therefore the "fullness" of the social body insofar as it is *ethnos*, *Volk*, people).[5] It is also, using a seemingly different terminology, a good, a value, an essence, which depending on the case in question, can be lost and then refound as something that once belonged to us and that therefore can once again belong to us; an origin to be mourned or a destiny foreshadowed based on the perfect symmetry that links *arche* and *telos*. In each case, community is what is most properly our "own" [*il nostro più proprio*]. Whether it needs to appropriate what is common to us (for communisms and communitarianisms) or to communicate what is most properly our own (for the ethics of communication), what is produced doesn't change. The community remains doubly tied to the semantics of *proprium*. On this score, it isn't necessary to touch on the post-Romantic mannerism of

Ferdinand Tönnies's *Gemeinschaft*, which differs from *Gesellschaft* on the basis of the originary appropriation of its own proper essence. It's enough to recall in this regard Max Weber's most secularized community in order to find highlighted, albeit in a denaturalized form, the very same figure of belonging: "The *communalization* of social relationships occurs if and insofar as the orientation of social behavior—whether in the individual case, on the average or in the idea type—is based on a sense of solidarity: the result of emotional or traditional attachments of participants."[6] That this possession might refer above all to territory doesn't change things at all,[7] since territory is defined by the category of "appropriation," as the originary matrix of every other property that follows.[8] If we linger a little and reflect on community without invoking contemporary models, the most paradoxical aspect of the question is that the "common" is defined exactly through its most obvious antonym: what is common is that which unites the ethnic, territorial, and spiritual property of every one of its members. They have in common what is most properly their own; they are the owners of what is common to them all.

My first intention in this work lies in distancing myself from this dialectic. Yet if, as we say, this dialectic constitutively inheres in the conceptual language of modern political philosophy, the only way to escape from it resides in locating a point of departure, a hermeneutic support, that is both outside and autonomous with respect to such a dialectic. I've searched for this point, in a manner of speaking, within the origin of the very thing itself under investigation, in the etymology of the Latin term *communitas*. In order to do so, I had to proceed along a path that was anything but easy, one that moves across lexical traps and difficulties in interpretation, but that can lead to a notion of community that is radically different from those that have been dealt with up to now.

Indeed, as dictionaries show, the first meaning of the noun *communitas* and of its corresponding adjective, *communis*, is what becomes meaningful from the opposition to what is proper. In all neo-Latin languages (though not only), "common" (*commun, comun, kommun*) is what is *not* proper [*proprio*], that begins where what is proper ends: *Quod commune cum alio est desinit esse proprium.*[9] It is what belongs to more than one, to many or to everyone, and therefore is that which is "public" in opposition to "private" or "general" (though also "collective") in contrast to "individual" [*particolare*]. In addition to this first canonical meaning, which is already traceable to the Greek *koinos* (and also translated in the Gothic *gemein* and its derivatives *Gemeinde, Gemeinschaft, Vergemeinschaftung*), there is still another meaning to be added, one, however, less obvious because it transfers properly within itself the larger semantic complexity of the term from which it originates: *munus* (its archaic form is *moinus, moenus*), which is composed of the root *mei-* and the suffix *-nes*, both of which have a social connotation.[10] This term, in fact, oscillates in turn among three meanings that aren't at all the same and that seem to make it miss its mark, or at least to limit the emphasis, the initial juxtaposition of "public/private"—*munus dicitur tum de privatis, tum de publicis*—in favor of another conceptual area that is completely traceable to the idea of "obligation" [*dovere*].[11] These are *onus, officium,* and *donum.*[12] In truth, for the first two the meaning of duty [*dovere*] is immediately clear: obligation, office, official, position [*impiego*], and post. The third appears, however, to be more problematic. In what sense would a gift [*dono*] be a duty? Doesn't there appear, on the contrary, something spontaneous and therefore eminently voluntary in the notion of gift?

Yet the specificity of the gift expressed in the word *munus* with respect to the more general use of *donum* has the effect of reducing the initial distance and of realigning this meaning with the semantics of duty. The *munus* in fact is to *donum* as "species is to genus,"[13] because, yes, it means "gift," but a particular gift, "distinguished by its obligatory character, implied by its root *mei-*, which denotes exchange."[14] With respect to the circular relation between gift and exchange, one can't help referring to Emile Benveniste's well-known studies and, even earlier, to Marcel Mauss's famous essay on the relationship.[15] But let's stay for a moment longer with the element of being obliged [*doverosità*]: once someone has accepted the *munus*, an obligation (*onus*) has been created to exchange it either in terms of goods or service [*servizio*]. Once again the superimposition between "gift" and "office" comes into view, which in addition are distinctly joined in the expression *munere fungi.*[16] It's true that Benveniste, following Mauss's lead, traces the necessity of the exchange, of the "counter-gift," even before in the root *do-* and therefore in the derivatives *doron, dorea,* and *dosis*; from there we find the doubly crossed direction of "give" [*dare*] *and* "take" [*prendere*], "to take (to give) to" [in English.—Trans.], which are transposed in *donum* [gift], and situates in Benveniste's view the specificity of the latter in a present [*regalo*] that is potentially unilateral. By this I mean that it does not require an equal return or remuneration, as is shown in the late Thomistic expression *donum proprie est "datio irredibilis," id est quod non datur intentione retributionis.*[17] Yet it is in this withdrawal from being forced into an obligation that lies the lesser intensity of the *donum* with respect to the unrelenting compulsion [*cogenza*] of the *munus*. In short, this is the gift that one gives because one *must* give and because one *cannot not* give. It has a tone so clearly of being obliged [*doverosità*] as to modify or even to interrupt the one-to-one correspondence of the relation between the gift giver [*donatore*] and the recipient [*donatario*]. Although produced by a benefit that was previously received, the *munus* indicates only the gift that one gives, not what one receives.[18] All of the *munus* is projected onto the transitive act of giving. It doesn't by any means imply the stability of a possession and even less the acquisitive dynamic of something earned, but loss, subtraction, transfer. It is a "pledge" or a "tribute" that one pays in an obligatory form. The *munus* is the obligation that is contracted with respect to the other and that invites a suitable release from the obligation. The gratitude that *demands* new donations. *Munus*, in this sense, and even more *munificus*, is he who shows the proper "grace," according to the equation of Plautus's *gratus-munus*:[19] giving something that one can *not* keep for oneself and over which, therefore, one is not completely master. I realize that I am forcing slightly the concept of "gratefulness," which is more literally expressive of the *munus*. Yet what else does the "one obliged" [*il riconoscente*] accede to if not that he unequivocally "owes" something of which he was the beneficiary and that he is called to acknowledge in a form that places him "at the disposition of" or more drastically "at the mercy of" someone else? What predominates in the *munus* is, in other words, reciprocity or "mutuality" (*munus-mutuus*) of giving that assigns the one to the other in an obligation [*impegno*]. But let's also add in a common oath: *iurare communiam* or *communionem* in the sacred bond of the *coniuratio*.

If we relate this final meaning of *munus* to the collective *communitas*, we can draw forth a new force with respect to the classic duality "public/private," one that calls into question (or at least problematizes) the widespread but rather dubious homology between *communitas* and *res publica*, which in turn produces the equally problematic synonym *koinonia-polis* (originally authorized by the Aristotelian *koinonia politike*, which is translated most frequently in Latin as *communitas* and not as *societas*).²⁰ The semantic disparity registered in this making homologous of *res publica* and *communitas* concerns, on the one hand, the excessive vagueness of the attribute *publica*, but especially, on the other hand, the "quality" of the *res*. What is the "thing" that the members of the community have in common, and is it really "something" positive? Is it a good; is it wealth? Interest perhaps? Dictionaries provide us with a clear answer. Despite their warning that we aren't dealing with a certified meaning, they do tell us that the ancient and presumably originary meaning of *communis* had to be "he who shares an office [*carica*], a burden [*carico*], a task [*incarico*]." From here it emerges that *communitas* is the totality of persons united not by a "property" but precisely by an obligation or a debt; not by an "addition" [*più*] but by a "subtraction" [*meno*]: by a lack, a limit that is configured as an onus, or even as a defective modality for him who is "affected," unlike for him who is instead "exempt" [*esente*] or "exempted." Here we find the final and most characteristic of the oppositions associated with (or that dominate) the alternative between public and private, those in other words that contrast *communitas* to *immunitas*. If *communis* is he who is required to carry out the functions of an office—or to the donation [*elargizione*] of a grace—on the contrary, he is called immune who has to perform no office [*immunis dicitur qui nullo fungitur officio*], and for that reason he remains ungrateful [*ingratus*].²¹ He can completely preserve his own position [*sostanza*] through a *vacatio muneris*. Whereas the *communitas* is bound by the sacrifice of the *compensatio*, the *immunitas* implies the beneficiary of the *dispensatio*.

The contentious result of this etymological journey with respect to the various philosophies of community cannot be ignored. As the complex though equally unambiguous etymology that we have till now undertaken demonstrates, the *munus* that the *communitas* shares isn't a property or a possession [*appartenenza*].²² It isn't having, but on the contrary, is a debt, a pledge, a gift that is to be given, and that therefore will establish a lack. The subjects of community are united by an "obligation," in the sense that we say " I owe *you* something," but not "you owe *me* something." This is what makes them not less than the masters of themselves, and that more precisely expropriates them of their initial property (in part or completely), of the most proper property, namely, their very subjectivity. We thus come 180 degrees back to the synonymy of "common-proper," which the philosophies of community unconsciously presuppose, and to the restoration of the fundamental opposition: the common is not characterized by what is proper but by what is improper, or even more drastically, by the other; by a voiding [*svuotamento*], be it partial or whole, of property into its negative; by removing what is properly one's own [*depropriazione*] that invests and decenters the proprietary subject, forcing him to take leave [*uscire*] of himself, to alter himself. In the community, subjects do not find a principle of identification nor an aseptic enclosure within which they can establish transparent communication or even a content to be communicated. They don't find anything else except that void, that distance, that extraneousness that constitutes them as being missing from themselves; "givers to" inasmuch as they themselves are "given by" [*donati da*] a circuit of mutual gift giving that finds its own specificity in its indirectness with respect to the frontal nature of the subject-object relation or to the ontological fullness of the person (if not in the daunting semantic duplicity of the French *personne*, which can mean both "person" and "no one").[23]

Not subjects. Or subjects of their own proper lack, of the lack of the proper. Subjects of a radical impropriety that coincides with an absolute contingency or just simply "coincides," that falls together. Finite subjects, cut by a limit that cannot be interiorized because it constitutes precisely their "outside"; the exteriority that they overlook and that enters into them in their common non-belonging. Therefore the community cannot be thought of as a body, as a corporation [*corporazione*] in which individuals are founded in a larger individual. Neither is community to be interpreted as a mutual, intersubjective "recognition" in which individuals are reflected in each other so as to confirm their initial identity; as a collective bond that comes at a certain point to connect individuals that before were separate. The community isn't a mode of being, much less a "making" of the individual subject. It isn't the subject's expansion or multiplication but its exposure to what interrupts the closing and turns it inside out: a dizziness, a syncope, a spasm in the continuity of the subject. The common "rose" of its being "no subject." No one's rose [*Niemandsrose*], or even better, "no person's rose" [*rose de personne*], as the greatest poet of the twentieth century would have said about community, abandoning himself [*deponendosi*] to the ultimate *munus*.[24]

Naturally, the subject who experiences this exposure (or devotion, the *munus* of self) doesn't perceive it as painless. Exposure, which pushes him into contact with what he is not, with his "nothing," is the most extreme of its possibilities but also the riskiest of threats, as was largely implicit in the always risky (when not conflict-producing) semantics of the *donum-damnum*, expressed with extraordinary clarity in the Virgilian *timeo Danaos et dona ferentes*, that is, not in spite of the fact that they bring gifts but *because* they do.[25] That which everyone fears in the *munus*, which is both "hospitable" and "hostile," according to the troubling lexical proximity of *hospes-hostis*, is the violent loss of borders, which awarding identity to him, ensures his subsistence.[26] We always need to keep these two faces of *communitas* uppermost in mind: *communitas* is simultaneously both the most suitable, indeed the sole, dimension of the animal "man," but *communitas* is also its most potentially disintegrating impetus for a drift in meaning of that dimension of the animal "man." Seen from this point of view, therefore, the community isn't only to be identified with the *res publica*, with the common "thing," but rather is the hole into which the common thing continually risks falling, a sort of landslide produced laterally and within. This fault line that surrounds and penetrates the "social" is always perceived as the constitutive danger *of* our co-living, more than in it. We need to watch out for this without ever forgetting that it is *communitas* itself that causes the landslide; the threshold that we can't leave behind because it always outruns us as our very same (in)originary origin; as the unreachable Object into which our subjectivity risks falling and being lost. Here then is the blinding truth that is kept within the etymological folds of *communitas*; the public thing [*res publica*] is inseparable from no-thing [*niente*]. It is precisely the no-thing of the thing that is our common ground [*fondo*]. All of the stories that tell of the founding crime, the collective crime, the ritual assassination, the sacrificial victim featured in the history of civilization don't do anything else except evoke metaphorically the *delinquere* that keeps us together, in the technical sense of "to lack" and "to be wanting";[27] the breach, the trauma, the lacuna out of which we originate. Not the Origin but its absence, its withdrawal. It is the originary *munus* that constitutes us and makes us destitute in our mortal finiteness.

The grand philosophical tradition has always intuited that the question of community borders on death to such a degree that one could read Plato and Machiavelli, as different as they are, precisely by the optic that such an equation between death and community creates. Yet it's only in the modern period, let's say at the end of the *res publica christiana*, that this fact begins to appear as a problem, indeed as *the* fundamental problem that political philosophy is obliged to interpret and resolve. Before seeing how it does so, we need to turn for a moment to the Christian conception of community if we are to complete the categorical and semantic frame that functions as the presupposition for the communitarian genealogy under examination here. Things are made more difficult by the double move—historical-institutional and theological-philosophical—the term *communitas* undergoes when it is interwoven with that of *koinonia*, especially in the New Testament.[28] The first vector would seem to follow an itinerary of the increasing erasure of the originary ancipital character of the *munus* in the direction of that "appropriating" drift in meaning to which the *lectio difficilior* of *communitas* is still sacrificed. In all of the medieval lexicons, in fact, the lemma *communitas* is associated with the concept of "belonging," in its contemporary subjective and objective meaning: the community is that which belongs to a collective *and* is that to which it belongs as its own properly essential type [*genere*]: *communitas entis*. Over time, however, the particular [*localisitico*] character of this totality always takes on the shape of a fixed territory, as emerges in the nearness of usage between the concept of *communitas* and those of *civitas* and *castrum*; the latter having an obvious military inflection, signifying the defense of proper borders. It's true that this meaning initially takes on a noninstitutional force, unlike the parallel expression *universitas*.[29] Yet slowly, and above all in France and Italy, those *communia* that before signified a simple rural or urban collection now begin to acquire the increasingly formal traits of a true juridical-political institution, until *communia* designates, from the twelfth century on, the features that autonomous cities possess both factually and legally, which is to say, they are the proprietors of themselves.

Nonetheless, this drastic simplification that *communitas* undergoes juridically, especially in the early centuries, is accompanied (and subtly contradicted) by the semantic complexity that concerns the theological term *koinonia*. In reality it isn't completely equivalent to *communitas* nor to *communio*, to which it's often joined in the translations. Nor does it coincide with *ekklesia*, to which it's just as often confused. Indeed, one could argue that it is the arduous relation that the *koinonia* has with the originary form of *munus* that distances it from its strictly ecclesiastical inflection. How so? We know that at least from Acts of the Apostles (2:42), but especially from Paul's entire letter to the Corinthians (and then following along the entire course of Patristic literature), the "common place" [*luogo comune*] of the *koinonia* is constituted by the Eucharistic participation in the *Corpus Christi* that the Church represents. Yet the problem posed lies in these two joined (though nevertheless distinct) figures of "representation" and "participation." The most perceptive commentators have always underscored that what is not to be lost in the latter notion is the vertical dimension that unites man and God, but also separates them due to the infinite heterogeneity of substance.[30] Indeed, it is God and man since only God is entitled to subjectivity, to being the initiative of the relation, to which man can't be anything but receptive. Man receives the gift (here surfaces once again the *munus*) that God, through the sacrifice of Christ, makes to him, a gift that is both free and overabundant.[31] Against a purely anthropological reading, one that is completely horizontal, one needs to respond firmly that it is only this first *munus* from on high that puts men in the position of having something in common with each other. And it is precisely this "given"—what is given to us, we ourselves as "given," "donated," born from a gift—that stands in the way of any hasty translation of *koinonia* into a simple *philia*—"friendship," "fellowship" [in English.—Trans.], "camaraderie," or "*Freundschaft*." Yes we are brothers, *koinonoi*, but brothers *in Christ*, in an otherness that withdraws us from our subjectivity, our own subjective property, so as to pin it, subjectivity, to a point that is "void of subject" from which we come and toward which we are called, just as long as we remain "grateful" so as to respond to that first *munus* with a corresponding gift. This, nevertheless, doesn't alter the fact that our giving is inevitably inadequate, wanting, purely reactive with respect to the only gift that is truly such, because it is unconditional, which has already come to us from the Creator (1 Cor. 1:9; 2 Cor. 9:15). From this, however, we can deduce that what we offer isn't a true gift or that the gift is not completely ours (1 Cor. 4:7). We can deduce that the possibility of the gift is withdrawn from us in the precise moment when it is given to us; or that it is given to us in the form of its withdrawal. This gift-giving [*donativo*] inflection of "participation" restores to the Christian *koinonia* all of the expropriating drama of the ancient *munus*; what one participates in isn't the glory of the Resurrection but the suffering and the blood of the Cross (1 Cor. 10:16; Phil. 3:10). Any possibility of appropriation is diminished; "taking part in" means everything except "to take"; on the contrary, it means losing something, to be weakened, to share the fate of the servant, not of the master (Phil. 3:10–11). His death. The gift of life, offered in the communitarian archetype of the Last Supper.

One will want to say that Augustine "inflects" Paul's message in a direction that is even more contradictory. Also, the *dilectio proximi* is thought from the essence of a created being, as finished, as heteronymous, and nonsubjective. What joins us in the same "community of destiny," in a communal future, is our being *morituri*;[32] therefore the *communis fides* that we share with those like us can be experienced only in the bitter solitude of the singular relation with God.[33] That, however, isn't anything other than the consequence of an earlier *communitas* that Augustine doesn't hesitate in describing as "the community of guilt" since "Totus ergo mundus ex Adam reus."[34] The community coincides with the complicity established initially by Adam and fixed by Cain even *before* the moment when Abel constituted the city of God: "Natus est igitur prior Cain posterior Abel."[35] On this point Augustine is terribly explicit—it is the sedentary Cain and not the pilgrim Abel who founds the human community.[36] And that first fratricidal violence inevitably refers to every future founding of community, as that of Romulus confirms with a sort of tragic punctuality.[37] What this means is that the human community is in close contact with death, "a society from and with the dead."[38] This second origin (an origin through birth) remains stuck like a kind of thorn or poisoned gift in the first origin (*the Creation*); as testimony to a "doubleness," to the duplicity of the origin, from which it will no longer be possible to free oneself, not even when men will be called to the *sanctorum communio*. The reason is that the past, *that* past, cannot be erased by a *caritas* [love] from which it logically descends.[39]

Yet Augustine says something else that introduces us into the modern, Hobbesian, perception of community: the love for one's neighbor is directly proportional to the memory of common danger (*communis periculi*) that we share.[40] If the community of sin from which we originate is marked by fear, no one can be secure in this life, which is literally besieged by death; but also the *communitas fidei*, which, structured so as to be the salvific compensation of the first, inevitably remains prey to the fear [*timore*] no less acute of another, and even more definitive, death. Caught in the grip of this double danger, the *communitas* (on the Christian side as well, we should note) acknowledges its constitutive alliance with nothing. "Eating up time [*devorans tempora*] as I was myself eaten by it [*devorata temporibus*]":[41] *communitas* seems to defer the gift of life at the unbearable abduction of the fear of death.

Modern political philosophy attempts to respond to this unacceptable *munus*. How? Here reappears that category of "immunization" that we saw as constituting the most incisive semantic counterpoint of *communitas*.[42] The thesis I would like to advance in this regard is that the category of immunization is so important that it can be taken as the explicative key of the entire modern paradigm, not only in conjunction with but even more than other hermeneutic models, such as those we find in "secularization," "legitimation," and "rationalization," terms that hide or diminish the lexical significance of modernity. The reason is that, yes, there are echoes in these models, distant with respect to the premodern past, but not of the prospective inversion and the negative power [*potenza*] of the negative that juxtaposes directly *immunitas* and *communitas*. The "immune" is not simply different from the "common" but is its opposite, what empties it out until it has been completely left bare, not only of its effects but also of its own presupposition; just as the "immunitarian" project of modernity isn't directed only against the specific *munera* (class obligations, ecclesial bonds, free services that weigh on men in the earlier phase) but against the very same law of their associated coexistence [*convivenza*]. The modern individual, who assigns to every service its specific price, can no longer bear the gratitude that the gift demands.[43] The term "absolutism" also carries within it this meaning of "decision," which means violent breaking of his roots. There is no need to hypothesize any sort of former idyllic community, no primitive "organic society" that exists only in the Romantic *imagerie* of the nineteenth century, to see how modernity is affirmed in its violent separation from an order in which the benefits no longer balance the risks that these same benefits require as the two inseparable faces joined in the combined concept of *munus*—gift and obligation, benefit and service rendered, joining and threat. Modern individuals truly become that, the perfectly individual, the "absolute" individual,[44] bordered in such a way that they are isolated and protected, but only if they are freed in advance from the "debt" that binds them one to the other; if they are released from, exonerated, or relieved of that contact, which threatens their identity, exposing them to possible conflict with their neighbor, exposing them to the contagion of the relation with others.[45]

As will emerge in the following pages, the philosopher who first and more radically than anyone else followed this logic to its extreme theoretical consequences was Thomas Hobbes. His extraordinary hermeneutic force lies in having extended the semantic complexity of the common *delinquere* to its bare literalness of collective "crime"—to the society of Cain, which Hobbes in theological terms unconsciously incorporates into his own lexicon at the same time that he attempts to free the lexicon precisely from the theological. What men have in common, what makes them more like each other than anything else, is their generalized capacity to be killed: the fact that anyone can be killed by anyone else. This is what Hobbes sees in the dark depths of the community; this is how he interprets community's indecipherable law: the *communitas* carries within it a gift of death. From it inevitably arises the following: if community is so threatening to the individual integrity of the subjects that it puts into relation, nothing else remains for us except to "immunize us" beforehand and, in so doing, to negate the very same foundations of community. The keenness of Hobbes's observation is matched by the drastic nature of the solution. Since the common origin threatens to drag down with it into the vortex all those that it attracts, the only way to save oneself is by breaking cleanly from it; by limiting it in a "before" that cannot be joined to what comes "after"; to institute between before and after a border that cannot be crossed without catastrophically falling back again into the condition from which one had wanted to escape. What is to be loosened is the link with the originary dimension of common living (Hobbes will say "natural" living) via the institution of another artificial origin that coincides with the juridically "privatistic" and logically "privative" figure of the contract. Hobbes perfectly registers its immunizing power with regard to the previous situation when he defines the statute through the juxtaposition with that of the gift: above all, the contract is that which is *not* a gift; it is the absence of *munus*, the neutralization of its poisonous fruits.

Naturally, the immunitary, and more generally, the modern option in Hobbes has a price, indeed a terribly high price. What is cut and expelled in the sovereign decision is the very same content of the new form, which in any case is inevitable given the homeopathic nature of the remedy: occupy the void of the *munus*, the originary fault line, with an even more radical void [*vuoto*]; eliminate [*svuotare*] the danger of the *cum* by utterly eradicating it.[46] In fact, the Leviathan-State coincides with the breaking of every communitarian bond, with the squelching of every social relation that is foreign to the vertical exchange of protection-obedience. It is the bare [*nudo*] relation of no relation.[47] If the community entails crime, the only way an individual can survive lies in the crime of the community. Here is sketched for the first time in its most theoretically accomplished form that "pyramid of sacrifice," which in a certain sense constitutes the predominant feature of modern history.[48] What is sacrificed is nothing other than the *cum*, the relation among men, and for that reason as well, in some way men themselves are sacrificed. They are paradoxically sacrificed to their own survival. They live *in* and *of* their refusal to live together [*convivere*]. It's impossible not to recognize here a remnant of irrationality that is subtly introduced into the folds of the most rational of systems: life is preserved through the presupposition of its sacrifice, the sum of refusals out of which sovereign authorization is made. Life is sacrificed to the preservation of life. In this convergence of the preservation of life and its capacity to be sacrificed, modern immunization reaches the height of its own destructive power [*potenza*].

Nevertheless, modernity doesn't entirely coincide with the sacrificial mechanism to which it also gives rise. It's true that modernity is self-legitimating, cutting itself off from every social bond, from every natural link, from every common law. Yet there also emerges from within modernity itself the tragic knowledge of the nihilistic character of this decision. The Hobbesian uprooting [*taglio delle radici*] is lived therefore with a sense of "guilt" with respect to a community, both whose absence and necessity one recognizes. It is this vector of self-problematization, running like a subterranean river through modern philosophy that is the object of the pages that follow. What I have tried to reconstruct is that line of thought, which from Jean-Jacques Rousseau to Georges Bataille, moving through Immanuel Kant and Martin Heidegger, reintroduces the question of community that modernity seemed to have completely closed off, but also the radical transformation that community experiences in this transition from Rousseau's semantics of "guilt" [*colpa*] to that Kantian one of "law," until we arrive at the "ecstatic" opening of Heidegger and the "sovereign" experience of Bataille. It needs to be said straightaway that we're dealing with an extremely subtle kind of thought—a "broken path," a space that is always on the point of being closed off, not only because it is objectively restricted by the "immunizing" vocation of the most substantial part of the modern project but expressly because this kind of thought is completely jeopardized by a mythic drift that accompanies it like an originary risk or a slippery slope across the entire arc of its development.

This myth is generated when the constitutively concave character of *communitas* is displaced by its affirmative entification. All of the figures of identity, fusion, and endogamy that the representation of community will assume in modern political philosophy are nothing other than the unavoidable result of this first conceptual short-circuit. If the *communitas* is the escape or release from the individual subject, its myth is the interiorization of this exteriority, the representative doubling of its presence and the essentialization of its existence.[49] Nevertheless, there's no need to look at this excessive superimposition only as a subjective "error" on the part of the interpreter. It does nothing other than express the objectively inherent interval of difference with regard to the semantic double bottom of the concept of *munus*, to the structural ambiguity of its constitutively equivocal figure. The mythological inclination that all philosophies of community experience as the irresolvable blind spot of their own perspective consists in the difficulty of taking on and supporting the void of the *munus* as the object of philosophical reflection. How are we to think the *pure relation* without supplying it with subjective substance? How do we fix our gaze on it, without lowering it from the nothing that surrounds and traverses the common *res*? Notwithstanding all the theoretical precautions intent on guaranteeing the void of pure relation, that void tends to present itself in almost irresistible fashion as fullness; it tends to reduce the generality of "in common" in the specificity of *a* common subject.

Once identified, be it with a people, a territory, or an essence, the community is walled in within itself and thus separated from the outside. This is how the mythical reversal takes place. The Western tradition is literally hammered by this *koine*-centric conversion, almost like a recurring countertendency, more than a simple residue, a tradition on which is imprinted its growing immunitarian impulse. Yesterday as well as today (indeed more so today than yesterday), community appears to be marked, indeed saturated with communitarianism, patriotism, and local and factional interest that with regard to *communitas* constitute not only something different but the clearest kind of negation; both the paroxysm and parody that are produced every now and then in the "impropriety" of the common, when the reference to the "proper," or the voice of the "authentic," or the assumption of being pure, reappears. It's useful here to consider that *communis* (always referring to its earliest meaning) meant in addition to "vulgar" and "of the people," also "impure": "dirty services" [*sordida munera*]. We could say that this mixed or hybrid element, together not only with common sense but also political-philosophical discourse, is unable to endure when the search for its own proper and essential foundation is taken up again. Then what is simply exposed, namely, the *cum*, takes on the characteristic of a presupposition that is destined to be actualized. It is the dialectic of lost and found, of alienation and reappropriation, of flight and return that joins all *philosophies* of community in a mythology of origin. If the community belongs to us as our deepest and most proper root, we can, in fact we must, find it again or reproduce it, in line with its originary essence.

It's not by accident that the grand thought of community coincides with the deconstruction of this dialectic. What Rousseau previously had refused is the idea of an origin fully reproducible as such through the course of history. He was the first to register the fracture of difference that cuts the beginning [*inizio*] through an irrecoverable difference into a logical commencing [*cominciamento*] and a historical genesis and therefore was the first to withdraw the concept of community from its affirmative entification. Community appears to be definable only on the basis of the lack that characterizes it. It is *nothing other* than what history has negated, the nonhistoric backdrop from which history originates in the form of a necessary betrayal. The fact that Rousseau's discovery of the originary fracture is always on the point of falling prey again to the myth of a naturally incorrupt dimension (with all the aporetic consequences that ensue) doesn't erase the critical potential with regard to modern immunization.

Kant, more than any other, appears to have understood both the importance and the limit of these discoveries when he shifts the definition of community from the anthropological level of will to that of the transcendental one of law. The result of this move is a further and more powerful destructuring of the philosophy of the origin. Caught between the antinomical conjunction of freedom with evil, the origin literally becomes impenetrable in the precise sense that it cannot be defined except by the otherness that separates it from itself. It is from this perspective that, together with the mythologeme of the state of nature, every recompensatory dialectic between origin and later accomplishment fails. Kant criticizes it not only for the irremediably unsocial character of human nature but above all because the law of community isn't feasible as a matter of principle. That the categorical imperative doesn't dictate anything other than its own proper obligingness—it has no fixed content—means that its object is in and of itself unattainable or that our "thing" is inhabited by no-thing; that men are united by a "not" that joins them in a difference that cannot be lessened. Thus, Kant registers for the first time the antibiological character of *communitas*: its being a gift that does not belong to the subject, indeed that weakens [*reduce*] the subject and that hollows him out through a never-ending obligation, one that prescribes what is prohibited and prohibits what is prescribed.

In the case of Kant, nevertheless, the thought of community doesn't lack for contradictions and subtle wrinkles of meaning. The reason is not only that his transcendental perspective is shown to be open to a return of sorts to empirical anthropology, and therefore to a latent superimposition between the radical language of community and a more traditional intersubjective semantics, but also that the same reduction of community to its unattainable law discloses a residue of teleology. It is the underlying claim that Heidegger makes with respect to Kantian criticism, albeit in a reading that recovers and valorizes more than all of Kant's other interpreters his tense problematic with respect to subjectivity. Not even the law is to be made absolute as the very origin, because it is in turn preceded by an "out-law" [*fuorilegge*] even more originary that is precisely that *cum* to which we always belong with respect to temporal existence: *coexistence.* This means that the community is unattainable because it is barred by a cruel *nomos* that blocks our access and because of the simple fact that it is already given, here and now, in its constitutive withdrawal. For this reason community is neither promised nor to be disclosed beforehand, neither presupposed nor predetermined. Community doesn't require a teleology nor an archaeology since the origin already lies in its after; the origin is already perfectly contemporaneous with what follows. It is the opening of being that is given by and in its withdrawal, and that draws back when it is offered, in the very trembling of our existence.

There's no need to recall that Heidegger's thinking of community is anything but sheltered from a return to myth, and indeed from one of the most terrible of all political myths. This was obvious when he was tempted to reinstate the *munus* within the horizon of the proper, and indeed of the property, of a single people—losing the *munus* together with the *cum* that constitutes it as our "we-others" [*noi-altri*]. This is exactly the knot that Bataille cuts in an extreme combat with that thought, thanks to the formulation of a "non-knowledge" that decidedly exceeds the sacrificial horizon of political philosophy. Yet even more of interest in the economy of our work is Bataille's positioning of this excess in such a way as to drive him to the final, or better, the first meaning of that *munus*, which was our starting point from the central void of community; to the gift of self to which the subject feels driven by an unavoidable obligation because it is one with the subject's own proper desire.[50] Here one finds the most explicit contradiction of that process of immunization that beginning with Hobbes is put forward as the prevalent vector of meaning in the modern paradigm. That which Bataille contrasts with the "restricted economy" of a *conservatio vitae*, which culminates in the compulsory sacrifice of all who emerge as nonfunctional to such a preservation of life, is a conception of negative energetic excess that pushes the individual beyond his own limits while risking his life. In a flash that relation between community and death is displayed, which the *munus* carries from its inception as its fiery and unapproachable nucleus. It is the *non-being individual* of the relation; the *continuum* that originates out of and to which we are drawn by a force that is directly counterposed to the instinct for survival; the wound that we cause or from which we emerge when we ourselves are changed when we enter into a relation not only with the other but with the other of the other, he too the victim of the same irresistible expropriative impulse. This meeting, this *chance*, this contagion, more intense than any immunitarian cordon, is the community of those that manifestly do not have it, when not losing it, and losing themselves in the very same process of flowing away from it.[51] What this flow might mean, and above all if it doesn't risk, in turn, falling again upon a different but specular sacrificial logic, is the question on which the book closes. No answer is given except in the form of a further, final question: If existence cannot be sacrificed, how are we to think the originary opening to it?[52] How are we to fight the immunization of life without making it do death's work? How are we to break down the wall of the individual while at the same time saving the singular gift that the individual carries?

1

Fear

More than the thousand books that crowd the immense, official bibliography for Thomas Hobbes, a short text in the form of an aphorism from Elias Canetti introduces the secret heart of Hobbes's thought:

Hobbes. Thinkers not bound to any religion can impress me only if their thinking is extreme enough. Hobbes is one of these; at the moment, I find him to be the most important. Few of his thoughts strike me as correct . . . Why, then, does his presentation so greatly impress me? Why do I enjoy his falsest thought as long as its expression is extreme enough? I believe that I have found in him the mental root of what I want to fight against the most. He is the only thinker I know who does not conceal power, its weight, its central place in all human action, and yet does not glorify power, he merely lets it be.[1]

In Hobbes, hate and love, sharing and refusing to share, attraction and repulsion are based on a singular mixing that has at its origin the same element. The element in question is fear: "He knows what fear is; his calculation reveals it. All later thinkers, who came from mechanics and geometry, ignored fear; so fear had to flow back to the darkness in which it could keep operating undisturbed and unnamed."[2] It is the centrality of fear that explains for Canetti both Hobbes's greatness and his unbearableness. It is what makes Hobbes necessary analytically and unacceptable prescriptively; what makes him almost our contemporary and at the same time distances us from him as what is and indeed *needs* to be other from us. Or better: what places us in relation and in struggle with something that is already within us but which we fear can be extended to the point of taking us over completely. This something that we feel is ours (and for precisely that reason we fear it) is fear. We are afraid of our fear, of the possibility that fear is *ours*, that it is really we ourselves who have fear; whereas it is the courage to have fear that Hobbes teaches us, which comes most profoundly from *his* fear: "I am still attracted by everything in *Hobbes*: his intellectual courage, the courage of a man filled with fear."[3] Hobbes has the courage to speak to us about fear without subterfuge, circumlocution, and reticence; that fear is ours in the most extreme sense that we are not other from it. We originate in fear. In his Latin autobiography Hobbes writes that his mother was so frightened by the impending Spanish invasion that she gave birth to twins—himself and fear—and that in fear we find our most intimate dwelling. Indeed, what does it mean that we are "mortals" if not that we are subjects above all *to* fear? Because the fear that traverses us or rather constitutes us is essentially the fear of death; fear of no longer being what we are: alive. Or to be too quickly what we *also* are: mortal insofar as we are destined, entrusted, and promised to death. Hobbes says it with glacial clarity: "For every man is desirous of what is good for him, and shuns what is evil, but chiefly the chiefest of natural evils, which is death."[4]

Hobbes here examines the fear of death from the point of view of its complementary opposite, which is to say that instinct for self-preservation [*conatus sese praeservandi*] that constitutes the most powerful psychological foundation of man. But the instinct for preservation is nothing but another affirmative mode of inflecting the same fear of death: one fears death because one wants to survive, but one wants to survive precisely because one fears death. Leo Strauss had already assigned this logical-historical primacy of the fear of death with respect to the will to survive to the circumstance that is identifiable with a *summum malum* and not a *summum bonum*, the order of good not having any real limit: "Hobbes prefers the negative expression 'avoiding death' to the positive expression 'preserving life': because we feel death and not life; because we fear death immediately and directly . . . because we fear death infinitely more than we desire life."[5]

The fact is that fear comes first. It is *terribly originary*: the origin for that which is most terrible about fear. Even if in daily life fear is never alone, it is also accompanied by what man opposes to it, namely, hope, in the illusion that hope is its opposite, while instead hope is fear's faithful companion. What, in fact, is hope if not a sort of fear with its head hidden? Hobbes admits as much when in *De homine* he explains that hope is born from conceiving an evil together with a way of avoiding it, while fear consists, once a good is in view, in imagining a way of losing it. From this we read his conclusion, which sounds like a substantial identification between fear and hope: "And so it is manifest that *hope* and *fear* so alternate with each other that almost no time is so short that it cannot encompass their interchange."[6] Isn't it hope that pushes men to trust in themselves, carrying them right up to the edge of the abyss?

When one moves to the realm of politics, the role of fear becomes even more decisive. Nowhere more than here is its founding *fundamentum regnorum* revealed. Fear isn't only at the origin of the political, but fear is *its* origin in the literal sense that there wouldn't be politics without fear. This is the element that for Canetti separates Hobbes from all the other political philosophers past and present, and not only from those who belong to the so-called idealist or utopian line of thought but also from those to whom is traditionally assigned the term "realist." But why? What is it that isolates and pushes forward Hobbes with respect to his and to our current theoretical scenario? Above all, there are two intuitions and both concern fear. In the first instance, Hobbes raised what was unanimously considered the most disreputable of the states of mind to the primary motor of political activity. Compare in this regard Hobbes's position on fear to those of his greatest contemporaries. René Descartes expressly excludes the utility of fear, whereas Spinoza assigns the task of liberating us from fear to the state.[7] Hobbes's second intuition was to have placed fear at the origin not only of the degenerate or defective forms of the state but above all, its legitimate and positive forms. Here one finds all of the original power of Hobbes's thought as well as the cause for the very real ostracism to which that thought has been subjected for more than two hundred years, beginning with those same authors who derived their thought from Hobbes. Seen from this perspective, all wither when compared with Hobbes, that is, with the hardest rock, the sharpest blade, the coldest metal.

Certainly, others from Plato to Xenophon, to Machiavelli, accentuated the political role of fear. Then there is Montesquieu, who made fear the principle itself of the despotic regime.[8] But here lies the point: for Hobbes fear is bounded by the universe of tyranny or despotism. It is the place in which law and ethics of the best regime are founded. At least potentially, fear doesn't only have a destructive charge but also a constructive one. It doesn't only cause flight and isolation, but it also causes relation and union. It isn't limited to blocking and immobilizing, but, on the contrary, it pushes to reflect and neutralize danger. It doesn't reside on the side of the irrational but on the side of the rational.[9] It is a productive power [*potenza*].[10] It is this functional side of fear that distinguishes it from terror, from immediate fright or absolute panic. It's no accident that Hobbes never confuses *metus* and *pavor*, or fear [in English.—Trans.] and terror [in English.—Trans.], as sometimes his Italian and French translators do; in the sense that the second term—the Italian *terrore*, the French *terreur* (or *crainte*), and the German *Entsetzen*—connotes a completely negative and therefore paralyzing sensation, the first—the Italian *paura* (or in a more attenuated form, *timore*), the French *peur*, and the German *Furcht*—is also considered to be an element of strength because it forces one to think about how best to escape a situation of risk. In fact, Hobbes responds to his critics who accuse him of making fear out to be a unifying rather than a disunifying power that they confuse apprehension [*timore*] with terror [*terrore*], fear [*metuere*] with being terrified [*perterreri*].[11] Once he subtracts fear from the negative semantics of terror, Hobbes makes it the base of his entire political anthropology, the very presupposition of the social covenant as Carl Schmitt synthetically represents it: "The terror of the state of nature drives anguished individuals to come together, their fear rises to an extreme: a spark of reason (*ratio*) flashes, and suddenly there stands in front of them a new god."[12] And this in the sense that fear not only originates and explains the covenant but also protects it and maintains it in life. Once tested, fear never abandons the scene. It is transformed from "reciprocal," anarchic fear, such as that which determines the state of nature (*mutuus metus*), to "common," institutional fear, what characterizes the civil state (*metus potentiae communis*). Fear does not disappear, however. It is reduced but doesn't recede. Fear *is never forgotten.* As already noted, fear is a part of us; it is we outside ourselves. It is the other from us that constitutes us as subjects infinitely divided from ourselves.

It is this permanence of fear even within the condition of its modern "overcoming" that attracts Canetti to Hobbes, which makes him see Hobbes as the undisputed head of those "dreadful" thinkers that "look at reality point-blank and never fear calling it by its name."[13] This is true from Joseph de Maistre to Friedrich Nietzsche, for whom the longest of all the epochs is that of fear since "fear is a human being's original and basic feeling; from fear everything can be explained,"[14] including morality, whose "mother" is fear.[15] To these names we could easily add Guglielmo Ferrero, who considered fear "the soul of the living universe." He goes on:

The universe cannot enter into the sphere of life without becoming afraid . . . The highest living creature is man, who is also the most fearful and the most feared creature. He fears and is feared more than any other because he is the only creature with the idea, the obsession, and the terror of the great dark gulf of death into which the torrent of life has been pouring ever since the beginning of time.[16]

Ferrero's presupposition is Hobbesian, that is, the fear of death not only as the angle with which to look upon life but also as the "political" conclusion that inevitably derives from it:

Every man knows that he is stronger than certain of his fellows and weaker than others; that, living alone in a state of complete anarchy, he would be the scourge of the weaker and a victim of the stronger, and would live in perpetual fear. That is why in every society, even the crudest, the majority of men give up terrorizing the weaker so as to be less afraid of the stronger—such is the universal formula of social order.[17]

This is exactly how Hobbes reasons. The texts are well known in which this transition from an originary fear emerges, that of everyone toward each other, to the derived and artificial fear with respect to the state, which can protect but only in proportion to the continuing threat of sanctions. But it's worth recalling at least that text according to which "the origin of all great and lasting societies consisted not in the mutual good will men had towards each other, but in the mutual fear they had of each other," for the force with which Hobbes casts aside all the positive anthropology (of the Aristotelian sort) of the natural sociality of man.[18] This is how the infinite dialectic of fear begins and unravels: to escape an initial and indeterminate fear, men accept an amount of fear and indeed institute a second and certain fear with a covenant. They organize the conditions for rationally stabilizing fear by defining it as the normal state. For this reason it is a legitimate power [*potere*]. What distinguishes a despotic state from a legitimate one is not, therefore, the absence of fear or its lessening, but the uncertainty (or certainty) of its object and its limits, according to Franz Neumann's well-known distinction between neurotic *Angst* and *Realangst*.[19] The state's task is not to eliminate fear but to render it "certain." This conclusion opens a tear of unusual analytic depth in the entire paradigm of modernity. That the modern state not only does not eliminate fear from which it is originally generated but is founded precisely on fear so as to make it the motor and the guarantee of the state's proper functioning means that the epoch that defines itself on the basis of the break with respect to the origin, namely, modernity, carries within it an indelible imprint of conflict and violence. Note well: I am not speaking of the simple secularization of a more ancient nucleus, nor am I speaking about a "memory" that is temporarily necessary for reactivating an energy on the verge of exhausting itself. Rather, I have in mind something more intrinsic that could be defined as the *modern archaic* [*l'arcaicità del moderno*]. By this I mean the permanence of the origin at the moment of its leaving. Here lies the double layer that is least visible in the Hobbesian text. Differently from what is generally held, the political-civil state is not born against or after the natural one but through its reversed inclusion in terms of an emptiness rather than a fullness.[20]

This is what the liberal interpretation in all its possible inflections is unable to grasp: it is true that state order puts an end to natural disorder, but within the very same presupposition. What this might be isn't difficult to recognize because it also constitutes at the same time the reason and the object of that fear that we have identified in the same form of the modern archaic. We are dealing with the relation between equality and the capacity to kill:

The cause of mutual fear consists partly in the natural equality of men, partly in their mutual will of hurting: whence it comes to pass, that we can neither expect from others, nor promise to ourselves the least security. For if we look on men full grown, and consider how brittle the frame of our human body is, which perishing, all its strength, vigour, and wisdom itself perisheth with it; and how easy a matter it is, even for the weakest man to kill the strongest: there is no reason why any man, trusting to his own strength, should conceive himself made by nature above others. They are equals, who can do equal things one against the other; but they who can do the greatest things, namely, kill, can do equal things. All men therefore among themselves are by nature equal.[21]

What men have in common is the capacity to kill and, correspondingly, the possibility of being killed: a capacity for killing [*uccidibilità*] generalized to such a degree as to become the sole link that joins individuals who would otherwise be divided and independent. This is Hobbes's discovery that makes him the most tireless adversary of community. The *res publica* is nothing other than a form of life that is preserved or lost according to changing and uncontrollable relations of force. We can say that the entire Hobbesian anthropology is constructed on this fixed principle: "Men by natural passion are divers ways offensive one to another."[22] They are united by the common desire to injure one another since they aim at the same objective constituted by power. But because power isn't measured except in relation to another's powerlessness [*impotenza*], all are focused on mutually destroying each other. The reason is that men are *essentially* "against": forever and always "in the state and posture of gladiators; having their weapons pointing, and their eyes fixed on one another."[23] They encounter each other in battle; they develop relations in violence; they face each other in death. They are "those who clash," the "opponents," the "competitors" based on the image of the running to the *death*, moving toward death, and giving oneself over to death, which constitutes the most fitting figure of the community of the crime: "Continually to out-go the next before, is felicity. And to forsake the course, is to die."[24] For this reason "men are accustomed to hasten to the spectacle of the death and danger of others,"[25] because "the delight is so far predominant, that men usually are content in such a case to be spectators of the misery of their friends";[26] and because "the way of the competitor to the attaining of his desire is to kill, subdue, supplant, or repel the other."[27] The fundamental reason for all of this is "metaphysically" planted in that terrible dialectic between power [*potere*] and survival, whose ancestral, anthropological roots Canetti analyzed with unmistakably Hobbesian overtones: "The situation of survival is the central situation of power," to the point that the pleasure that each "draws from surviving grows with his power; power allows him to give his consent to it. The true content of this power is the desire to survive ever greater numbers of men."[28] Power doesn't need life any less than life needs power.

For this reason—and here it is Hobbes who speaks—we fear "death, from whom we expect both the loss of all power and also the greatest of bodily pains in the losing"[29] One can ensure life, which is the first necessity, only by accumulating power, which is the first passion. Yet one can accumulate power only at the expense of others; at the cost of *their* life; living in their place, at the cost of their death. After all, Hobbes sees in war—not necessarily one fought openly but the one that is latent—men's very same "condition" and their "time," with respect to which peace is nothing but an exception, a parenthesis, a contretemps.[30] This means that the relation that unites men does not pass between friend and enemy and not even between enemy and friend, but between enemy and enemy, given that every temporary friendship is instrumental ("Friendships are good, certainly useful") with regard to managing the only social bond possible, namely, enmity.[31]

It is at this point that Hobbes's response jumps out at us in the form of a specular inversion or a homeopathic cure of the infinite crises of the interhuman relation. If the relation between men is in itself destructive, the only route of escape from this unbearable state of affairs is the destruction of the relation itself. If the only community that is humanly verifiable is that of crime, there doesn't remain anything except the crime of the community: the drastic elimination of every kind of social bond. Naturally, Hobbes doesn't express himself in these terms: his discourse has an intonation and an intention that is "constructive." He intends to build the new state in a form that is in itself outside mutual conflict. Yet, and this is the decisive point, such a form is that of absolute dissociation: only by dissociating themselves from any relation can individuals avoid lethal contact. This is the most extreme etymological meaning that is to be attributed to Hobbesian absolutism: it is the principle of dissolution of everything that is still "bound," of any relation that is not that of dissociation itself. We need to look at this from each side and at the same time from within the contradiction that holds it together. Men now are associated in the modality of reciprocal dissociation, unified in the elimination of every interest that is not purely individual, artificially united in their subtraction from community. Schmitt also perceives this when he observes that the covenant "is conceived in an entirely individualistic manner. All ties and groupings have been dissolved . . . The assemblage of men gathered together by the fright of fiends cannot from the presuppositions of their gathering, overcome hostility."[32] Such hostility that returns again, and indeed that never disappears from the Hobbesian scenario because it constitutes his horizon, is what we have defined as the Archaic or the Elementary, that originary violence that precedes and also embraces the project of its modern "domestication," in the sense that rather than disappearing, it simply changes level. It is transferred, we might say, from the level of content to the form of relation that is also negative: it becomes its absolute "non" and is a relation of irrelation. This is how we should understand the prohibition of any association internal to the state, which for Hobbes is integral to the functioning of the model. Not only would it threaten the sovereign power but it would constitute its logical negation since sovereignty coincides with dissociation. It is its normative institution. We are not dealing with two distinct and successive moments but with the same constitutive *and* dissociative act: the state is the desocialization of the communitarian bond [*legame*]. It is with this radicality in mind that we ought to understand Hobbes's repeated warning that "this word body politic . . . signifieth not the concord, but the union of many men."[33] Union but not concord because it is at the same time much more: the incorporation in the sole, sovereign power. But also (and for this reason) union is infinitely less than any form of communitarian relation: unity without relation, the suppression of the *cum*. That body isn't simply different or other from the community but is its opposite: the production and not the simple inclusion of its void.[34] The covenant is made from this lack, of the many "nons" whose sum cannot be anything except the nothing of community: for this reason the Leviathan isn't only "like a creation out of nothing" but also *of* nothing.[35] Subjects of such a sovereign are those that have nothing in common since everything is divided between "mine" and "yours": division without sharing [*condivisione*].

This is what "immunizes" from the risk of death that is contained in the community, according to that opposition between *immunitas* and *communitas* that organizes the entire modern project. When Helmuth Plessner or Arnold Gehlen, explicitly referring to Hobbes's " *fame futura famelicus*,"[36] locate in the "exoneration" or in the "exemption" (*Entlastung*) the functional criterion for the reduction of dangers connected to the "risky" situation of the animal man, they do nothing other than reformulate the logic of the Hobbesian pact, both with regard to the freeing of the

modern individual from all that is tiring and dangerous and with regard
to the "burdens" that weigh on the preceding condition: and with respect
to his institutional confinement to a framework that is rigidly exclusive
of any communitarian figure because he is characterized by the "same
diversity" of egoism.[37] It is this irremediable separation that puts an end to
that form of originary *munus* that had still characterized the precontrac-
tual social relation. From this perspective, the structural homology that
Marshall Sahlins sees between the archaic paradigm of the gift and the
Hobbesian contract is unconvincing. When, following Mauss, he declares
that "the primitive analogue of social contract is not the state, but the
gift," he isn't completely wrong, but only on the condition that he identifies the gift with a surreptitious form of exchange (and therefore undoes
the principle of the gift itself, which is to say its gratuity).[38] Hobbes avoids
committing this error when he juxtaposes the free and unilateral logic of
the gift to that of the bilateral and self-interested contract: "When a man
transfereth any right of his to another, without consideration of reciprocal
benefit, past, present, or to come; this is called free gift . . . When a man
transfereth his right, upon consideration of reciprocal benefit, this is not
a free gift but mutual donation; and is called contract."[39] Therefore, the
contract does not coincide with the gift, nor does it derive from it. Rather,
it is its most direct negation: the passage from the communitarian level of
gratitude, which according to Hobbes is unbearable for "modern" man, to
that of a law, which is subtracted from every form of *munus*.[40] Indeed, it is
destructive of that *cum* to which the *munus* is semantically oriented in the
figure of the *communitas*. The sovereign exchange between protection and
obedience responds to this power [*potenza*] to undo: to preserve individuals through the annihilation of their relation.

Seen in the light of such a rationalization, the Hobbesian project
seems perfectly realized. If relation carries mortal danger, the only way
to escape is to suppress relations through the institution of a Third with
whom all relate without any further need of relating among them. Yet the
logical rigor of this deduction uncovers an unresolved node, similar to a
remnant of irrationality. Previously, the move that we have reconstructed
from the state of fear to the fear of the state creates more than some per-
plexity. Can a system sustain itself only on fear without exploding or imploding? What kind of politics is it that can be completely encapsulated in

blackmail? Despite his refined logical constructions and his consummate argumentative ability, Hobbes doesn't furnish a convincing answer to this underlying question. Indeed, to the degree that we proceed in the reading of his "story," a series of difficulties, inconsistencies, and real contradictions become increasingly evident, which the Hobbesian text, even in its continual adjustments, is never completely able to hide.

As is often emphasized, the most controversial point remains that of the conceptual passage from the renouncement of the right of resistance to the formation of the sovereign person. How is a positive power derived from the sum of so many negations? How is it possible that from a totality of passivity an active principle might spring? And from the perspective of subjects, why should they ever renounce what they already have in favor of an entity that is external to them? In what way would that rejection not only remain completely unilateral, without any certain counter to it, but be configured as a sort of preventive sacrifice that no hypothetical future advantage would be able to compensate? Hobbes himself saw this incongruity and tried to remedy it in his greatest work through the so-called theory of authorization, according to which individuals not only give up their right but in fact authorize a representative person to act in their place, thus preserving the role of subject for each of his actions.[41] This formulation, nevertheless, rather than resolving the difficulties just described, sharpens them. In the first instance because the objective result certainly isn't that of ensuring subjects from eventual impositions on the part of the sovereign, but on the contrary, of freeing the latter from the control of the former. The criterion of legitimacy is subordinated to that of implementation. It is true that the pact logically precedes sovereignty, but sovereignty is what renders it historically, which is to say, factually possible, since any pact is ineffectual without a sword to enforce it. It is the juridical that founds the political, but the political that subordinates and then exceeds the juridical. The same can be said of the relation between order and decision, norm and exception, universality and contingency: sovereignty is both the superimposition of the two terms and the surplus of the second with respect to the first. I noted this earlier: the state of nature is not overcome once and for all by the civil, but it resurfaces again in the same figure of the sovereign, because it is the only one to have preserved natural right in a context in which all the others have given it up.

Now the contradiction reaches its apex: it is the theory of authorization that seems to absolutize sovereign power to an extreme degree, a theory assigned to eliminate the transcendence of sovereign power over the contracting parties. How is this possible? The explanation for such a paradox is to be sought in the double valence of the concept of identification. Or better: in the exchange of subjectivity between its two terms. To identify with another can mean to bring the other to the self, but also to carry the self to the other. Here Hobbes oscillates continually between these two possibilities, but the logic (though it would be better to say the force) of his discourse moves entirely in the direction of the second. To be identical to the sovereign means to give completely one's own subjectivity to him. It means to renounce any margin of autonomy with respect to his actions, precisely because they are considered as one's own [*come proprie*].

Therefore, from this point of view (and differently from what we might suppose), it isn't the distance or the transcendence but the identity of the sovereign with respect to the subjects [*sudditi*] that sets in motion that sacrificial *dispositif* that the authorization should have blocked. Instead, it ends up increasing it to the utmost. What greater sacrifice on the part of these subjects authorizes their own expropriation: that interiorizes their own alienation; that identifies them with their own loss of identity? This consideration is true as a matter of principle for any action of the sovereign but acquires a particular weight as soon as it is turned *against* the subject [*soggetto*] subjugated [*assoggettato*] by the sovereign. Not even in this case can that subject contest the action, not only because the only objective measure of judgment remains the one adopted (and indeed instituted) by the sovereign but, above all, because, if the act in question were subjectively held to be unjust, it could not be logically disapproved of by the one who by definition is its author: "Every particular man is author of all the sovereign doth; and consequently he that complaineth of injury from his sovereign complaineth of that whereof he himself is author."[42] For this reason, "to resist the sword of the commonwealth in defense of another man, guilty or innocent, no man hath liberty."[43] Neither is one free, moreover, to defend oneself without breaking the pact that binds one to an unconditional obedience. Here the unmistakably sacrificial character of the Hobbesian paradigm comes directly out into the open:

And therefore it may (and doth often) happen in common-wealths that a Subject may be put to death by the command of the sovereign power, and yet neither do the other wrong, as when Jeptha caused his daughter to be sacrificed (in which, and the like cases, he that so dieth, had liberty to do the action for which he is nevertheless without Injury put to death). And the same holdeth also in a sovereign prince that putteth to death an innocent subject.[44]

Yet Hobbes in *Elements of Law* had previously said with regard to children (whose Latin name, in the height of irony, is "*liberi*, which also signifieth freemen") that "they may alienate them, that is, assign his or her dominion, by selling or giving them in adoption or servitude to others; or may pawn them for hostages, kill them for rebellion, or sacrifice them for peace, by the law of nature, when he or she, in his or her conscience, think it to be necessary."[45] It is true that such an arrangement refers less to the state instituted by the covenant than to that "paternal" or "despotic" one. The decisive element is constituted by the fundamental balance that Hobbes institutes between the two types of regime. What links them is a shared origin of fear: sovereignty through acquisition "differeth from sovereignty by institution only in this, that men who choose their sovereign do it for fear of one another, and not of him whom they institute; but in this case they subject themselves to him they are afraid of. In both cases they do it for fear."[46] Certainly such a worry [*timore*] produces varied effects in the two cases, insofar as the subjects that the sovereign represents are different, but not with regard to the "mastery" [*padronanza*] of life that is nevertheless sacrificed to its immediate preservation. What the two situations share is that in both cases life can be subtracted from death only by entrusting it to the one who has the right to take it away, based on the terrible conjunction that gives him the power "of life *and* of death." It is as if life were saved only because it belongs to death, acting in death's name and on death's behalf:

And that which men do, when they demand (as it is now called) *quarter* (which the Greeks called *zogria, taking alive*) is to evade the present fury of the victor by submission, and to compound for their life with ransom or service; and therefore he that hath quarter hath not his life given, but deferred till further deliberation; for it is not a yielding on condition of life, but to discretion. And then only is his life in security, and his service due, when the victor hath trusted him with his corporal liberty. For slaves that work in prisons, or fetters, do it not of duty, but to avoid the cruelty of their task-masters.[47]

The identification of the victim with his own persecutor marks the height of a sacrificial mechanism set in motion originally by mimetic desire and subsequently institutionalized in the political exchange between protection and obedience.

Certainly, the reversal of protection into persecution constitutes a limit point, which the logic of Hobbes's discourse tends to push to the outermost margins. In the state created by the covenant, "the infliction of what evil soever on an innocent man" appears as the exception to a rule that generally always situates the enemy on the outside.[48] We are concerned here, however, with an exception that restores the "abnormal" assumption on which the same norm is based, the coincidence of the preservation of life and the capacity to sacrifice it in a framework predefined by the primary relation of enmity. Sacrificing life to its preservation is the only way of containing the threat that menaces life. Yet this is the equivalent of preserving and perpetuating as well life's capacity to be sacrificed; to "normalize" the possibility if not the reality, of its sacrifice. The community is literally prey to this dialectic. From one side it is the community of sacrifice in the sense that René Girard expressed it: "The sacrifice serves to protect the entire community from *its own* violence; it prompts the entire community to choose victims outside itself."[49] The community can survive the violence that traverses it only by shifting violence onto an enemy that is able to attract it. Nevertheless, in this shift a transfer of the same "common ground" is produced from within to without: "It remaineth therefore still that consent (by which I understand the concurrence of many men's wills to one action) is not sufficient security for their common peace, with the erection of some common power, by the fear whereof they may be compelled both to keep the peace amongst themselves, and to join their strengths together against a common enemy."[50] It is as if the victimizing mechanism suitable for maintaining the community were to determine at the same time an absolute exteriorization that subtracts community from itself: the "common" now describes in fact the enemy that attacks it and the power that keeps it united against the enemy. But that power, which is founded precisely on the impossibility of suppressing the enemy, can keep the community united only by dividing it, eliminating it as community. This is how the community of sacrifice is turned inside out or doubled in the sacrifice of the community. What the community sacrifices to its own self-preservation isn't other from itself. It is sacrificed in the sacrifice not only of the enemy but also of every single member of community, since every member finds in his own being the originary figure of the *first* enemy. Sacrifice responds to this origin, to the fear that the origin provokes: infinitely reactivating it in a circle from which we still have not emerged.

Excursus on Hobbes

The circle perfectly expresses the insolubility of the question of the origin. What came first: fear or sacrifice? Which of the two terms is the origin of the other? To this point we have kept Hobbes's explicit theorization in mind: it is fear of violent death that determines the sacrifice of basic instincts, of freedom, of desire. In this sense sacrifice is second; it logically follows fear. There is, nevertheless, another hermeneutic key that invites us to reverse the relation of precedence between fear and sacrifice, traceable this time outside the Hobbesian text. It concerns a pre-text that is capable of explaining it as well as its most jarring antinomies in the light of a "symptomal" reading that places sacrifice before fear; that suspends what for Hobbes is first to an ignored, implicit, and latent origin, which is nevertheless operative in the analytical cadences and the argumentative rhythm of his discourse. Which one is it? What is this preoriginary origin, this Ur-origin that resides on this side of fear and what in fact determines it? What is that fear born from that is apparently primary but in reality is already second with respect to another event, to another scene, which it is more the cause of than the effect?

Before responding directly to this underlying question, let's put forward a further consideration. When Hobbes alludes to the fear that rouses the state institution, he always speaks of terror and never of fear: "punishment . . . serveth to the benefit of mankind, because it keepeth men in peaceable and virtuous conversation by the terror";[51] the sovereign "hath so much power, as by the terror of it he can conform the wills of particular men unto unity and concord";[52] "the laws of nature . . . of themselves, without the terror of some power to cause them to be observed, are contrary to our natural passions."[53] The reason is that the fear [*timore*] that frightens the state doesn't have to be of the kind that makes one reason and ready a response, but of the kind that immobilizes before one is even able to conjure up a form of resistance. This observation offers us another useful element for identifying the nature of that first sacrifice on which the entire social edifice was built. What we are concerned with here cannot be anything except something as terrifying as it is horrifying, for which state terror needs to provide cover and at the same time a counterweight. What event has those characteristics of unbearableness if not the murder of the father on the part of the hordes of brothers that Freud describes in *Totem and Taboo*?[54] Clearly, I do not want to argue that Hobbes might have guessed beforehand what Freud "discovered"; nor do I want to suggest that Freud might have intentionally wanted to complete Hobbes's account in reverse, providing the reasons for Hobbes's lacuna, giving voice to the not-said. With that said, however, not only the conceptual but even the semantic concordances between the two authors are remarkable, especially with regard to the theory of natural aggressivity, for which Freud takes up even the letter of the Hobbesian formula (which was already present in Plautus) of the *homo homini lupus*, as well as the apparent contradiction between the state of nature and the civil state: "For the principal task of civilization, its actual *raison d'être*, is to defend us against nature."[55] Rather, the problem I want to pose is that of, in a manner of speaking, the structural logic of the sacrificial paradigm that leads Freud to insist so strongly (and with absolute fidelity) on Hobbes's itinerary:

Human life in common is only made possible when a majority comes together which is stronger than any separate individual and which remains united against all separate individuals. The power of this community is then set up as "right" in opposition to the power of the individual, which is condemned as "brute force" . . . The final outcome should be a rule of law to which all—except those who are not capable of entering a community—have contributed by a sacrifice of their instincts, and which leaves no one—again with the same exception—at the mercy of brute force.[56]

Here, too, the only possible community is the one cemented by sacrifice: community of sacrifice that cannot be anything but the sacrifice of the community as well, but with a supplement with respect to the Hobbesian framework, which, modifying the times, renders it in the end as reason: sacrifice is not only the result but also the presupposition of *pactum societatis*. It isn't just any sacrifice, however, but that first and most terrible sacrifice, that "principle and primal crime of humanity as well as of the individual" whose sensation of atavistic fear dominating the Hobbesian world can be related only in ontogenetic terms.[57] From this perspective, therefore, the real, the phantasmic object begins to come into focus, of that otherwise inexplicable "fear" [in English.—Trans.] that would force everyone to give up everything in favor of only one man. We aren't dealing with fear of death in general but of *a* death; or better, of its return as death for all those, namely, the brothers, who once killed and then forever made that death one that belonged properly to them [*per sempre fatte proprie*].

The return of what is most familiar (and who is more familiar than the father) is the same essence of what is "uncanny," what is troubling, and what creates fear: "For this uncanny element is actually nothing new or strange, but something that was long familiar to the psyche and was estranged from it only through being repressed . . . something that should have remained hidden and has come into the open."[58] Uncanny isn't, therefore, death but death's return, according to the well-known maxim that "the postman always rings twice"; where death's return cannot be anything else but what is killed in reality or in thought. This, however, isn't what counts in Freud's view.[59] What matters instead is how this event, be it real or imaginary, might structurally explain the impossibility of eliminating fear, once it is considered to be not first but second with respect to the event, as well as its paradoxical associative effect. The effect arises out of the "historical" circumstance that the homicidal brothers join together in a founding pact, despite the fear that really ought to keep them apart, because they were *already* united by a hatred and violence of the father that is *more originary*. This Freud had already noted in the incomplete sections of *Overview of the Transference Neuroses*: "The next change could only consist in the fact that the threatened sons avoided castration by means of flight and, allied with one another, learned to take upon themselves the struggle for survival. This living together had to bring social feelings to the fore."[60] We can see this especially in the third essay of Freud's *Moses* in which the steps of this archi-political event are reconstructed with extraordinary adherence to Hobbes's argumentative machinery:

It is reasonable to surmise that after the killing of the father a time followed when the brothers quarreled among themselves for the succession, which each of them wanted to obtain for himself. They came to see that these fights were as dangerous as they were futile. This hard-won understanding—as well as the memory of the deed of liberation they had achieved together and the attachment that had grown up among them during the time of their exile—led at last to a union among them, a sort of social contract (*eine Art von Gesellschaftsvertrag*).[61]

It is the commonality first of expulsion and then of the conspiracy, of the common oath *cum-iuratio*, that makes possible and motivates the pact that fear imposes: the "common fear" that in both Hobbes and Freud follows from the "reciprocal fear" of the natural state; with the difference that in Freud reciprocal fear is itself preceded by a movement backward, without end, away from "paternal fear" (the origin always remains further behind with respect to where it is represented): first of the father alive and then of the father dead, of his violent death and of the emotional ambivalence that it sparks in the murdering sons that hate and admire him at the same time. It is precisely this admiration that explains the father's symbolic reconstruction in a mytho-totemic figure, which, substituting for the father, generates even more fear, but a fear that is more bearable because it is produced by the same brothers. This explains, therefore, the otherwise paradoxical birth of law and morality from the most illegitimate and immoral act, but nevertheless always "sacred" (as every ritual sacrifice is etymologically "sacred"):

Thus there came into being the first form of a social organization accompanied by the renunciation of instinctual gratification; recognition of mutual *obligations*; *institutions* declared sacred, which could not be broken—in short the beginnings of morality and law . . . The memory of the father lived on during this time of the "brother horde." A strong animal, which perhaps at first was also dreaded, was found as a substitute.[62]

The temptation to identify this "strong animal" with what Nietzsche will call "the coldest of all cold monsters," the Leviathan, is great, given that "the relationship to the totem animal retained the original ambivalence of feeling towards the father."[63] Isn't this exactly the relation of respect mixed with fear that informs the relation of subjects with a Leviathan state that is neither friend nor enemy? "But, Hobbes' image of the Leviathan has another, altogether different meaning. In contrast to the later Behemoth, it does not depict an enemy; it shows a god that assures peace and security. Nor is it a political friend-enemy. It is too horrible and terrible for that."[64] Doesn't something that can no longer be but that is absolutely needed, such as the ancient paternal coercion, substitute for that of Hans Kelsen's "totemic mask"?[65] It's simply enough to read what the qualities are that a "great man" possesses (which in the Freudian myth occupy the father's position) to recognize that they are exactly the same as those of the Hobbesian *Leviathan*. That is absoluteness, irresistibleness, and lacking in conditions: "The conviction that his power was irresistible, the subjection to his will, could not have been more absolute with the helpless, intimidated son of the father of the horde than they were here."[66] Yet there is as well the identification with death because it is from death that the *makros anthropos* acquires authority and power. This is the case both in Hobbes, who constructs his state precisely on the fear of violent death and who preserves it through the fear of the pain of death, and in Freud for whom "the dead now become stronger than the living had been."[67] It isn't happenstance that Hobbes calls the Leviathan a *Deus mortalis*, as what belongs to death and that still carries death within, having already once cut it into pieces and eaten it: "According to cabbalistic views, the leviathan is thought of as a huge animal with which the Jewish God plays daily for a few hours; however, at the beginning of the thousand-year kingdom, he is slaughtered and the blessed inhabitants of this kingdom divide and devour his flesh."[68]

It is for this reason that the Leviathan can still be a god: "[H]is 'deus mortalis' is a machine whose mortality is based on the fact that one day it may be shattered by civil war."[69] This makes clear the sense of Schmitt's observation that "the accumulated anguish of individuals who fear for their lives brings about a new power, but it affirms rather than creates this new god."[70] What does the fact that the "new god" is more "affirmed" than "created" out of nothing mean if not that it resided in another part in a sinister past that can neither be remembered nor forgotten, but precisely only "evoked" as one does a dead person, who always returns in the living's obsession with it?

Nevertheless, in another sense that god is "mortal." Not only as one who brings death because he is always already dead from the archi-origin on but also as the one who gives death back, who every day returns death to those from whom he had previously received it and that had in the same body devoured it: "One day the expelled brothers joined forces, slew and ate the father . . . Now they accomplished their identification by devouring him and each acquired a part of his strength."[71] This force, born from identifying with the dead father, is itself a force of death. It is no accident that it is inexpressible except in the negativity of renunciation, and indeed of a double renunciation. For each of them renounces the desire to assume the role of the father and renounces the women guaranteed by the role:

Thus there was nothing left for the brothers, if they wanted to live together, but to erect the incest prohibition—perhaps after many difficult experiences—through which they all equally renounced the women whom they desired, and on account of whom they had removed the father in the first place. Thus they saved the organization which had made them strong.[72]

The force of sovereignty created in such a fashion is, therefore, directly proportional to the renunciation precisely of its exercise. Such a result is the last step in a sacrificial logic carried to its extreme consequence: first the sacrifice of the father and later the sacrifice of the same brothers to the sacrificed father. A double sacrifice, sacrifice squared. Blood but also inhibition; the interiorization of the prohibition in the form of a conscious self-imposition. As we saw, this is what Hobbes reveals to us, what he discloses and covers over at the same time, in the formula of the authorization: personally taking on one's own guilt. Here Hobbes's riddle is revealed, the secret, the curse that Canetti warned of without completely explaining: the authorization of one's own guilt is nothing other than the juridical figure of self-sacrifice that is interiorized in the act of incorporating the dead father. What the brothers voluntarily surrender isn't only women and power, but more than that (and prior to that), their own identity in favor of an identification with someone who is no longer but who is still able to pull them down into the void.[73] Making themselves brothers *in* guilt, they lose once and for all their own political subjectivity and commit themselves to deliver their subjectivity over to what remains of the ancient father—to the "remnants." Identifying themselves with him who is dead, they must deliver themselves over to that death that they gave and ate and that now, in turn, eats them: "One has wished another person dead, and now one *is* this other person and is dead oneself."[74] What the Freudian *Urszene* activates in the "repetition" of the Hobbesian pact is a figure of absolute reciprocity. The incorporation of the father on the part of the sons corresponds to the incorporation of the sons of the part of which, upon the death of the father, substitutes for him. What else does the celebrated image of the Leviathan represent, composed as it is of many small human forms wedged in together one against the other in the shape of a scale of impenetrable armor, if not the inclusion again of the murderous sons on the part of the "second" father *in one's own body*?[75] Isn't the sacrificial relation between fathers and sons always reversible and cyclical in all of classical mythology? Fathers that devour their sons and sons that devour their fathers along the originary chain that sees Cronus kill his father, Uranus, before in turn being killed by his son Zeus. A text from Canetti captures this infinite killing instantaneously in a terrible moment:

He roasts and devours them with relish, delighting in their sweet flesh. One day, however, their flesh turns to grubs in his bowels. These start to eat their father from within and so he is finally devoured by his own slaughtered sons. This case of self-consumption has a curious climax: *The thing which is eaten eats back.* The father eats his sons and these same sons eat him whilst he is still in the process of digesting them; it is a double and mutual cannibalism.[76]

2

Guilt

The first great adversary of Hobbes, Jean Jacques Rousseau, had already argued that the inevitable result of a politics of sacrifice would be the death of the community.[1] Furthermore, he did so employing a modality of reversed assimilation or negation by incorporation not unlike Canetti's, which we have just analyzed: "It is not so much what is horrible and false in his political theory as what is just and true that has rendered it odious."[2] As was the case with Canetti, what is at stake here is not simply appreciating Hobbes as "one of the greatest geniuses that ever lived" but something more that transpires in Rousseau's repeated designation of him as a "sophist" in the same text. This suggests that Rousseau evidently attributes to himself the role of philosopher.[3] Yet the sophist isn't a mere external enemy for the philosopher but rather is the alter ego that the philosopher always carries within, even fighting him intestinally. Rousseau fights against himself through Hobbes in those modern categories, but especially the individualist paradigm, which not only is an integral part of Rousseau's lexicon but in a sense is what he carries forward to even more extreme results than those obtained by his predecessor. Yet this use of the individualistic paradigm takes place in a problematic framework that radically changes his points of view. Here then is what the philosopher does when faced with the sophist: he takes on the "Enlightenment" theses until he reverses them into a different truth.

What is this ignored truth that Rousseau traces in the "dangerous reveries" of Hobbes?[4] What is there of "justice and truth" in his "horrible system?"[5] The response that I will attempt to advance here is that such a truth has to do precisely with what is most terrible in that common crime that we identified when we superimposed Freud over it as the explicative key of the entire Hobbesian construction: the political is born marked by an originary guilt that can be atoned for only by introjecting that guilt in a renunciation, according to the sacrificial and self-sacrificial dynamic over which we have lingered here. We can say that the ultimate sense of Rousseau's discourse is to be found in the separation between the premise and the outcome of this passage; between a taking on (and in) of guilt and the command of the sacrifice. Naturally, such an abridgement presupposes a very different characterization of guilt itself: it is no longer the ritual murder of the father committed by the community of brothers but, rather, is the antecedent that withdraws the possibility of community's own realization from itself. Here too a "crime," but only in the objective sense of *delinquere*—to be wanting. The community isn't definable except on the basis of the lack from which it derives and that inevitably connotes it, precisely as the absence, as the defect of community. For Rousseau, all of human history carries with it this wounding that consumes and empties it from within. History isn't interpretable except with regard to this "impossible," of what it is *not* and can never be, from what, nevertheless, it originates in the form of a necessary betrayal.

But if things really stand this way, if "the offense" [*colpa*] was never committed by anyone; if it is nothing other than the transcendental criterion of the negativity of history and indeed of history insofar as it is negative, this then means that guilt [*colpa*] can never be atoned for through any kind of sacrifice.[6] And it can't be for the very simple reason that sacrifice doesn't do anything except repeat and therefore multiply to the nth power the guilt that it should remove. This is the true breaking point with the Hobbesian model: its identification as a sacrificial *dispositif* not only that is by necessity internal to guilt but in fact is guilt's direct expression.

It's sufficient to note the vocabulary that Rousseau uses when defining Hobbesian men. They are not precisely men but demons that rage against their victims: "The intolerant person is Hobbes's man; intolerance is war with humanity. The society of the intolerant is like that of demons; they only agree in order to torment each other . . . it is purely a matter of chance that the victims are not the executioners."[7] Or they are wolves—and here the Hobbesian reading of *homo homini lupus* is apropos—intent "to devour one another with clear conscience,"[8] when they aren't able to divide up equitably their prey: "which is also [the opinion] of Hobbes. In this way we have mankind divided like herds of cattle, each of which has a master, who looks after it in order to devour it"; similar to how "the Greeks confined in the cave of the Cyclops lived peacefully until their turn came to be devoured."[9] Here we are utterly in the realm of Canettian language: power and devouring. It is the act of devouring, according to the dream of the sole survivor, duly noted by Rousseau:

> What is most singular is that the less natural and pressing the needs, the more the passions increase and, what is worse, the power to satisfy them; so that after long periods of prosperity, after having swallowed up many treasures and ruined many men, my hero will end by butchering everything until he is the sole master of the universe. Such in brief is the moral portrait, if not of human life, then at least of the secret pretensions of the heart of every civilized man.[10]

Not only, therefore, does civilization not wipe clean such a state of affairs but civilization itself produces this state through successive postponements of the sacrificial dialectic: from instincts to institutions, from fear to subjection, from imposed servitude to voluntary servitude, as La Boétie had already denounced.[11] First, there were the wealthy who "had no sooner known the pleasure of domination than before long they disdained all others . . . like those ravenous wolves which, on having once tasted human flesh, reject all other food and desire to devour men only"; and then those who "saw the need to be resolved to sacrifice one part of their liberty to preserve the other, just as a wounded man has his arm amputated to save the rest of his body"; and finally that despotic "monster" in which it isn't in the least unfair to recognize the terrifying features of the Leviathan: "in the end everything would be swallowed up by the monster, and the peoples would no longer have leader or laws, but only tyrants."[12]

Once again Rousseau follows all the moves of Hobbesian discourse in order to contest better their internal logic, the productive relation between preservation and sacrifice: a community preserved by sacrifice is for that reason promised to death. It originates in death and to death it returns, not only because the sacrifice always calls forth another sacrifice but because sacrifice as such is the work of death. Sacrifice *to* death, precisely when community should protect from death: "[I]f we are to understand"—here too Rousseau can't help referring to the passage quoted previously from Hobbes—"that it is lawful for the government to sacrifice an innocent man for the good of the multitude, I look upon it as one of the most execrable rules tyranny ever invented, the greatest falsehood that can be advanced, the most dangerous admission that can be made, and a direct contradiction of the fundamental laws of society."[13] What in Hobbes was allowed in so as to safeguard the state is seen in Rousseau exactly as the presupposition of the state's dissolution, insofar as the interest of the few is sacrificed to the many as the interest of the many is sacrificed to the few. Nevertheless, this is what occurs in all societies: "The multitude will always be sacrificed to the few, and the public interest to particular interest. Those specious names, justice and order, will always serve as instruments of violence and as arms of iniquity."[14]

Always [*sempre*]: in this adverb is condensed both Rousseau's agreement with and opposition to Hobbes, his "truth" and his "error." If one has for ages [*da sempre*] been sacrificed, if all historical societies sacrifice and continue to do so, then Hobbes is right in seeking the solution within the sacrificial paradigm. History as such is history of sacrifice in the strong sense that history belongs to it. But the originality of Rousseau's approach is this: history isn't man's only dimension. Rather, history requires a non-historical margin with respect to which it can carve out a space (and also simply if history is to be defined). Here, according to Rousseau, is the blind spot of the Hobbesian system: not the sacrificial characterization of history but its extension to the nonhistorical dimension from which it is born. Hobbes, in other words, doesn't err with regard to content but with respect to time, not only because he attributes features of the civil state to the state of nature (for which Rousseau repeatedly reproaches him) but especially because Hobbes historicizes the ahistorical commencing of history. In a word Hobbes errs because he confuses cause and effect, presupposition and result, origin and elaboration. Neither is the contract originary nor is the *Urszene* that in Freudian fashion precedes him; instead, both are derived from something that isn't temporally definable because it isn't inclusive of time, or at least of that linear and progressive time of history that articulates the different phases of human civilization. What Rousseau challenges in Hobbes isn't the "unsocial" character and indeed decisively conflictual character that Hobbes attributes to the state of nature (as John Locke and Samuel von Pufendork will) but the fact that Hobbes conceives such unsociability already as a social figure, even if it is negative, and for the same reason not truly natural.[15] According to Rousseau, "naturalness," however, isn't to be understood as a peaceful or bellicose modality of relations between men but instead in terms of lack of respect. It is here that the differential perspective is concentrated with regard to the Hobbesian model: the non-relation isn't the product of a civil state that is destructive of the social bond but is what precedes the one and the other—non-state *and* non-society. It is this absolute precedence that subtracts the man of nature from any moral qualification: "Hobbes did not see that that same cause preventing savages from using their reason, as our jurists claim, is what prevents them at the same time from abusing their faculties, as he himself maintains. Hence we could say that savages are not evil precisely because they do not know what it is to be good."[16]

This is the *pointe* of Rousseau's reasoning. Neither the cruel Hobbesian origin nor all the other peaceful origins imagined by philosophers are the true Origin for the same reason that they each give the origin a name, a title, a positive definition. From this perspective, whether such a name be either peace or war, harmony or opposition, changes little: in each case one begins with men and not with the Man, with fact and not law [*diritto*], with history and not logic. In order for this not to be the case, we need to dwell on pure negativity: the state of nature is *nothing other* than non-society, non-state, non-history. As soon as one moves from this negativity to any kind of affirmation, one falls again into the illusion of philosophers, plunging into the flux of social time, while reproducing the historicization of the origin. One thinks of the origin and speaks of its genesis. Paradoxically though, the origin is nameable only beginning from the perspective of history that negates it, just as nature is named only from the side of its necessary denaturalization. As soon as the gaze shifts directly onto that absolute "first," it is lost. It vanishes. It is confused with its "after." Innocence as such isn't to be thematized except by beginning with the angle of vision opened by loss of innocence: from the guilt that distorts and deforms it.

If this is the case; if it is true that the origin is recognizable only in the shade that projects its opposite; if the origin is inhospitable to any further definition than that furnished by its negation in opposition to it, we ought to conclude that the origin coincides with its non-being: there is nothing to be found where the origin is [*all'origine*] except the trace of its withdrawal. Or better: withdrawal is the only modality of origin's being. It is important to note immediately that Rousseau doesn't undertake this extreme move, which the logic of his own discourse pushes. Indeed, he explicitly denies it with all of the contradiction that such a retreat carries with it. In fact, we can say that his entire work (and not simply the two *Discourses* on the origin of inequality and on that of languages) are aimed at defining positively the origin that would take place by lamenting the disappearance of the origin. It is true that on more than one occasion he warns that "it is no light undertaking to separate what is original from what is artificial in the present nature of man, and to have a proper understanding of a state which no longer exists, which perhaps never existed, which probably never will exist." Still, this doesn't prevent him from concluding that "about which it is necessary to have accurate notions in order to judge properly our own present state."[17] Here already in this proposition begins to be delineated that route, that false scent, that pushes Rousseau down the path of irresolvable antinomies. How, for instance, can one have the correct idea of what isn't and has never been if not by giving a factual consistency to a pure, logical presupposition? Certainly, as has often been observed, Rousseau's research into the originary essence of human nature responds to an interest that is largely concentrated on the present, to a critical demand with regard to what exists [*dell'esistente*]. Yet this doesn't find another way of being formulated except in the onto-phenomenological question of the identity of the origin: what is the origin? What is the nature of man? How is his principal essence configured? Such a fundamental interrogation of the foundation appears to Rousseau as the only way of removing the sophist, Hobbesian short-circuit between fact and law [*diritto*], force and merit [*valore*], appearance and reality. Rousseau, however, cannot avoid falling into another form of aporia, that of seeking the only modality of "positive" community precisely in that state that precedes and is alternate to society; that sees men as naturally isolated one from the other. Paradoxically, the community is made possible only by the lack of a relation among its members. Indeed, it is from this lack that the community's features of immediacy, transparency, and innocence that connote it are derived, even before that entire series of successive mediations on which civilization is built, namely, language, power [*po-tere*], money, writing, laws, and so on, pervert and infect it. Before. This temporal element already expresses the imperceptible but decisive slippage from logic to history: in the "first" there cannot but follow an "after" in the form of a necessary degradation. The nexus that joins them together is the "fall": the "first" *falls* in the "after" and in this way degenerates. The accidental, that which happens [*accade*], strikes the origin and pulls the origin outside itself. It grabs hold of the origin and then loses it. This is how history, society, and technology [*tecnica*] are born. Time: death. Time *is* death: the origin of every evil insofar as it superimposed, superseded, and is subsequent to the first origin. Time is the origin's supplemental exteriorization or repetition. Rousseau's condemnation of representation in all its forms, be it theatrical or political, is explained by the element of exteriority implied with regard to the presence of the origin, of the origin as pure presence. Representation cannot represent itself but is always something other. This is how originary presence is already altered, decentered, and separated from what it is. It is condemned to difference and therefore negated in its identity.

This is the logic of Rousseau's discourse. A logic charged with a clear antinomy that places it in continual opposition to its own initial presupposition. Simply shift attention from the general argumentative apparatus to the individual details and we become aware of it.[18] Furthermore, Rousseau never describes the man of nature, and how could he? He describes instead a series of substitutes (above all the Caribbean native) but always with the clear knowledge that similar examples are inadequate with respect to the unreachable Exemplar. Here too the represented origin—so named because it is subject to the doubling enacted by representation—is outside itself; it is secondary with respect to itself. "However important it may be," Rousseau justifies himself, "in order to render sound judgments regarding the natural state of man, to consider him from his origin and to examine him, so to speak, in the first embryo of the species, I will not follow his nature through its successive developments . . . I will suppose him to have been formed from all time as I see him today: walking on two feet, using his hands as we use ours, directing his gaze over all of nature, and measuring with his eyes the vast expanse of the heavens."[19]

Yet this actualization of the first man isn't by any means irrelevant with respect to its natural characterization, if by "nature" we understand, as Rousseau does, something in opposition to everything that is historical-social and technical-artificial. As André Leroi-Gourhan observes, in debate with Rousseau, the reason is that the freeing of the hands and the face from the earth, marking anything but an originary condition, is the result of a long history, a diffuse socialization, and a technical development of man, which rather than being its early author is in fact its belated result.[20] Nothing changes when Rousseau underscores the preinstrumental, indeed almost passive features of those hands: "Natural arms, which are tree branches and stones, were soon found ready to hand," he writes in the second *Discourse*.[21] In *The Origin of Languages* he adds: "No one knew or desired anything other than what was at hand."[22] Yet can a hand be only receptive of something that is spontaneously offered to it? Or is not the same hand *already* an instrument, a means, a technology [*tecnica*] of precisely "manipulation"? Can it be an organ of prehension and not, at the same time, of construction, of work, and of production? Isn't it a sort of natural "prosthesis" and therefore something artificial as well? Here a second origin already seems to absorb the first, but what precisely is an origin that is always secondary if not a non-origin, just as the fall "comprises" creation, and technology, nature? where by technology we ought to understand in an Aristotelian sense exactly that which doesn't possess the principle of its own movement; what doesn't have, in fact, any principle: what is *without origin*.

Something still more intrinsically contradictory may be found in Rousseau's attempt to isolate the man of nature from his social-cultural context. I am speaking of freedom [*libertà*]. On many occasions Rousseau points to freedom as that quality that more than any other distinguishes man from animal and for that reason is most basic to an original human nature. Nevertheless, freedom is also that which, entrusting man to his own destiny, separates him from his own environment, moving him in a direction that cannot be anything other than that of civilization. Thus, man in his essence is free to betray his own essence: this is the inevitable price of freedom. What else does this mean if not that the denaturalization of man is already potentially within the natural origin, that denaturalization is not only the negation of the natural origin but also its necessary conclusion? In other words, that that origin is one with its own downfall, with its loss, with its originary defect? That denaturalization is precisely *nature's* origin, the origin of the end of the origin, in the end the non-origin? It isn't by accident that the natural features in all the examples Rousseau cites are always introduced by an "almost" (as "almost naked"), by an "only" ("armed only with a bow and arrow"), by a "like" or by a conditional verb: zero isn't representable except as an "almost one," one as "almost two," and so forth because of the inexpressible limit that separates as well as unites "already" with "not yet": already *and* not yet history, still *and* no longer nature, according to the ambivalently constitutive logic of the "supplement" that interrupts every knowledge of the origin with its internal deconstruction.[23] This tells us that the origin, cut by its "non," is *also* non-origin, difference from itself and therefore the in/original articulation of that from which it originates.

The same ambivalence that keeps Rousseau's "discovery" of the in/originary still within the mythology of the origin crosses and stretches the figure of community: on one side it is conceived unconditionally as an originary lack, a defect in the origin, a shared [*comune*] not having originated [*inoriginarietà*]; on the other side, intent on a final attempt [*tentativo*]—urge [*tentazione*] to be realized. That such an attempt might be doomed to failure doesn't lessen the force that it exercises with respect to the entire philosophical-political tradition that precedes it. Rousseau's work constitutes the first demand of the community as our own truth, notwithstanding the contradiction that subtracts community from itself. As impossible as it is, the community is necessary. It is our *munus* in the exact sense that we deeply carry responsibility for community. Here then we can distinguish the lines that separate it from the Hobbesian sacrificial mechanism. When Rousseau observes that "when isolated men, however numerous they may be, are subjected one after another to a single person, this seems to me only a case of master and slaves, not of a nation and its leader; they form, if you will, an aggregation, but not an association, for they have neither public property nor a body politic,"[24] he is in fact imputing to Hobbes not only the absence but the violent expulsion of every idea of community, and this at the exact moment and the same measure in which the English philosopher joins together individuals that are naturally in conflict in the great body of the Leviathan. What joins them isn't anything but shared fear. The result that directly follows can only be a shared servitude [*una comune servitù*], the contrary of community. It is this community that is sacrificed on the altar of individual self-preservation. Hobbesian individuals can save their own lives only by putting an end [*mettendo a morte*] to their own shared good, "immunizing themselves" from it. All of the evocations of this good (Liberty, Justice, Equality) that are articulated in Rousseau's work have this contentious objective vis-à-vis immunization, deliver this condemnation of it, and complain of community's absence: the human community is missing from itself. It does nothing other than *delinquere*, in the double sense of the expression.[25] It is what we most need since our existence is completely one with it. There is no existence except in relation to the existence of others: "Our sweetest existence is relative and collective, and our true *self* is not entirely within us."[26] Here too Rousseau's repeated declaration of his own solitude, which he obsessively stresses above all in the final phase of his work, has the tone of a silent revolt against the absence of community. He is alone because there is no community, or better, because all the forms of community that exist are nothing other than the opposite of an authentic community. Solitude protests against such a situation; it is the negative of an absolute need to share, which in Rousseau is manifested by extreme paradox in communication, of its own impossibility of being communicated, which takes place through writing, where writing takes on precisely the features of a "solitude for others," of the "substitute of the human community unrealizable in social reality."[27]

Note, however, that community is unrealizable since Rousseau's communitarian criticism of Hobbesian individualism, as Émile Durkheim observed, in effect remains within the same paradigm: that of the individual fully and perfectly closed.[28] It is true that Rousseau breaks up the decisive nexus between individualism and absolutism that Hobbes had established, but he does so by redefining the state of nature understood now in an even more absolutely individualistic key. Certainly, the Rousseauean man isn't naturally given to conflict as is the Hobbesian man, but only because he never actually faces his equals; or when he encounters them, he moves to separate himself from them as quickly as he can. Seen from this perspective, Rousseau's criticism of Hobbes has nothing in common with that of Locke or Montesquieu. Rousseau doesn't begin, as they do, from the Aristotelian presupposition of man's natural sociability but from the hypothesis of an unsociability even more extreme than that of Hobbes. For Rousseau, men in the state of nature aren't *even* united by war with each other, even if they are otherwise amoral and potentially given to conflict like the Hobbesian wolf-men. It's not happenstance that the sovereignty originated by the Rousseauean contract will be equally and, if possible, more absolute than that of the Leviathan. What is to be underscored, however, is that the underlying motive of a like convergence with the Hobbesian model (and despite all of Rousseau's best efforts at contesting it) isn't of the political but of the philosophical sort. It is born from a conception that makes commensurate the grade of perfection of the individual with the level of self-identification that he reaches with himself. Effectively therefore, the cause and the condition of primitive man's happiness are located in the adherence to what is most proper and intimately essential to him: "Natural man is entirely for himself. He is a numerical unity, the absolute whole which is relative only to itself or its kind."[29] Civil man too is evoked in opposition to such self-appropriation as the only one capable of sheltering man from those contradictions that divide what is and what must remain precisely individual: "I aspire to the moment when, after being delivered from the shackles of the body, I shall be *me* without contradiction or division and shall need only myself in order to be happy."[30]

The constitutively aporetic character of Rousseauean communitarianism lies precisely in such a question, that is, how can this kind of unity enter into contact with the other? How is it possible to derive a philosophy of community from a metaphysics of solitude? Can the absoluteness of the individual closed in on his own existence be "placed in common," and what kind of community would result? Unlike those who see in Rousseau a complementary relation between *"solitude et communauté,"* it seems to me that such an antinomy can't be resolved. The interval, not only lexical but theoretical between presupposition and result, is insurmountable, if the price isn't to be a forcing that gives the Rousseauean community those intolerable features for which Rousseau has been reproached by his severest critics, from Benjamin Constant to Jacob Talmon.[31] The line that Rousseau on more than one occasion is tempted to cross is the one that passes between the demand of community present in the negative in the critical definition of an existing society and its affirmative formulation. Or better: between the "political" determination of the absence of community (community as defect, lack, as boundless debt in relation to the law that prescribes it) and its political realization. Said concisely: beginning with those metaphysical presuppositions, namely, the individual closed in on his own absoluteness, the political formulation of community in Rousseau inevitably drifts toward a possible totalitarianism. Naturally, I am not referring to the specific category of "totalitarianism," which grows out of the experiences of the last century and to which the category is indissolubly linked. First, because of the great ease in demonstrating how anxious Rousseau was to protect the individual from every abuse of state power, the individual who remains the subject as much as he is a citizen but not as a man, according to the distinction between public and private that twentieth-century totalitarianism will attempt to suppress. And second, thanks to the fact that Rousseau adopts the concept of "general will" as an automatic corrective against any authoritarian temptation with regard to the individual [*singolo*]. Being integral to it, the individual is guaranteed by the fact that every order of the general will was issued by himself.

Yet isn't this automatism, that is, the presupposed identity of every one with everyone else and all with every one, exactly the totalizing mechanism in which the many are reduced into the one?[32] Wasn't it precisely this prejudicial identification that trips the sacrificial wire, the "trap" of the Hobbesian authorization? How else are we to understand, if not in objectively sacrificial terms, the well-known passage in which Rousseau prescribes "the total alienation to the whole community of each associate with all his rights," so that "in return each member becomes an indivisible part of the whole"?[33] Or for that matter another passage in Rousseau, according to which "he who dares undertake to give institutions to a nation ought to feel himself capable, as it were, of changing human nature; of transforming every individual, who in himself is a complete and independent whole, into part of a greater whole, from which he receives in some manner his life and his being?"[34] Where the proto-totalitarian risk in Rousseau seems most evident isn't in the juxtaposition of the communitarian model to that of the individual but in their reciprocal interpenetration that awards to the community the profile of the isolated and self-sufficient individual. And so: the route that takes us from the individual one to the one collective must flow through the waters of organicism [*alveo organicistico*]. It is as if both the individual and the community are unable to escape from themselves that they do not know how to welcome or receive the one without absorbing and incorporating it without making it a part of themselves. What in fact is Clarens if not an absolutely individual community, perfectly insular, and fully self-sufficient? "In an imaginative flight," writes Jean Starobinski apropos of Rousseau, "he transposes the ideal of the self-sufficient ego into a myth of the self-sufficient community."[35] Every time that this ideal takes form in a collective reality, be it small country, city, town festival, the demand that torments Rousseau for community is reversed into the myth of community. It is a myth of a community that is transparent to itself, in which every one communicates with the other one's own communitarian essence, without mediation, filter, or sign to interrupt the reciprocal fusion of consciousnesses. There is no distance, discontinuity, or difference with regard to another that is no longer other, because the other too is an integral part of the one. Indeed, it is already the one that loses itself (and finds itself) in its own *proper* alterity.

Rousseau seems to recognize a similar risk when he holds off transposing this "community of the heart" into a political community. It's important that we too refrain from reading *The Social Contract* as the political translation of the community of Clarens. Certainly, that community prefigured in the *Contract* is a democracy of the identity that excludes any distinction between the governed and those that govern, between the legislative and the executive, and between the prince and the sovereign. Yet it is for this reason that community is declared to be unrealizable except for a "people of gods." "Taking the term in its strict sense, there never has existed, and never will exist any true democracy."[36] If it were to exist, it could become the faithful realization of its opposite. This is the critical distance that the author takes up with regard to his stated intention to reclaim the Rousseauean community from its incipient mythical drift, but at the price of an antinomy that doesn't allow itself to be reconciled: the community is both impossible and necessary. Necessary and impossible. Not only is it given as a defect (it never is fully realized) but community is defective, in the specific sense that what is held in common is precisely *that* defect, *that* default, *that* debt, or also our mortal finitude, as Rousseau himself anticipated in an unforgettable passage from *Emile*: "Men are not naturally kings, or lords, or courtiers, or rich men. All are born naked and poor; all are subject to the miseries of life, to sorrows, ills, needs, and pains of every kind. Finally, all are condemned to death. This is what truly belongs to man. This is what no mortal is exempt from."[37]

Excursus on Rousseau

A question, however, requires a more thorough discussion. It has been said that Rousseau is the first modern thinker of community as well as the first to have constructed a myth of community, the first to think community together with and within its myth in a knot that isn't easy to untie. In what sense? Why in Rousseau is the community always on the point of slipping into the myth of community? An answer, indeed a double response, which enjoys a persuasive simplicity, has for some time been formulated and repeated under various guises. Rousseau mythologizes the community, they say, because he folds it into the absolute domination of the totality over the single elements that are incorporated therein without any remainder, parts that ought to compose it. This is the thesis I mentioned in the preceding pages of a Rousseauean "totalitarianism" that Talmon himself and his followers put forward, who come to see in Rousseau's critique of the sacrificial paradigm in Hobbes a new and more intense community of sacrifice.[38] This is a suggestive reading, especially as it relates to the undeniable tendency that is expressed in particular in those pedagogical writings in which Rousseau comes to theorize that "there is no subjection so perfect as that which keeps the appearance of freedom."[39]

This interpretation, which sees the perversion of the thought of community in the ascendancy of the whole over the part, is contrasted with another interpretation that infers the same perversion from the autonomization of the part vis-à-vis the whole (though clearly it mirrors it as well). Seen from this perspective, Rousseau is the philosopher of the part and not the whole, of partiality as belonging to limited and shared spaces: the small homelands [*patrie*] that break apart the universal idea of community into many small, unified micro-communities, opposed by definition to each other by ethnic, linguistic, and cultural identity, based on a perspective that today is urged forward again by those *communitarians* who, not by accident, find in Rousseau the most relevant theoretical forerunner.[40] Although we could obviously cite other texts, the principal text that authorizes this kind of reading is the one in which Rousseau argues against an abstract cosmopolitanism that dispenses with "having to love his neighbors."[41] Looking at it from the side of the "whole" or the "part," the Rousseauean community appears to be oriented toward an inevitable authoritarian tendency, which occurs paradoxically to the degree in which Rousseau rejects the absolute separation between "public" and "private" in Hobbes. Repairing that fracture that prevented Hobbes and, in general, all of modern political philosophy from thinking any thought of the community, Rousseau ends up deactivating that thought of community in its own myth. He abandons the absolute individualism that safeguarded the *foro interno* from the violence practiced by public power without moving beyond it in a different paradigm. He remains stuck midway: neither ancient individualism nor new universalism, or better, the one in the other: the one reversed and both negated and made stronger in the other. An individual universalized, which is the general will, and a universal individualized, which are small homelands [le piccole *patrie*]. It is as if the critique of absolutism were continually on the point of giving way to a new mythology of the absolute, of the whole and of the part, of the whole as part and of the part *as* the whole.

Still, our perspective remains too far removed from the question of community. To move forward in the reconstruction of this closely tied knot between thought and the myth of community requires a retreat of sorts in perspective from that "philosophy of existence," to appropriate the title of that exceptional essay by Pierre Burgelin, that is found more in the autobiographical and narratives texts than in the political and pedagogical ones.[42] Let's begin with a general formulation that is far too clear-cut: Rousseau is the first thinker of community because he presupposes the subject in its existence and not in thought. Here is the real breaking point with modern philosophy initiated by Descartes, even if Rousseau does take on again formally the same language. Existing [*l'esistere*] is a truth of the heart, of feeling, of passion, of suffering more than it is of the mind: "In the first place, I know that I exist, and have senses whereby I am affected.

This is a truth so striking that I am compelled to acquiesce in it . . . To exist is, with us, to be sensible. Our sensibility is incontestably prior to our intelligence, and we were possessed of sentiment before we formed ideas."[43] The opposition of sensation [*sentimento*] and idea cuts across Rousseau's entire work, but, and this is what matters, it is always linked to the claim that existence is originary with respect to any other condition from which it is derived, and it is in some way always reductive when not corruptive: "To live is not to breathe; it is to act; it is to make use of our organs, our senses, our faculties, of all the parts of ourselves, which give us the sentiment of our existence."[44] The sensation of existence coincides, therefore, with the dimension of life, not, note, in the sense of its continuation but in that of its intensity. In fact, Rousseau's text is explicitly intended to dispute those philosophies of the individual preservation, because they seal it off in a mechanism intent on its material continuation:

[H]e who by dint of concentrating all his affections within himself hath arrived at the pitch of having no regard for any one else, is no longer capable of such transports. His frozen heart never flutters with joy; no sympathetic tenderness brings the tears into his eyes; he is incapable of enjoyment. The unhappy wretch is void of sensibility; he is already dead.[45]

It is because such a wretch is concentrated on the self-preserving attempt to live more that he winds up living less; indeed he doesn't even live since "time spent in preserving life, lost for use, must be subtracted from it."[46] His life passes by *imperceptibly*, outside that *common, shared feeling* [*sentire comune*] that is existence.

Our attention is brought to bear on "common." What kills life, separating it from existence, is its purely self-referential character, or better, its "absolute" quality, the lack of relation with a larger and better-articulated totality of the individual subject. If individuality is the modality of life protected from death that is deferred, the community is the modality of vital existence, of life as pure existence. We can add something else: the community isn't other from existence, if existence (to the degree it is *ex-sistentia*) is a stretching out [*protendersi*] of the individual's life outside itself, a remaining [*stare*] beyond itself, a substance that continually exceeds its own proper site. Rousseau of course doesn't express it in these terms, but the link between community and existence, existence as a specific modality of the "common," emerges clearly in more than one text: "He is the only created being here below to join . . . the sentiment of a general existence [*existence commune*] to that of the individual."[47] A passage from the "Geneva Manuscript" is even more explicit:

Certainly the term *human race* offers to the mind only a purely collective idea which assumes no real union among the individuals who constitute it. Let us add to it, if you wish this Supposition, and conceive of the human race as a moral person having—along with a feeling of common existence which gives it individuality and constitutes it as one—a universal motivation which makes each part act for an end that is general and relative to the whole. Let us conceive that this common feeling is humanity, and that natural Law is the active principle of the entire machine.[48]

The text I've just cited is significant not only because it carries the thought of community to the extreme limit as the sense of existence, *coexistence* as a shared consenting, but because it reveals in the same set of expressions the contemporaneous slippage into myth. The junction is constituted by the transition in the concept of existence from community to individuality and unity. This is exactly how Rousseau's autobiographical writing (though not only there) reconstitutes the individual subject, entrusting existence to him, that existence that ought to have outstripped him [*eccederlo*], pushing him toward the other, deflecting him toward an outside that is irreducible to the solidity of the *ego*. It is as if the *ex* of existence were folded upon itself in order to recover a unity within that is ever more properly its own. Furthermore, the decisive relation is in fact the one between existence and "ownership" [*proprietà*]. Existence, as such, is shared in common, but this "common" is also always ownership, what is most *properly* owned by him who experiences [*sente*] his own existence: the *subiectum* as what cannot allow anything in that isn't properly of the substance that substantiates it.

It is here that we find one of the reasons for Rousseau's continuing exhortation to return to oneself, not to lose oneself, to find oneself again, all of which functions as a counterpoint to the same communitarian texts I referred to earlier. Indeed, it constitutes a unity so close to its proper essence [*il proprio essere*] as to protect it from any risk of alienation, exteriorization, or estrangement. The I, the ego, the *moi* must not leave anything of itself outside; it must fill every space that is capable of undermining the fullness of its own existence; block every escape toward the other that doesn't include a return even more decisive to the *proprium*: "I am whole, complete where I am," writes Rousseau in 1767 to Mirabeau: "*in* me, *with* me, *for* me."[49] From this side of things, which I repeat coexists in contradiction to the first, the same critique of abstract thought comes to coincide with the rejection of the split of the ego in the mirror of its own reflection. Where the reflection divides, feeling [*sentimento*] unifies, which is to say reunifies with itself. Feeling restores its own unity when threatened or lost through that exiting from itself, which civilization and history itself constitute generally: "We no longer exist where we are; we only exist where we are not . . . O man, draw up your existence within yourself, and you will no longer be miserable."[50]

One can see the thing in question in relation to temporality. It is seen as the space of existence coincides with that of life but not with its time. The difference isn't immediately obvious, nor is it clearly in evidence. It is the question of an extremely slight and yet decisive rotation of the angle of view that we might express thusly: existence is life held [*fermata*] in the instance of its pure presence. Life is existence subjected to the continuity of time, unfolded in duration, and so inclusive of, therefore, its necessary unity: the unity of a life and of that retrospective relation to the past as well as the perspective on the future that, consolidating existence with respect to its constitutive fragility, reinforces it at the same time (though in another sense removes or deprives it of existence). If we were to hazard a risky formula, life is *the interiority of the exteriority of existence.* For this reason life is the proof of existence, of life's consolidation and its negation.

Let's return to Rousseau. He always begins by critiquing any stance that sacrifices the present to the past and to the future. Past and future are evil [*male*] because, altering the presence of the present, they carry presence outside itself. Binding existence to blackmail of desire as well as to abduction of memory, past and future move presence from the level of being to that of having, or wanting, or, for that matter, of representing. They make simple presence the representation of the past or the prefiguration (which is still a representation) of the future. Thus, they double presence and re-present it, annulling presence insofar as it is pure presence. Nevertheless, without such a backward and forward expansion, pure presence would remain too fragile, literally inconsistent as to make itself come alive [*farsi vita*]; to *persist* [*permanere*] in life; to locate and determine, in the pronoun *I*, the mobile and transient waves of existence. In other words, in order to survive its own constitutive inconsistency, presence needs to be made "present to" itself as a subject: the subjective consciousness of existing that moves beyond an unreflecting existence by duplicating it. How? Through that form of reconstructing the self that is constituted by memory. So while the boy is "whole in present being, and enjoying a fullness of life which seems to want to extend itself beyond him,"[51] "memory extends the sentiment of identity to all the moments of his existence; he becomes truly one, the same."[52] Memory unifies and destroys the multiplicity of existence. It makes the other the same; it makes the outside inside; the many, one. While it strengthens existence, memory subtracts its originary void of essence from existence, filling it up with subjective substance. The subject, in this sense, is stronger than the time that traverses and decenters him. Rather than time exteriorizing the subject, it is the subject that interiorizes time. The subject wants to be present for everything that happens; such a wanting reinforces the subject ontologically, so as to find another—one-self—within but also beyond the events that befall the subject. In other words, to have control over what occurs by chance [*accidente*], which is in what the subject's existence consists, including that final chance event [*accidente*] that is death:

Everything I see is an extension of my being, and nothing divides it; it resides in all that surrounds me, no portion of it remains far from me; there is nothing left for my imagination to do, there is nothing for me to desire; to feel and to enjoy are to me one and the same thing; I live at once in all those I love, I am sated with happiness and life: O death, come when thou wilt! I have no more fear of thee, I have lived, I have anticipated thee, there are no new sentiments for me to experience, there is nothing more of which thou canst cheat me.[53]

This state is precisely "ecstatic"—*extatique*—here too in the double sense of being internal and external that defines the term. It isn't an accident that when discussing Rousseau, one speaks both of a "cosmic ecstasy" and an "ecstasy of ego" to signal the two opposing movements of expansion and contraction that mark the phenomenology of existence.[54] The point on which our attention ought to be concentrated, however, in direct relation to the question of community is not their opposition but rather their complementarity and simultaneity. This is so much the case that perhaps we ought to speak of a singular movement that expands and contracts at the same time, and as such is both diffusive and reductive in the specific sense that the expansion occurs through contraction, and vice versa, according to that undetectable passage, which, in the final analysis, is recognized the thought and myth of community in the same form. If by "community" one understands the exteriorization of existence, its mytholigization can be referred to as the interiorization of this exteriority. George Poulet reads this dialectic through the metaphor of the "circle" and "the center."[55] On the one hand, the center always tends to step outside itself, pushing its own rays to the extreme limits of circumference. It is attracted by what is exterior to it to the point that it must be divided from itself. When this exterior isn't nature (with which the Rousseauean ego is irresistibly pushed to identify itself) but another, and indeed, *the others* inasmuch as they are other, then can the word *community* be employed. The ego [*io*], as we have already seen, cannot live outside the community. Nor does the ego and perhaps especially, when, disappointed, live in isolation because that isolation expresses in a reversed form the irreducible need for sharing [*condivisione*]. "No," Rousseau writes in the "Seventh Walk," "nothing personal, nothing which concerns my body can truly occupy my soul. I never meditate, I never dream more deliciously than when I forget myself. I feel ecstasies and inexpressible raptures in blending, so to speak, into the system of beings and in making myself one with the whole of nature."[56] His ego coincides with the impulse to be reflected outside itself: "to be shared" with the other in the profound sense of sharing the other's alterity. His existence, from this point of view, isn't anything except the irrepressible radiating and spilling out in what doesn't belong to his existence, but of which it nevertheless is a part. This is the reason that Rousseau cannot bring himself to hate even those whom he believes are persecuting him. The impossibility of doing so isn't properly ethical but essentially ontological. How can one hate someone, even one's worst enemy, when each participates in what is constitutively shared [*comune*]? "In short, I love myself too much to be able to hate anyone whatever. That would be to constrict or repress my existence, and I would rather extend it over the whole universe."[57] After all, Rousseau's works don't do anything except reintroduce in different contexts and languages this final tendency or direction to move to the extreme. Existence tends toward its own extreme until existence is lost in its other. The center makes itself completely one with its ultimate circumference.

But, and here is the other side of the coin, the circle makes itself one with its opposite. The center is in the circumference in the same measure and through the same modalities with which the circumference is always in the center. The circumference is produced by the center and turned toward the center. The object—alterity—in which the subject is given expression, is always *its* object, as Karl Barth has observed: "It is thus that Rousseau can still say that he feels as if he were *brulant d'amour sans objet*. He yearns for a kind of happiness *sans en savoir démeler l'objet*. He thinks it is again the limitation imposed upon him to the feelings of his own heart which alone enables him to taste the sweetness of existence."[58] And this, one notes well, not in opposition to but because of what has been said. Not because his *âme expansive* isn't continually involved in radiating into the furthest periphery until it loses itself there, but because it is that; because it is the subject of this operation and therefore subject of its own loss. After all, what is a "proper" loss if not what is dearest to him who *feels* himself lost? "The more sensitive a soul a contemplator has," Rousseau writes some pages later with regard to the spectacle of nature, "the more he gives himself up to the ecstasies this harmony arouses in him. A sweet and deep reverie takes possession of his senses then, and through a delicious intoxication he loses himself in the immensity of this beautiful system with which he *feels* himself one."[59] When Rousseau describes the feeling of pity, of compassion for the other as a constitutive element of our nature, he does so in a way that directly uncovers the primacy of the ego with respect to what it also receives, but with a view to a more interior regrouping that is assembled. "But when the strength of an expansive soul makes me identify myself with my fellow, and I feel that I am, so to speak, in him, it is in order not to suffer that I do not want him to suffer. I am interested in him for love of myself, and the reason for the precept is in nature itself, which inspires in me the desire of my well-being in whatever place I feel my existence."[60] Here the movement of existence from a modification of the self to the identification of the other is made completely explicit. From this we ought to conclude that the thought of community is born within the terms of its own closure. Why then don't we also say that such a closure always holds in check the first thought of community?

3

Law

The contradiction in which Rousseau's thought is entangled is the very same object of Kant's philosophy. Eric Weil's statement that "one needs Kant in order to think Rousseau" could easily be interpreted this way, namely, that all of Kant's works are completely dedicated to attempting to bring to thought the community that Rousseau leaves exposed to the intrusiveness of myth.[1] So Kant in an important passage answers his predecessor when he recognizes in Rousseau the merit of having brought him back from a solitary individual search to a larger interest for the world held in common.[2] Not because there is anything more important than truth—a friend, one's fellow men, one's neighbor—but rather because truth isn't thinkable apart from the question of community. Kant says so explicitly: "But how much and how accurately would we *think* if we did not think, so to speak, in community with others to whom we *communicate* our thoughts and who communicate their thoughts to us!"[3] We can't think truth outside the context of community because community forms, more than the object of thought; thought's very own foundation: we are of this world even before ourselves. It is this implicit presupposition of Rousseau that Kant will be fully conscious of, that is, the constitutively communitarian characteristic of thought. In its broadest meaning of a relation among human beings, the community isn't just one of any number of possible contents of philosophy, nor is it a problem of philosophy, but rather community is the very form of thought, since thought—even the most original or singular thought—doesn't have a sense apart from the communal horizon in which it is situated: "But does one demand that a cognition concerning all men surpass common understanding and be disclosed to others only by philosophers? . . . and that in respect of the essential ends of human nature the highest philosophy can accomplish no more than the guidance with which it has endowed the commonest understanding?"[4] Yet, if the problem of community forms the area of contact and comparison between the two philosophers, what is the conceptual path that they both travel? What is the category that introduces and defines that path? The first response originates with Hegel and concerns the formalism of the will, or better, of that unconditionality of "*the free will which wills the free will.*"[5] Without lingering over Hegel's critique of Kant, let's dwell on the hermeneutic effects that this definition produces in its relation to Rousseau. In a word, what links the two philosophers is the primacy of will, even if it is articulated differently. Kant remains within a Rousseauean semantics: the Kantian categorical imperative here is nothing other than the interiorization of Rousseau's principle of the freedom of willing [*volere*]. A different reading, which is explicitly neo-Kantian, reacts to this first interpretation, which we'll call philo-Rousseauean, now reversing literally the hierarchy between the two authors. According to Ernst Cassirer, who is its most authoritative exponent, the relation no longer concerns the preeminence of the will but that of law. "Rousseau's ethics is not an ethics of feeling but the most categorical form of a pure ethics of obligation (*Gesetz-Ethik*) that was established before Kant."[6] In this case it isn't Kant who is crushed into Rousseau, but Rousseau who is projected toward Kant.

Is such a move really legitimate? Don't we risk losing precisely what we were intent on finding, namely, the line separating the two philosophers? Of course, Cassirer insists on those passages in Rousseau that exalt the law as the necessary condition of a life beginning with that well-known passage of the *Social Contract* in which Rousseau evokes "civil state moral freedom, which alone enables man to be truly master of himself; for the impulse of mere appetite is slavery, while obedience to a self-prescribed law is freedom."[7] Essentially we're speaking of a connection between the law and freedom that returns especially in Rousseau's *Dissertation on Political Economy*. There he notes that "it is to the law alone that men are indebted for justice and liberty."[8] It is precisely in this text, nonetheless, that the inclusion of freedom within the sphere of the law (which is Kantian) is balanced and in a certain sense contradicted by a corresponding inclusion of the same law in that of the general will, which is not only shaped by the legislator but also referred to as its same "source."[9]

The question is entirely relevant because it is one that defines the relation between Kant and Rousseau, by which I mean characterizes and delimits it. Both link law and will together in a knot that moves beyond every kind of psychological or utilitarian conception of ethics. Both do so thanks to the medium of freedom. On the one hand, Rousseau has the law originate in a will free of any form of external conditioning of its full deployment; on the other hand, Kant submits the will to a law that in some way calls forth the same freedom. But in that case, to whom does freedom belong: to will or to the law? Who or what is the subject of freedom, and what does it mean to be a subject of freedom? As we will shortly discover, these are all questions that profoundly belong to how we want to think community. For now let's simply say that while Rousseau assigns the role of subject to will—it is the will that, when seen collectively, "makes" the law—Kant sees in the law the transcendental border within which the will itself is constituted.[10] The principal consequence of this logical displacement is the opening of a gap within will. Unlike in Rousseau, the will in Kant is no longer itself; it is no longer absolute, in the sense that it depends transcendentally on something that both comes before and comes after, cutting it like a razor's edge. It is this difference within will that Kant permits, which pulls the community away from a pending relapse into myth, or as I noted earlier, that pushes what remained unexamined in the thought of community into the light. Isn't the self-identification of will with its very own object, and the identification of all the subjects in a same willing, what pushes Rousseau's community into a mythological loop from which it can escape only by taking on a contradiction? Moreover, wasn't it too much immanence or too much transparency that sets community on the road to its totalitarian destination, which an interpretation inspired by liberalism couldn't wait to roundly criticize?

The Kantian semantics of the law operates to block this elaboration [*declinazione*] or tendency [*inclinazione*]. It's the law and not the will that is at the origin of community, so much so that one could even say that the community is identical to the law: to the law *of the community*, in the dual sense of the genitive case. The law establishes the community, which in turn constitutes those areas in which the law is applicable. The law is an ordering of things in the sense that it is the *nexus*, the *logos*, the *Ur-form*, that holds them together. It is the foremost gift of world as the "common place" of men: the *Es gibt*, the original giving of itself in which what is diverse appears and exists in relation with that which is other from itself.[11] Now, however, a preliminary question demands our attention. What does the phrase *Es gibt* mean? What is the "material" of the relation? What kind of content do these diverse elements have in common? Here we really should avoid an excessively optimistic reading of the text, one that relates both to the former one I gave of Rousseau, as well as any reading that presumes some kind of idealistic affiliation of Kant. Indeed, Kant is at his most acerbic when he responds to both possible readings. His answer is *Es gibt Böse* [there is evil]. That which is given is, above all else, evil [*male*]. It is the most common way of relating different elements to each other. We could even say the following: the principal reason for the need for having laws is that evil exists in all relations between men and that men relate to each other thanks to this language of evil. In the same way that without the law we wouldn't be able to perceive evil, so too without the possibility of evil there would be no need to have laws. We have here a radical development with respect both to the extralegal relation of be- ing able to be killed by everyone else (which is the Hobbesian argument) and as the non-relation of the state of nature in Rousseau. For Kant the relation between men is never separated from the possibility of doing evil. Yet that doesn't mean the presence of the law is somehow withdrawn but rather that the law entails the presence of evil. When Kant adopts the celebrated metaphor of the *legno torto* in *What Is Enlightenment?*—that is, that the law must and at the same time can never completely remedy the wrong—the reference is to this dialectic: on the one side, the "guilt" that it is given to us beforehand, which we cannot say no to because it is so inti- mately connected to our nature. On the other hand, this destiny becomes visible only by contrasting it with the law. This is the decisive line that separates Kant from Rousseau: the law doesn't dictate a return to nature because human nature contains within it a seed that is the exact opposite of the law. That is the reason why Kant never thought the community in Hegel-Marxian terms as a reappropriation on the part of man of his own essence, because that essence is configured from the outset as a debt, as a lack, as a *negativum* not produced by history and which therefore it cannot somehow remedy. Indeed, history can't even lay hold of this *negativum* since history itself is always already preceded by it. In this sense, we can't say that the origin (here human nature) has declined over the course of history, but if anything that history itself has fallen, plunging through the cracks of the origin.

Kant poses the question in his *Conjectures on the Beginning of Human History* where, appearing to follow Rousseau's genealogy in all its twists and turns, in the end he reverses direction. The point of departure the two philosophers share vis-à-vis ancient theodicy will be found in giving to man the responsibility for evil that before had been attributed to God, but with the difference that Rousseau comes up against the logical difficulty of making such an attribution and then assumes the original goodness of human nature. I don't think we can resolve the problem as Cassirer does by distinguishing between the single person [*uomo*] who is innocent and society that in its totality is guilty because what emerges as problematic (and indeed as aporetic) from Kant's point of view is precisely this distinction.[12] Does man exist prior to the formation of society? What is he really? Once again the question of the origin appears and the myth in which Rousseau envelops it. Kant will admit that, contrary to what is generally believed, Rousseau thinks that a return to a state of original purity is impossible, but that this impossibility is to be inferred not only from a sweeping consideration that one cannot run history backward but, above all, based on that fundamental consideration that any kind of similar origin doesn't exist as such. We find Kant both agreeing and opposing Rousseau. When he says that man is not "entitled to ascribe his own misdemeanors to an original crime committed by his earliest ancestors" but rather "has every justification for acknowledging the action of his first ancestors as his own, and that he should hold himself wholly responsible for all the evils which spring from the misuse of his reason; for he is quite capable of realizing that, in the same circumstances, he would have behaved in exactly the same way," he is in fact unsettling Rousseau's narrative of the "fall" as something that follows in succession and in opposition to the purity of the origin.[13] This is where Kant thinks beyond Rousseau: at the origin of man there is that freedom, which already carries within it the possibility of evil: "Thus, the history of *nature* begins with goodness, for it is the work of God; but the history of freedom begins with evil, for it is the *work of man*."[14]

Yet this "precedence" of evil is anything but simple: in no way does it appear to be a form of predetermination. From the outset evil marks human nature only because it is inextricably joined to our freedom. But if that's true, then are we inescapably led to do evil since it is part and parcel of the same freedom? How is this freedom to be reconciled with the naturalness of evil? This is the question that Kant takes up in *Religion Within the Limits of Reason Alone* by using a modality of logic that pushes the deconstruction of Rousseau's myth of the origin to its ultimate limits. Kant opens with a definition that is also a distinction, almost as if to signal that the origin cannot be defined except through the otherness that separates it from itself: "An origin (a first origin) . . . can be considered either as an *origin in reason* or as an *origin in time*. In the former sense, regard is had only to the *existence* of the effect; in the latter, to its *occurrence*, and hence it is related as an event to its *first cause in time*."[15] Such a marked duplication allows Kant to make compatible the principle of the naturalness of evil with that of absolute freedom. We can think them together because they originate together. It's true that evil, being innate, exists [*sta*] before the act that brings it into being. Yet its preexisting is to be read according to a criterion that is rational but not temporal. In order to avoid contradicting the principle of freedom, with freedom inasmuch as it is an origin, we also need to think the principle of evil, not as a decisively natural impulse but rather as the maxim, in this case of the worst sort, that free will gives itself. Free will, or freedom, thus becomes the same principle by which and from which, simultaneously, freedom itself originates: the origin of its own origin, an origin that is (in)original, having originated from that which originates:

But since the ultimate ground of the adoption of our maxims, which must itself lie in free choice, cannot be a fact revealed in experience, it follows the good or evil in man (as the ultimate subjective ground of the adoption of this or that maxim with reference to the moral law) is termed innate only in *this* sense, that it is posited as the ground antecedent to every use of freedom in experience (in earliest youth as far back as birth) and is thus conceived of as present in man at birth—though birth need not be the cause of it.[16]

On the one hand, Kant's discourse, as it slowly moves forward, multiplies its own antinomies, but rather than hiding or finessing them, makes them even more obvious. The beginning [*principio*] doesn't coincide with its commencing, the cause with birth, the foundation with its starting [*inizio*]. The origin is always outside itself: it comes before and follows another origin that is nevertheless co-present with it. Evil is innate and nevertheless is to be completely ascribed to our free choice. It is freely innate and necessarily free. Neither of the two points of view can be sacrificed to the other. Nor can they be superimposed over each other as in the biblical story that would have sin appear as that which remains after an initial moment of innocence (thereby confusing a temporal sequence with a causal one), caused, namely, by an entity that is outside human nature. The result is to lose, together with the assumption of guilt, that of freedom to which it is logically connected.

On the other hand, if freedom originates in guilt, how can it be that guilt derives from freedom? The contradiction can't be resolved: the only thing that Kant can do is openly recognize that the origin is impenetrable: both that temporal origin, which is multiplied by the presence of beginnings that inhabit it and then make it collapse, and that rational origin, since it becomes necessary to imagine a good origin that can be logically opposed to it (this so that a product of our free will can be declared evil). This is how that tendency to do evil that is innate within us requires at least (if we are to see it as such) the possibility of an inclination to do good that can be corrupted:

> Evil could have sprung only from the morally evil (not from mere limitations in our nature); and yet the original predisposition (which no one other than man himself could have corrupted, if he is to be held responsible for this corruption) is a predisposition to good; there is then for us no conceivable ground from which the moral evil in us could originally have come.[17]

We're in a tight spot with the "transitional phrase" that places us on an ethical footing with regard to that law that both explains and complicates the constitutively aporetic dialectic between freedom and evil. It's really the final and strongest blow against the presumed solidity of the origin. If freedom is defined only starting from the possibility of evil that is present in it, evil in turn can be recognized and opposed only according to a law that has to precede it as an arch-origin that comes before its own quality of being original [*originarietà*] (its own innateness). And yet it is synchronous with it, based on the principle of co-beginnings, which infinitely reproducing the origin, break down every presumption of unity from within. It is the paradox that informs all of *Critique of Practical Reason* and is to be set off from what Kant states in more traditional fashion in *The Metaphysics of Morals.*[18] Whereas in the latter Kant tries again to deduce transcendental-ly the ethical principle from freedom of will, in the former he upends the proceedings, moving free will after the primary "fact" of the law. That the law is precisely a *Faktum* that cannot be theoretically inferred means that it isn't to be derived from any criterion that precedes it nor from the dis-tinction between good and evil, which far from establishing the law, now is derived from it.[19] The law is, in point of fact, the only measure that can de-termine whether a given action, or more simply a principle, is good or bad. Thus, law has to logically come before freedom since such an action or principle originates precisely in the law. Therefore, when we ask ourselves, "whence *begins* our *knowledge* of the unconditionally practical, whether it is from freedom or from the practical law?" we need to agree that it is "the moral law, of which we become directly conscious (as soon as we trace for ourselves maxims of the will), that first presents itself to us and leads directly to the concept of freedom."[20] Once again, however, this doesn't mean that the law imposes its will on freedom. Furthermore, Kant himself doesn't fail to highlight more than once that "the moral law expresses noth-ing else than the autonomy of the pure practical reason; that is, freedom; and this is itself the formal condition of all maxims, and on this condition only can they agree with the supreme practical law."[21] Thus, it is the moral law that leads us first to the concept of freedom, but freedom is the formal condition of moral law. We are close to that "vicious circle," one Kant ac-knowledged in *Groundwork*, between the two related concepts, neither of which can be "used to explain the other or to furnish the ground for it."[22] The only way of getting to the heart of the relation without sundering it completely lies in distinguishing two distinct levels, first the epistemic and second the ontic that determine two different standards of precedence: the first, a *ratio cognoscendi*, according to which the law spells out the meaning of freedom; and another, *ratio essendi*, which would have freedom be an-tecedent to the law. The answer that Kant himself saw as more elemental lies though in the fact that freedom concerns a being, that is, man, who simultaneously belongs to two orders: the intelligible order of ends and the sensible order of productive causes. Thus, where in the first, freedom and moral law have to coincide on the basis of the shared principle of reason, in the second they must undoubtedly move apart. It is in this second sense that the concept of freedom plainly contradicts that of the law, to which it would otherwise correspond. It is as if a passage were to be opened in freedom, or that a dark side of freedom were manifested that stops it from claiming to be the conscience of the law and which instead forces a disavowal on the part of law. Certainly, such a negation is a way for freedom to be exercised, but it is precisely the way in which freedom in its being exercised destroys itself.

The political is organized so as to contain this power [*potenza*] of destruction within acceptable limits. Limit, yes, but not doing away with since not only does the political carry the trace of such a power within but also, in a certain sense, the political can be said to be derived from just such a power. For this reason all of the attempts to trace the origin of politics back to the blind spot when power becomes right [*diritto*], decision becomes a norm, and force becomes reason are bound to fall prey to that nothingness from which the political would like to free itself. Kant's polemical reference to Rousseau is obvious: rather than presupposing an original contract that can provide a juridical foundation to power, Kant instead makes the contract the result of an interplay of forces that power limits itself to legitimating a posteriori:

> Since therefore there must come into existence, over and above the variety of the particular will of all, such a uniting cause of a civil society in order to bring forth a common will—something which no one of all of them do—the *execution* of the idea [of eternal peace] in practice and the beginning of a lawful state cannot be counted upon except by *force* upon the compulsion of which the public law is afterward based.[23]

That this kind of reflection is part of an international project for "perpetual peace" in which is expressed more than anywhere else the Enlightenment spirit speaks volumes about the limits the thinking of an effective political community comes up against. Notwithstanding all the reasons that make a project of perpetual peace necessary, such a possibility remains thoroughly blocked by the same law that sets it out. If mankind is united by the universal form that brings men together, they are irreparably separated by the material interests of which they are the content, so that their sociability is balanced and contradicted by an overpowering unsociability. For this reason the community cannot become a reality or a concept; it needs to remain only an idea of reason, an utterly unreachable destination. The Kantian statement, "the sublime, yet never wholly attainable idea of an ethical commonwealth dwindles markedly under men's hands," is a powerful rejoinder to every dream or attempt to translate ethics immediately into politics, and vice versa.[24] Politics cannot be thought in the light of the good, just as practice is different from theory. It's true that the ethical community could, if we're speaking purely hypothetically, "exist in the midst of a political commonwealth"; but the political community can't force citizens to be a part of the ethical community, except by risking the destruction of both.[25] Certainly, Kant goes on, it would be nice to imagine the two together, but it's foolhardy to suggest anything of the sort. Ethical formulations can't be joined to political ones except by using weak phrases such as "as if." But between the political and the ethical a gaping abyss opens. The relation between them remains purely analogic: it can be expressed through symbols, signs, emblems (for instance, as enthusiasm for the revolution), but not through proofs or examples taken from history (which instead continually disprove them).[26] The political is organized so as to include nothingness; it is as if the political were included within itself, its terms fixed in such a way that they define the political precisely by separating it from that "being-in-common" that the political is not and can never hope to be.

Is this Kant's final word on community? Doesn't declaring its impossibility decisively block every approach to it? Is there another approach, a final door, a fold in his discourse that opens to community, essentially by means of such a closing to community? I have the impression that such a breach shouldn't be sought in those places where traditionally readers of Kant have stubbornly been conducting their excavations, namely, outside that frightening law that dictates what is allowed and allows what is dictated. Rather, it should be sought within the same law. From this point of view, neither the religious reference to "kingdom of ends" nor the aesthetic one that refers to the judgment of taste allows us to think community effectively, because these references as a matter of principle escape the negative power, the prohibitions that the law places on those who are subject to it. In both cases, we are speaking of an increase, an empowering of subjectivity, which in the first instance is vertical and in the second horizontal. If in *Kingdom of Ends* [*Reich der Zwecke*] the subject, who is beyond the social world as well as the world of phenomena, enters in relation with others through the shared reference to the transcendence of an invisible *corpus mysticum*, in aesthetic judgment that relation is in point of fact taken to be the subject's transcendental condition. As I noted earlier, some interpreters of Kant, especially Hannah Arendt, have argued along the lines of the communitarian character of judgments of taste.[27] Where in the other two *Critiques*, the category of plurality doesn't have any relevance since the "validity" of experience is determined with the measure of objective universality, that of aesthetics requires a sort of paradoxical "subjective universality." It is based, in other words, on a consensus made possible only by the preexistence of a "common sense" (*Gemeinsinn*) or communitarian sense (*gemeinschaftliche Sinn*) that we share with everyone else. This means that if the subject of theory is the I and that of ethics is the Self, the subject of aesthetics is We. Indeed it is We-others, a We that is constitutively open to relations with others. Isn't the preliminary condition of judgment perhaps that of adopting the point of view of others, of overcoming the particularity of our own perspective? If communicability forms both the presupposition and the ultimate goal of aesthetic judgment, then the communitarian discourse finally finds a basis that is neither simply objective (true), nor exclusively subjective (individual), but fully intersubjective. The bridge between them has been found; the door is open. Community appears on the horizon and indeed in a certain sense is already here among us.

Yes, but is this how things really stand? Is it possible that such an "easy" conclusion is really Kant's conclusion? If there's any doubt to be found here, it does not concern only the leap that this reading makes between the purely transcendental level (that of communicability as an a priori condition of judgment) and the phenomenological (that of effective communication). Nor is it only a matter of reducing empirically and anthropologically the entire critical Kantian apparatus when we immediately read politically what Kant offers as a pure formal possibility. More than anything else the doubt concerns the "humanistic" layering of intersubjectivity and community. The community would correspond in this case to the multiplication of subjectivity for an indeterminate number of individuals, just as the individual would constitute a fragment of community that is simply waiting to have a relation with others so as to completely come into its own. Transitioning from one to the other is linear, and no obstacles are encountered. In order for the community to be realized, there wouldn't even be the need for the law that for no good reason complicates matters: it's enough simply to put together what before, namely, by Hobbes and Rousseau, was thought separately or in contradiction to community. But the question, which in this way gets skipped over, remains exactly where Kant's two predecessors had left it, precisely because they weren't able to answer it within the individualistic-subjective paradigm that they had at their disposal. They couldn't resolve it because the individual subject, undivided, and far from being an unconscious part of the community, is what bars the way and in fact is defined exactly by its own incommunicability: what lives *in* and *of* the inexistence of the other; that exists, subsists, and persists as if the other didn't exist. In brief, that *survives* it.

For this reason Kant's approach to the community has to be sought elsewhere and not in the subject and every form of presumed intersubjectivity. Your attention please: by elsewhere I don't mean "outside," since the subject remains the key axis around which all of Kantian criticism turns, but rather in the subject's empty spaces, pauses, and its external, but above all internal, border; in precisely that limit that traverses the subject and cuts it, marking its finiteness and its fragility. A limit that abandons the subject to the abyss of its other or pushes the other within the subject. This means that the other thought *of* the community in Kant—the only thought, I want to say, by which the community is not limited to being an object, but in some way is made subject—is to be sought even in the first edition of *Critique of Pure Reason* in those passages, but especially in the *Dialectic*, where subjectivity withdraws, is subtracted, escapes from itself. Community becomes indefinable as subject to the degree that it loses substance so as to become a simple formal proposition; a pure function that cannot subsist on its own or in itself unless by making itself other than itself: "I think," *Er*, *Es*, but not Subject (if by subject is understood a being that is completely continuous with itself; a constancy or a persistence in identity with itself in space and time), which themselves are subjective-objective forms (and therefore *neither* objective *nor* subjective) that are challenged by the unfathomability of the Object with which the subject also attempts to identify itself, and in the process once again loses its identity by making itself "thing" (*das Ding an sich*) or "being" (*das Wesen selbst*) that eludes its own thought: "[I]n the consciousness of myself in mere thought I am a being, though this consciousness does not present to me any property of this being as material for thought."[28]

That this work of desubjectification of the ego, which takes place principally in the critique of the paralogisms of substantiality and personality, leads Kant to hypothesizing a relentless transfer of ego [*egoità*] from one to another isn't just the final result that referring to reason's indestructible limits achieves, but also reconfirms the correspondence between the semantics of community and the critique and/or crises of subjectivity.

If such a correspondence is still implicit in the first *Critique*, it is made utterly manifest in the second, in the sense that the correspondence between the semantics of community and the crises of subjectivity acquires the formal statute of a real law. Indeed, that this law is one with the thinkability of the community as the withdrawal of the subject. We might say that community coincides with the nonsubjective character of the law, with the widening gap between the form of the law and the content of its subject. Contrary to all those readings that emphasize how the law belongs to the subject, the fact should be underscored that in Kant, if anything, it is the subject who belongs to the law, who appears in its presence before the law [*Vor dem Gesetz*] as in Franz Kafka's short story.[29] The reason isn't only that the law is self-legislating, a law unto itself since it has no subject as its author, not even God, who is neither guarantor nor sovereign, but simply executor; but rather that the subject is constitutively incapable of "understanding the law."[30] The subject is always in debt, is always somehow defective or guilty vis-à-vis the law, in spite of and *indeed the more* the subject tries to conform to the law.[31] This aporetic dialectic between conforming to the law [*Gesetzmässigkeit*] and sense of guilt [*Schuldgefühl*] isn't to be toned down in any way: the subject cannot carry out the law not only (and not so much) because he or she cannot fight the temptation to break it but because it is the law itself, the categorical imperative, that is incapable of being actualized insofar as the law sets out nothing other than its own prerogative, no content other than the formal obligation to obey.[32] This we know: the law imposes a mode of behavior that constitutes in turn our desire for the principle of universal legislation, but the law fails to tell us how to go about it. In fact, the law's enjoining force resides precisely in what it doesn't say. Here we find then what the descriptor "categorical" in categorical imperative really means: on the one side, its absolute, unconditional, and irrevocable sovereignty; on the other, its aporetic withdrawal from any attempt at performing the law. Seen from this perspective, the categorical imperative isn't only incapable of being accomplished but it is Non-Accomplishment or Non-Actualization itself. It's important to establish this point without losing any intermediate step. We cannot carry out the law that admonishes us because we didn't give birth to such laws. The law in no way can be said to be the product of the subject, even if the subject is subjected to it.

Here I am speaking only of the passive modality of "subjection," "of being subjected to," and not of the active modality of "subjectivity." In fact, the law corrodes; it ensnares us; it breaks down [*scompone*] our subjectivity. It comes from outside ourselves, and it carries us outside ourselves both in the sense that one cannot make laws for oneself and, more radically, that the law, which unconditionally commands its nonactualization [*l'inadempibile*], prescribes in a certain sense the impoverishment of the subject, with which it is concerned. It imposes on the subject a statute of permanently being unable to carry out the law: "Whatever a man may have done in the way of adopting a good disposition, and, indeed, however steadfastly he may have preserved in conduct conformable to such a disposition, *he nevertheless started from evil*."[33] The law, without any limit whatsoever, puts the subject in its debt. As I noted earlier, this doesn't mean that the law excludes the subject; nowhere do we find Kant rejecting or refusing the category of the subject, but on the contrary he includes it in the law's own exteriority. In fact, he places the subject at the center of his "system." Therefore, he subtracts the subject from any self-consistency, as Nietzsche well understood when he emphasized that Kant's categorical imperative was "dangerous to life";[34] not in the general sense that answering to the law eliminates in itself any subjective content—feeling, pleasure, and interest, excepting pain (*Leid*) and suffering (*Schmerz*), which instead are essential—in favor of complete submission to what is formally compelled. Rather, it is in the more specific sense that the law can be imposed, only "harming," "damaging," and "shaming" that inviolable nucleus of subjectivity that is constituted by the "love of self" (*Selbstliebe*), of "love proper" (*Eigenliebe*), and of "benevolence toward the self" (*philautia*):

> Now the moral law, which alone is truly objective (namely, in every respect), entirely excludes the influence of self-love on the supreme practical principle, and indefinitely checks the self-conceit that prescribes the subjective conditions of the former as law. Now whatever checks our self-conceit in our own judgment humiliates; therefore the moral law inevitably humbles every man when he compares with it the physical propensities of his nature.[35]

What the moral law humbles is precisely the pretext that subjectivity comes before the law and defines it, rather than being itself determined by, limited by, and defined in its limits. The subject is "obliged to," "owned by," and "constricted by." It is true that the high price the subject pays the law is in some ways returned to him by the conquest of "respect for self," but the same respect for self doesn't eliminate but in fact presupposes his finitude as a subject that is eternally incapable of carrying out the law (also leaving aside the conflict that such a pretension sets off in an "ego" that is ever more divided and contested by its opposing origins):[36] "Now it is to be observed as respect is an effect on feeling, and therefore on the sensibility, of a rational being; it presupposes this sensibility, and therefore also the finiteness of such beings on whom the moral law imposes respect."[37] This finitude, I noted, expresses the impossibility of community: it is when speaking about the actualization of community that we turn out to be irremediably finite. At the same time, though, the law also is what provides us with the possibility of thinking community for the first time. Or better: what is allowed to be thought about community. In this sense it has been said that the community isn't to be found outside the law but exactly within the limits of the law, even if this is what precludes its realization. There's no need to avoid the contradiction and the paradox that result because it is just this contradiction that constitutes the crucial tear that Kant represents with respect to all preceding philosophy, divided between those who deny even the question of community, as Hobbes does, and those who attempt to resolve the question through myth, as Rousseau does. That contradiction, one that only Kant will remain faithful to, says that declaring the impossibility of community is to be read in reverse: to say that the community is impossible means in fact that *that impossibility is community*. Community is the only one that men and women can experience if they accept its law: that of their finitude, which is to say, of community's impossibility. This is what they really share: they are joined together by the impossibility of community, by the impossible that is their common *munus*. They are united by a "non" that traverses them and outstrips them as their unattainable Object; as the Thing that it would be important to do but that cannot be done because it would then coincide with their own commonly held Nothing. This is the very object of the law of community: this nothing-in-common cannot be destroyed, reduced to a simple nothing as Hobbes wanted, since nothing-in-common precedes and encompasses every attempt at its own destruction. Moreover, it can't be actualized either, made substantial as Rousseau would seem to suggest, because the only way of producing a lack is that of maintaining it as such. The Thing is inseparable from Nothing. This is what the law of the community says: that the limit cannot be erased nor can one cross it.

Excursus on Kant

It is the reference to the limit that provides us with an occasion to return more forcefully to a question that I perhaps dealt with too quickly; it's that of judgment, especially in the "political" inflection that Hannah Arendt puts forward. We are concerned here with a theme that is entirely relevant because, beyond allowing us to dig deeper into the communitarian characteristics of Kant's philosophy, it is also of great help in shedding light on the none too obvious relation that Arendt herself maintains with the semantics of the community. Rather than risk a straightforward response to this profound question, I would like instead to take it up indirectly by way of her interpretation of Kant's *Critique of Judgment*. The least we can say in this regard is that we are concerned with a reading that moves the discussion of community forward, not only beyond where the earlier literature on Kant ends but also vis-à-vis more contemporary literature on Kant. I'm alluding, on the one hand, to the criticism (not only French) that is indebted to the work of Lucien Goldman in *La communauté humaine et l'universe chez Kant*, and on the other, to the theory of the "community of communication" that is to be found in Germany, especially in the work of Karl-Otto Apel and Jürgen Habermas.[38] Despite the obvious differences of emphasis and approach, we can say that what keeps all of them within the same hermeneutic horizon—which the Arendtian exegesis breaks with—is the "acquisitive" and at the same time "limited" modality with which both interrogate the Kantian text. The text, despite enjoying the recognition of having anticipated their respective positions—dialectical in the case of Lucien Goldman and ethic-discursive for Apel and Habermas—is judged incapable of moving beyond the objective limit that fixes it to an underdeveloped state of elaboration with respect to the double exigency of passing from the level of the singular to that of the collective, and from the formal level to that of content. The fact that making the sphere of sense homologous with that of meaning is prohibited by the Kantian community of the law doesn't seem to bear in the slightest in the exegetical claims of these critics. If Goldman "explains" it as the tragic price that Kant pays to the "individualistic-bourgeois" culture of his time, for Apel it's always possible to resolve the contradiction between "ideal community" and "real community" through a mediation of transcendental idealism.[39] This is how the "limit" of Kant's thought is understood as an obstacle to be removed rather than as the heart of his philosophy. These interpreters of Kant see the limit, the imposition of the law, only as that which renders the community elusive, rather than as the concave and syncopated modality of community's own presentation [*del suo darsi*]. It's for this reason the imposition of law is to be overcome, naturally in the direction of a dialectic between Hegel and Marx for Apel or in Habermas's terms through "this internal connection between morality and ethical life."[40]

It's this kind of genealogy established beforehand that Arendt will radically question: not only that the Kantian community isn't to be made replete with Hegelian content but is to be kept at arm's length from it. That the formulation of a clear-cut alternative between Kant and Hegel might even precede and almost introduce the text that Arendt explicitly dedicates to the critique of will raises the possibility that Arendt's opting for Kant rather than Hegel not only constitutes a general rejection of ancient (and not so ancient) philosophies of history, but represents a clear position with respect to the series of problems that coalesce around the idea of community, and even more precisely around the constitutive oscillation between will and law.[41] Arendt doesn't use this terminology, but it's not difficult to think that by opting for Kant and not Rousseau and Hegel (or better, a Rousseau who has been Hegelized), Arendt moves in the direction of an explicit withdrawal of the community from the semantics of the will. If will necessarily refers to unity (of the single subject or the entire political body), the community, for its part, is inseparable from otherness, and therefore from the limit that this inserts with regard to every hypothesis of fusion, namely, an organic form of unity. Such an option already furnishes us with an affirmative response to the question, which I intentionally left open earlier, concerning the degree to which Arendt belongs to a thinking of community. For now let's simply say that her thinking certainly is a part of that thought of community to the degree in which she joins the *cum* to a notion of distance as opposed to that of proximity. The community is what places all in relation to one another in the modality of their reciprocal difference, what Kant will call "respect" distinguishing it from love.[42] "To live together in the world means essentially that a world of things is between those who have it in common, as a table is located between those who sit around it; the world, like every in-between, relates and separates men at the same time."[43]

Nevertheless, such a reflection in no way responds completely to the underlying problem since it is precisely the reference to distance as *the* figure of community that implies another question with regard to the relation between such a difference and the subjects that community places in relation: is difference to be located outside or within subjects? Is it only space that separates them, keeping intact their individuality or that which calls into question their individuality, decomposing it as such? In other words, where exactly does the dividing line cross: near or within subjects? Depending upon how she responds to this question, Arendt is pushed toward one of the many philosophies of intersubjectivity or toward the thinking of community. Perhaps in Arendt's theoretical apparatus (but her figural and narrative ones as well), the two sides alternate and intermix. This leaves a residue of ambiguity that cannot be eliminated, especially when compared with the notion of "subject" as it appears in her texts, where she employs a range of different registers (phenomenological, existentialist, deconstructionist) broad enough to make it extremely difficult to find a definitive meaning.

What is for certain is that such an ambiguity not only is never resolved but in fact is strengthened by her reading of Kant.[44] The fact that the "place" of community is sought in the *Critique of Judgment* rather than in practical reason is the first indication that Arendt captures the structural connection with the universe of the law and therefore with the finitude of the subject. Yes, it's true that her critique of voluntarism works against every single notion of organic community derived by analogy from the development of the individual monad; but it's also true that this kind of antinomial polemic takes on more the characteristic of a multiplication than that of a contestation of subjectivity. Attention though: I am not saying that a community of plurality is opposed in principle to a finite community, because both in point of fact are crossed and constituted by difference. But the accent placed on birth in explicit juxtaposition to mortality winds up keeping such a difference well within the traditional area of the subjective *infra*, rather than projecting it into the internal folds of a subjectivity that is no longer such precisely because it has split with respect to itself. From here it isn't far to the humanist shades that color the same deconstruction of humanism. These are never more evident than in the essay "The Crisis of Culture: Its Social and Its Political Significance," in which Arendt's interpretation of Kant begins to take shape. It isn't my intention to minimize the fact that there she writes "taste judges the world in its appearance and in its worldliness; its interest in the world is purely 'disinterested,' and that means that neither the life interests of the individual nor the moral interests of the self are involved here. For judgments of taste, the world is the primary thing, not man, neither man's life nor his self."[45] Nor is it my intention to deny that this critique of *conservatio vitae* or of "immunization" of its dimension of a "free gift" refers also to the "inoperative" dimension of a political community that is distinct from other forms of activity for its unproductivity.[46] Leaving aside the problematic nature of the expression "political community," as well as the fact that Arendt had her encounter with community exactly at the instant when she was considering the "mental" forms of a withdrawal from the public scene, all of this still doesn't detract from the fact that the notion of taste emerges as more and more weighed down with explicit references to Ciceronian and Viconian tradition that reinstates taste within a categorical framework that is undeniably humanist. It's no accident that taste is defined as "the political capacity that truly humanizes the beautiful and creates a culture."[47]

Notwithstanding a series of relevant theoretical and interpretive shifts, we still cannot say that the later *Lectures* on judgment are completely free from the "essentialist" emphasis, if these—and here the reference is to the Kantian text on perpetual peace—conclude that "it is by virtue of this idea of mankind, present in every single man, that men are human."[48] This is in agreement with those who had respectfully described Arendt's thought as "a thinking concerned with health," by which they mean a thought inflected more toward protecting than calling radically into question the mythologeme of *humanitas*.[49] But the point I want to make is that this possible subjectivist tendency is developed within the communitarian thematic drawn in Kant's philosophy, and in particular with reference to that "common sense" that objectively constitutes both an unavoidable conduit for it and the most insidious obstacle for identifying it; in the first instance because common sense certainly alludes to a possible form of accord between entities—for now I have chosen to use this neutral expression—that are different. In the second instance, common sense is an obstacle because such an "agreement" in fact doesn't have in Kant's philosophy the sense of a "concordance" but of a perennial disaccord, an accord of disunity. This is due, moreover, to the fact that "hearts" that "agreeably do not agree" are neither "men" [*gli uomini*] nor subjects but the human faculties (imagination, intellect, reason) of the single subject who emerges less strengthened than disturbed from such an internecine battle. I've already highlighted how Kant doesn't always distinguish between these two possibilities: between that of a simple intersubjectivity and that of an "impossible" community. Indeed, in a number of different texts he is pushed to the point of superimposing the two possibilities, beginning with the fateful move in which "we must [here] take *sensus communis* to mean the idea of a sense *shared* by all of us, i.e., a power to judge that in reflecting takes account (a priori), in our thought, of everyone else's way of presenting [something]."[50] This is true even if later he will describe such an accord as a possibility, an aspiration, an obligation, but never as an empirical reality that is traceable or in which one is truly able to intervene. The fact is that Arendt tends to work more on the first than the second hypothesis, more on anthropologizing the transcendental based on the short-circuit that functions without interruption from communicability to communication and from there to the community.[51] "We were talking about the political implications of critical thinking and the notion that critical thinking implies communicability. Now communicability obviously implies a community of men who can be addressed and who are listening and can be listened to."[52]

As Jean-François Lyotard emphasizes more than once, it is this linear transition that is prohibited by the intrinsic logic of Kantianism, not only because communicability is a concept of reason that in itself is deprived of empirical correspondences but because generally the most penetrating meaning of the criticism resides precisely in the impediments, true abysses joined together only by the weak bridge of analogy, which block the free movement between different faculties; between phrases subjected to different and opposing regimes of sense such as those descriptive and others prescriptive, or ethical, political, and aesthetic. The aesthetic phrase, indeed, doesn't have a concept with which to present its own felt intuition: "It results from this that the universality invoked by the beautiful and the sublime is merely an Idea of community, for which no proof, that is, no direct presentation, will ever be found, but only indirect presentations."[53] With this perspective in mind, we can say that the *sensus communis* really has nothing to do with "good sense," but neither does it have to do with *intellectio communis* or *communitatis*, which is to say with a communal intelligence.[54] This in turn signals that we can capture its meaning only through the negative, in the form of that which is not. Wasn't this precisely the law of community, that of both a necessary and impossible (re)presentation? If that's the case, however, then we can infer that the category that can be assigned to it, more so than any other, isn't the beautiful but the sublime. This is the real blind spot of Arendt's reading of Kant, which is concentrated above all on the first part of the *Critique of Judgment*. She is reluctant to follow Kant down the inviolable road that brings us to the antinomical superimposition between community and law, because the sublime constitutes exactly the bridge between the felt area of the aesthetic judgment and the ethical-rational of the law as Kant himself underscores: "It is in fact difficult to think of a feeling for the sublime in nature without connecting with it a mental attunement similar to that for moral feeling."[55]

At this point the reason why Arendt doesn't deal with but flees from the sublime in her analysis of judgment becomes clear: the sublime puts in doubt the presupposition on which the analysis is based, which is to say the absolute separation between ethics and aesthetics that allows her to translate the communitarian thematic from ethics to aesthetics without any reservations and without any remnant. But this is possible only by canceling out the tight and risky passage to the sublime. It is a narrow passage because despite its moral vocation, the sublime always has to do with the faculty of the imagination and not of reason. It's risky because the only way to restabilize the predominance of imagination over reason—and thus respond to the call of the law—is by violently imposing the latter over the former, which passes for the "sacrifice" of sensibility and, therefore, for an infinite rip in subjectivity. As we know, the law in order to be actualized requires a separation from sensibility that carries with it unpleasantness, and even more intensely, pain. And this in turn explains the lexicon of war—"power," "fear," "domination," "alliance," "submission"—that Kant will every now and then deploy. As Lyotard narrates it, in order for the "sublime son" to be born, what is required is that the Father-Law impregnate the Mother-Imagination in the blood of sheer violence, such that the Mother, dying, can give birth to it.[56] But the most troubling aspect of all is that this violence is desired not by reason (since it is absent in the aesthetic sphere) but by imagination itself. It is the imagination that forces itself to imagine its own decimation in order to gratify a law of which it isn't a part: "in an aesthetic judgment about the sublime we present this dominance as being exerted by the imagination itself, as an instrument of reason."[57]

How are we to explain this sacrificial economy in which what is gained is the consequence of and coextensive with loss? And what kind of relation does sublime self-mutilation of the imagination enjoy with our theme of community? My impression is that it really concerns the question of the limit and therefore pertains to the veil with which the community is "uncovered," simultaneously displayed and protected by the law that shows it by barring it, that reveals it by blocking it. We know that while the beautiful expresses the formation of what doesn't have form, an ordering of chaos, the limitation of the limitless, the sublime for its part aspires, desperately so, to represent unlimitedness [*l'illimitatezza*]. I say desperately because its representation is suspended, held back, interrupted on the outside of a limit of the same law that it is forbidden from crossing. The sublime is born from the sensation of inadequacy when the imagination is faced with the task of making itself correspond to the Idea. The displeasure of not being up to the task is balanced, however, by the pleasure of seeing its ability of being up to the task as corresponding to its own inability. Still, what does this prove? What is it that both attracts and frightens the imagination? Why is the imagination blocked by what has need of imagination? The answer to these questions, this is the final question Kant asks, turns finally on the nature of the law. As we've said repeatedly here, the law is the law of the community. This means that on the one hand the community is given to us as our fixed abode, that it calls us with a voice that cannot go unheard because it originates from within us. That such a community is given in the restraining form of a law also means that we cannot directly come into contact with it without the filter of a *nomos* that at the same time separates us from it because the law isn't to be obeyed in full; indeed the law forces upon us moments of disobedience, if for no other reason than completely obeying the law would mean removing transcendence from it, making transcendence useless because it is already inscribed in the real. What requires emphasis is this: the Real as such, the "thing-in-itself," stays out of reach, not so much to defend the Real from us but to defend us from the Real, and from its terrifying truth that the sublime speaks without disclosing everything, "sublimating it" precisely through the impenetrability of the veil with which it "reveals" it.[58] This is the sense with which Kant remains intensely within the thought of the law: the community is to be defended by a protection [*diaframma*] that we cannot cross so as to not fall into it; so as not to be completely incorporated in an Object that would lose track of us as subjects, in a bottomless area in which every possible determination would become obscured.[59] Behind the limit here the face without any distinctive features of the *Ungeheure*, the monstrous [*mostroso*] appears, or also the unbearable display [*mostrarsi*] of a world without limits; literally an impure [*immondo*] world [*mondo*], which is what a community absolutely coextensive with itself can be, which is to say utterly indifferent to all difference.[60] Wasn't this the ultimate risk that Hegel, *from his point of view*, perceived when speaking of the "fury of destruction," of "pure terror"?[61] Isn't a community *of* the good possible? Hegel asks himself, and in the process drags Kant back to the point from which Kant had tried to distance himself. A community of the good that doesn't overturn the absolute intimacy of the subject with himself into the most devastating sort of evil? Here is the reason behind the interdiction that I spoke of earlier. But something else comes into view, that is, the reason behind the desire for breaking, for going beyond finiteness and experiencing the infinite. This is another way of saying coming into direct contact with the Thing, experiencing community on one's own flesh, taking pleasure [*godere*] in the Real beyond the imaginary and the symbolic, which is also how Lyotard describes it.[62]

Yet taking pleasure in the Real, which is to say realizing the law to the point of canceling it out, would also mean touching what in life can prefer death.[63] The person who leads us to this extreme step, one no longer within Kant's thought but residing in its opposite, is Jacques Lacan. He is the one who tells us that the Kantian sublime, the pleasure held in check by the sublime, was the latest, most important attempt to separate ethics from desire; to prohibit us from the self-destructive identification with the "all" of the community, and in so doing sublimating it, that "more of pleasure," which is no different from lack of being. Kant pushes traditional ethics to the extreme and makes it dependent on the necessity of further elaborating it, because for the first time he registers with a stark clarity that the topical site of morality isn't constituted by what is possible but rather by what is impossible. This explains why the law of the categorical imperative is absolutely unconditional, because the problem of that which one can truly do is never asked. This is where ethics, as it has been understood from Aristotle onward, culminates while also reaching a point of crisis that moves it beyond, along a road that Kant doesn't travel but that he points to, if only negatively. This is the road that will carry ethics beyond commandment and obligation, and therefore beyond the Pauline dialectic between law and sin—the law as the occasion or even the demand to sin. One doesn't free oneself from the law by transgressing it (which is in fact the best way to ratify it) but by shifting it to a different order of discourse dominated not by its language but by that of desire: "and when the law is truly present, desire does not stand up, but that is because law and repressed desire are one and the same thing."[64] If the law is the repression of desire, desire can do nothing other than push us to break with the word of the law. This is exactly the line that Kant doesn't cross. By removing every content from the law, Kant creates the empty space in which the enigmatic shadow of that Thing becomes visible. Not the thing (*die Sache*) but the Thing (*das Ding*) that fascinates us and paralyzes us like the face of Medusa.

4

Ecstasy

It might not seem risky to state that the only philosopher who took up Kant's question on the community was Martin Heidegger and not only in different fashion but *against* that line of thought that from Johann Fichte to Georg Wilhelm Friedrich Hegel is believed to have responded definitively to Kant's question, entering by force of arms the "fortress" that Kant had constructed.

This philosophy leaped over Kant with all due respect but did not overcome him. This could not be done, if for no other reason, because his essential foundation was not attacked but only abandoned. It was not even abandoned, because it was never taken; it was only skirted. Kant's work remained like an unconquered fortress behind a new front.[1]

That "fortress," Cassirer would have said polemically, can be stormed only *manu militari* by a "usurper, who penetrates, as it were, by force of arms into the Kantian system in order to subdue it and make it serviceable for his problem."[2] That Heidegger acted more as "usurper" than as a "commentator" is difficult to deny. It is hard to dispute the forcing, the rips, and the true and real violence with which Heidegger "subjected" Kant's philosophy throughout the course of his entire work: even if we consider only the clearly exaggerated role Heidegger assigns to the transcendental dialectic, to the receptive schematics of the imagination with regard to logic. But what presses in on Heidegger, and this is the point that moves well beyond Cassirer's loyal philology, isn't what Kant "truly" said but rather what he did *not* say. "To make visible in this way the decisive content of this work and thereby to bring out what Kant 'had wanted to say.'"[3] Furthermore, wasn't it Kant who called forth or at least authorized that "violence" when he stopped short before the door, which was opened in Kafkaesque fashion, of the law of the community without taking that final step that could have pushed him over the edge into its "abyss"?[4] "In the radicalism of his questions, Kant brought the "possibility" of metaphysics to this abyss. He saw the unknown, and he had to shrink back.[5]

What did Kant come face-to-face with that *made* him retreat? What did he see in that abyss, or what did he not *want* to see? We know Heidegger's response: that abyss is above all an abyss in or *of* subjectivity— "the abyss of being-a-self" (*Abgrund des Selbstseins*);[6] the empty space that Kant himself, especially in the first edition of the *Critique of Pure Reason*, had created in the compact fullness of the metaphysical subject; in its *permanence* as being-always-the-same, because that empty space is nothing other than time. It is the temporal structure that subtracts the *subiectum* from his identity, suspending him by a contingency or a finiteness that makes him no longer subject, a non-subject. Or it makes a form different from what the Cartesian tradition had seen in man as his essential property. Time—here is Kant's "un-said" that Heidegger "makes" him say—extends, "stretches" the subject to the breaking point, opening and exposing the subject to a constitutive alterity. Or better: time constitutes the subject in that alterity that transports him outside himself. This is what Heidegger in his polemic with Edmund Husserl's theory of consciousness means by "existence" or "ecstasy" of *Dasein* or *as Dasein*; the fact that what transcends is the subject and not the things in front of subject; and above all, that what is at stake here is a transcendence that is not contrasted with but within, coinciding with immanence: *the subject's excess,* that is, not a simple exiting from the self but a "being in self" in the form of its "outside." This explains why it is perfectly understandable that in a few short pages of *Letter on Humanism* Heidegger can write that existence is "an ecstatic inherence [*ek-statische Innerstehen*] in the truth of Being" and a "standing out [*Hin-aus-stehen*] in the truth of Being" because the point lies precisely in the change that the ontic constitution of the subject undergoes in relation to being.[7]

That all of this appears in Kant's work is certainly difficult to agree

to. Indeed, Heidegger doesn't really believe so either, or he thinks it together with its contrary, hence the oscillations in judgment one finds in
all of Heidegger's writings on Kant.[8] This means that, yes, Kant forces
the limits of metaphysical language, but *from within*, without ever really
crossing its foremost limit. It also means that Kant denies the possibility
to determine the I according to ontic categories but never arrives at its
ontological determination. Therefore, he still understands the *sum* of the
cogito according to the Cartesian semantics of *res cogitans*.[9] This doesn't
change the fact, however, that Kant translates *sum* in a new form, exposing it to that internal-external movement represented precisely by its intrinsic temporal dimension. This is true, it has been said, for the cognitive
subject, afflicted by the "passivity" of a too sensitive imagination, but also
(not less but perhaps even truer) for the ethical subject, as Heidegger noted
especially in the crucial course he taught in 1930.[10] The ethical subject is
the only one who, in the final analysis, is susceptible to an ontological
interpretation, an interpretation to which Kant, as we have seen, was never
really able to arrive. The subject is the only one who emerges as subjected
[*assoggettato*] in the form of a necessary lack [*inadempienza*]: "A creature
that is fundamentally interested in a duty knows itself in a not-yet-having-
fulfilled, so that what indeed it should do becomes questionable to it."[11]
This isn't just any old reflection; it means that ethics is "finished" *radicibus*,
in the double sense of the expression. Ethics is finished, terminated, closed
as a discipline of values that "surround" or "tower over" being, pointing
out the "correct way," based on the dialectic between "being" and "the
ought" that is described and rebutted in the *Introduction to Metaphysics*.[12]
Ethics is finite, limited, and determined by an otherness that changes it—
that depletes it *and* makes it complete at its ontological root.[13]

It is on this question that Heidegger's dispute with Cassirer hinges.
If for the latter the categorical imperative opens "a breach" that pushes
the subject to overcome his phenomenal [*fenomenica*] finiteness in order
to achieve the infinite universe of freedom, Heidegger radically overturns
the perspective:

In the Categorical Imperative we have something which goes beyond the finite
creature. But precisely the concept of the Imperative as such shows the inner
reference to a finite creature . . . This transcendence too still remains within the
[sphere of] creatureliness [*Geschöpflichkeit*] and finitude . . . I believe that we pro-

ceed mistakenly in the interpretation of Kantian ethics if we first orient ourselves to that to which ethical action conforms and if we see too little of the inner function of the law itself for *Dasein*.[14]

It seems to me that in reaffirming "the finitude of the ethical creature" in opposition to Cassirer's humanism, Heidegger is placing in relief that problem of precedence, or better, of presupposition, especially between subject and law.[15] As I've repeatedly stressed here, the subject, rather than preceding—producing—the law, presupposes it. The law comes *before*. It is the "before" of the subject that is subjected to the law. But—and this is the point at which Heidegger begins clearly to distance himself even from *his* own reading of Kant—we need to be careful not to make absolute or delimit even transcendentally the law itself. By this I mean that despite preceding the subject, the ethical law is in turn preceded by something other: by *an other* law, which is outside the law to the degree in which it in fact places law in *being*.[16] This is what Heidegger means when he writes that the "original ethics" [*ursprüngliche Ethik*] is always ontology.[17] It doesn't furnish moral, theological, or juridical commands inasmuch as these are derived from and second to a more originary instance that coincides with the being-law of every law, which is to say coincides with the very same possibility of the law.

Already this ontological declination of ethics constitutes a less than generic indication of the demarcating line that separates the Heideggerean analytic from Kantian criticism. And it is also the most explicit response to the question of the reasons for Kant's retreat from his own "discoveries"; what he *could* not see, what he was afraid of seeing, is precisely the *non*-originacy of the law, or put more incisively, the law's immanence to the subject that it, the law, "decides." It is what in *Being and Time* is expressed in the formula "the calls come *from* me, and yet *over* me," by which we understand an otherness that cannot be interpreted as either transcendence or as a transcendental.[18] The "call" is no longer an instance outside *Dasein* that demands obedience from the categorical imperative, but the exteriority or the extraneousness of *Dasein* from itself. It's for this reason that the call doesn't affirm anything but speaks instead in the mode of silence. For Kant too, certainly the law doesn't command anything that is other from its own obligatory categoricity. Yet this always takes place according to a lexicon that still prescribes the "realization" of the community, even if impossible. Here too for Heidegger the community cannot be realized in point of fact if not, as we will soon see, in its historical and fated corruption [*pervertimento*]. The reason isn't that it represents an unreachable target but simply that it *already* is given even before we place the lens in front of us. This means that the community isn't a destination, nor exactly is it a presupposition—archaeology coming together with teleology—if not in the arch-originary form in which the presupposition is a law unto itself. Therefore, it is no longer law in the sense of a *having* to be but in the sense of a *being* that is required. This is the way that the absolute identity of ethics and ontology is to be understood and the reason why it isn't nearly precise enough to argue, as Levinas does, that Heidegger more than once sacrifices the first to the second; nor is it precise enough to say that "ontology stands guard on the threshold of ethics" as Paul Ricoeur expresses it with some disapproval.[19] The truth is that we shouldn't speak strictly either of one or of the other because both expressions are overcome in that ethics *of* being that in the *Letter on Humanism* Heidegger will find both in Heraclitus's "character is fate" [*ethos anthropo daimon*] and in Friedrich Hölderlin's "Full of merit, yet poetically, man / Dwells on this earth." Both citations have as their theme the question of "dwelling in" [*abitare*], despite being elaborated differently; in both citations this "sojourn" (*Aufenhalt*) is situated in the dimension of language; of the world and of listening and therefore of "corresponding" (*ent-sprechen*) as the originary dialogue (*das ursprüngliche Gespräche*) that we do not begin but to which we belong in the very same opening of being.[20] We have seen how according to Heidegger this might be the abyss from which Kant retreated from, horrified, "barricading" himself by means of the law. Now we can further specify the nature of that "abyss." We said that it was nothing other than the "donation," the *munus*, of being that is expressed in the formula *Es gibt Sein*. Yet here we are dealing with a particular *munus*, because it is constituted precisely by its "with," as is already made clear by the most profound essence of the word: "the word not only stands in a relation to the thing, but this 'may be' itself is what holds, relates, and keeps the thing as thing; that the 'may be,' as such keeper, is the relation itself";[21] a *cum-munus* that is the same figure of community; its original foundation, the emptiness of the *subiectum*, in which every individual, understood one-dimensionally by subjectivist (and objectivist) metaphysics, including the Kantian one, gets lost. What else did Heidegger mean to say when he stated that "*the fundamental character of dwelling is this sparing and preserving. It pervades dwelling in its whole range,*" if not that our being-in-the-world (*In-der-Welt-Sein*) is exactly an "inter-being," as "being between" "in the in-between" of a commonplace?[22] Common: we need to be careful not to interpret these expressions anthropologically or intersubjectively, and not with respect to near opposites but rather to distant ones, of opposites like the stellar poles of the Fourfold, heaven and earth, divine and mortal rendered "a simple oneness" by their irreducible difference [*differire*].[23] But doesn't Heidegger also add that "on the earth" and "under the sky" "*also* . . . include a belonging to men's being with one another"?[24] Here is the ultimate sense of that law *before* the law, preceding the law *and* the "first" law itself, that is the original ethics of being that is given by withdrawing itself:

Nomos is not only law but more originally the assignment contained in the dispensation of Being. Only the assignment is capable of dispatching man into Being. Only such dispatching is capable of supporting and obligating. Otherwise all law remains merely something fabricated by human reason. More essential than instituting rules is that man find the way to his abode in the truth of Being. This abode first yields the experience of something we can hold on to. The truth of Being offers a hold for all conduct.[25]

If, therefore, the community shows itself to be the very place of that *Sinngebung*, of that gift of meaning that Kant could never see other than as barricaded by the prohibition of the law, it won't surprise anyone that in his *Anaximander's Fragment*, Heidegger defines justice as "jointure,"[26] as "original gathering";[27] nor that paraphrasing Hölderlin's "Since we have been a conversation," Heidegger writes, "We are a conversation, that always also signifies we are *one* conversation."[28] It's already clear that Heidegger is well inside the "fortress" that Kant had made impregnable. The Medusa cannot frighten us because the abyss is revealed as nothing other than the infinite *cum* of our finiteness.

It is this *cum* that Kant hasn't thought deeply enough or that he thinks in a modality that is missing the very object of its own thought: "At first, it appears as if Kant has abandoned the Cartesian position of a prediscovered isolated subject. But that is only illusion."[29] What escapes

Kant is "what is ontologically decisive . . . the fundamental constitution of the subject, of *Dasein*, as being-in-the-world," or more precisely the *being* of community.[30] That the community *is*: not as a pure potentiality to come nor as a law that is placed before our being there [*esserci*], but as that very being there in its *singularly plural* constitution. From this point of view, namely, of a philosophy of the community elaborated especially in the second half of the 1920s from the *History of the Concept of Time: Prolegomena* until *The Fundamental Concepts of Metaphysics*, Heidegger simply distances himself not only from the Kantian ethics of the law but also from political philosophy in all its forms, not only in that Hobbesian form of the destruction of the community but also in that Rousseauean and then Kantian form of its destination-presupposition. The community cannot be destroyed because even its destruction would be a modality of interhuman relation. Yet it cannot even be presupposed or destined as something that is outside and that precedes its actual placement [*porsi*]. It doesn't belong to either our past or to our future but to that which we *are* now. To our ecstasy, to us insofar as we are ecstatic. From this point of view, any effort to reach an objective isn't any less useless than that of reappropriating an origin that at a certain point was lost. The community isn't before or after society. It isn't what society has suppressed nor the goal that society has to place before itself. In the same way community isn't the result of a pact, of a will, or of a simple demand that is shared by individuals, nor is it the archaic site from which these individuals originate and then abandon for the simple fact that there are no individuals outside their being-in-a-common-world. This is the reason why all of the studies on Heidegger's "political philosophy" have been shown to be not only false but intrinsically groundless; this because Heidegger's isn't a political philosophy but, more specifically, the deconstruction of a political philosophy in the thought of community. Although political philosophy always begins with preconstituted individuals, to remain there or to found them in a larger individual that political philosophy will give the name of "community," the thought of community always begins with the relation of sharing [*condivisione*]: "On the basis of this *like-with* being-in-the-world, the world is always already the one that I share with the others. The world of Da-sein is a *with-world*. Being-in is *being-with* others. The innerworldly being-in-itself of others is *Mitda-sein*."[31]

This proposition, which appears in the decisive paragraph 26 of *Being and Time*, is to be taken absolutely literally. As Jean-Luc Nancy has said on more than one occasion, it means that all that exists, coexists; or that existence is the being whose essence is the "with," the "*mit*," the "*avec*"; or existence is "with," with-existence [*con-esistenza*], or doesn't exist.[32] The *cum* isn't something that is added from without to the being of existence. It is that which makes being that being that it is. For this reason, in Heidegger every possibility of an *I* or an *ipse* that isn't always already a we fails to come about; also in the case that "these beings are neither objectively present nor at hand" and also in that state of the most complete solitude, since "being-alone is a deficient mode of being-with, its possibility is a proof for the latter."[33] He notes as well that a certain kind of isolation—which doesn't coincide at all with the solipsism of the individual ego [*egoità*]—"is rather that *solitariness* in which each human being first of all enters into a nearness to what is essential in all things."[34] Existence, in other words, cannot be declined except in the first person plural: we are.

Careful though: this is not to be understood in the sense of intersubjectivity and even less in the sense of intentionality, according to which a given subject addresses himself to another, to the transcending first encounter. Heidegger decisively leaves behind the traditional problem of the passage from the immanence of me to the transcendence of the other, since in the analytic of existence, not only is there no place for the *ego* but neither is there, if we're being rigorous, for the other either, where such an "other" has the characteristic of another subject, of an alter ego, as precisely we are wont to say. From this perspective, Heidegger's position is incompatible with all the philosophies of alterity, as Levinas himself well understood, regardless of the fact that such alterity is connoted in terms of proximity or extraneousness. The reason is that in all these cases the other faces the one [*all'uno*] in a relation of necessary separation that can be bridged only by endeavoring to put one in the other [*immedesimazione*], which inevitably leads to the negation of the other's alterity.

It is precisely this . . . going alongside one another, as a particular way of being with one another and being transposed into one another, that creates the illusion that in this being alongside one another there is initially a gap which needs to be bridged, as though human beings were not transposed into one another at all here, as though one human being would first have to empathize their way into the other in order to reach them.[35]

Against this temptation for fusion and therefore for the sacrifice of the one *or* of the other (which paradoxically the philosophy of alterity arrives at), Heidegger refers to the originally singular *and* plural character of a shared existence, which is properly ecstatic: each [*ciascuno*] opens to all, not despite of but *inasmuch* as single, the contrary of the individual. The other cannot be brought near, nor can it be absorbed or incorporated by the one, or vice versa, because the other is already *with* the one given, on account of the fact that there is no one without the other. In this sense a "we" cannot even be spoken of that isn't always a "we-others." For Heidegger this means beginning not with "me" or with "not-me," but with *cum*, with "with": we are together with others not as elements [*punti*] that at a certain point come together, nor in the mode of a totality that is subdivided, but in that of always being the-ones-with-the-others and the-ones-of-the-others.

How are we to understand this "with" or "of"? Heidegger, one will object, never provides a satisfying or complete answer to this central question. Nevertheless, with this kind of criticism is hidden a misunderstanding that risks occluding or reversing the meaning itself of Heidegger's intention here. As has been rightly observed, those who rebuke Heidegger (as Karl Löwith does, but also Karl Jaspers and Arendt, despite Arendt's changing her mind later on) for never comparing the properly solipsistic categories with a fully elaborated theory of sociality, forget that the register of Heidegger's discourse is that of a fundamental ontology and not of sociology, political philosophy, or anthropology; that indeed his discourse explicitly rejects these.[36] It's true that the ontological question of being requires moving through the single expressive referent, namely, the being of man, but this doesn't deny that such an anchoring to the reality of *Dasein* (despite being methodologically necessary) isn't either the means or the object of Heidegger's analysis. It's no accident that Heidegger doesn't use the expression "humanity" (*Mitmenschlichkeit*) but rather "being-with" (*Mitsein*), "being-with there" (*Mitdasein*), or "with-world" (*Mitwelt*), so as to avoid that anthropological misreading that marks Löwith's discussion.[37] There is an even greater misreading, however, when Heidegger is accused of not having completed his thinking of the communitarian conception, that is, the failure to understand that such incompleteness isn't the limit but exactly the meaning of community: that the community is essentially unfinished, that its incompleteness is its essence; the essence, which is precisely and necessarily defective, of its existence, of its being *simple* existence. In other words, the Heideggerean community presents an interval just as originary with regard to its constitution, which doesn't allow community ever to coincide with its essence and which blocks its realization. In reality, however, this formulation is also insufficient because it suggests two parallel movements that neutralize each other.

It just isn't so, however. It isn't that on one side there is an affirmative movement and on the other a negative that interrupts or stymies the first. The interval doesn't cut the community from without because the community is nothing other than that interval, more precisely, that what human beings [*gli uomini*] share is just this impossibility to "make" the community that they already "are," which is to say the ecstatic opening [*apertura*] that destines them to a constitutive lack. It's not by chance that Heidegger writes that "it is precisely the absence in the lonesome of something in common which persists as the most binding bond *with* it."[38] We are not joined by a fullness but rather by an emptiness, by a defect, by a fall [*caduta*]. Viewed from this perspective, the community needs to be understood literally as "coincidence," as a falling *together* [*cadere insieme*], with the warning that such a fall, the "being thrown" [*gettatezza*], is not to be taken as the precipitous fall from a condition of prior fullness but as the sole and original condition of our existence. *Dasein* is neither the result nor the subject of the fall but the fall itself, the "there" of being thrown there [*il "là dell" essere gettata-là*]. All of these expressions, "debt," "guilt," "failing," which exhibit in Heidegger's parlance this defective condition, refer to the insurmountable incompleteness of an entity characterized by the nothingness of its own foundation. Our action, or better, the acting that we are, emerges as completely invested by this nothingness as well when the making constitutive sense of, which is expressed in action, is nothing other than the projected side of an underlying lack of sense.

Seen in this context, the juxtaposition between "authentic" and "inauthentic" loses relevance and meaning. As some have contended, Heidegger will stop short of examining the phenomenon of being-with at the level of the inauthentic without moving it to the sphere of authentic relations.[39] Aside from the fact that, as has already been established, the terms *eigentlich* and *uneigentlich* are not to be translated as "authentic" and "inauthentic" (since these terms are too charged with ethical connotations—if anything it would be more proper to translate them as "proper" and "improper"), the underlying question lies in the indivisibility and continual superimposition between these two levels, which traditionally are juxtaposed. The purpose of community, if it is admitted that one might speak of purpose, cannot be that of erasing community's own negative, that is, of bridging over the interval of difference, of achieving community's own essence, and not because community fails to aspire to be properly its own. The reason instead concerns that what is properly ours [*il nostro proprio*] doesn't reside anywhere else except in the knowledge of our "impropriety." We have to appropriate for ourselves the origin in the form of its negative, of what community is *not.* For us the origin coincides with its "not." That is why the first presupposition of philosophy can no longer be thought to be a pure I uncontaminated by the effective being-in-the world, as Husserl will do, but on the contrary is to be understood precisely as such a being there in the "inauthentic" form of an anonymous and impersonal "one." The "authentic" stance, in short, doesn't reside in the impossible unmaking of the "inauthentic" but in assuming it as such, and therefore in taking care of it. In fact, it is precisely the "cure" (*Sorge*) that is the modality in which more than any other the necessary opaque (and *not transparent*) nature of community shines through [*trapare*], in the sense that it is care and not interest that is central. The community is determined by care insofar as care is itself determined by community. You can't have one without the other: "caring-in-common." But, and here is the novelty of Heidegger's discussion with respect to all the preceding analyses, this means that the "task" of the community isn't that of freeing us from care but of looking after care as that alone that makes community possible. This is the approach that gives proper weight to Heidegger's distinction between two different and opposed modalities: on the one hand, of "taking care" of the other with whom we share existence, of substituting ourselves for the other, taking the other's place, so as to free the other from care; on the other hand, that of soliciting the care of the other, of freeing him not *from* but *for* [*alla*] care: "This concern which essentially pertains to authentic care; that is, the existence of the other, and not to a *what* which it takes care of, helps the other to become transparent to himself *in* his care and *free* for it."[40]

How is such a thing possible? What does it mean to "help" others? Heidegger's response is that with regard to the other only a noninvasive mode of helping others is to decide to "let the other be" in its alterity *from itself,* which is to say, in its authentic inauthenticity or most proper impropriety: "The resoluteness toward itself first brings Da-sein to the possibility of letting the others who are with it "be" in their ownmost po-tentiality-of-being, and also discloses that potentiality in concern which leaps ahead and frees. Resolute Da-sein can become the "conscience" of others."[41] This means that there is no positive, affirmative, "political," or "ethical" mode of relating to others that doesn't co-open [*co-aprirli*] to them, a co-opening of oneself to the common responsibility for one's own proper care (ours and theirs, inextricably linked). Neither are we dealing here with "making" a gift but of "re-placing" (*freigeben*) in the other the possibility of being-with in donation, or the self-sacrifice [*dedizione*] of be-ing. The community is and needs to remain constitutively impolitical in the sense that we can correspond to our being in common only to the de-gree in which we keep it away from every demand for historical-empirical actualization, that is, if we do *not* take on for ourselves the roles of sub-jects: the community cannot have "subjects" because it is the community itself that constitutes—that deconstructs—subjectivity in the form of its alteration.

The clarification is entirely relevant since the majority of misun-derstandings of the Heideggerean relation between philosophy and the political are born precisely from the incapacity to think community as implying the impolitical. Attention, however: I'm not speaking only of Heidegger's interpreters but also of a certain moment that dates to the first half of the 1930s and also of Heidegger himself. It is as if Heidegger misunderstood himself, as if he lost the most vital dimension of his own philosophy. How is it possible for a philosopher to lose a part of his own thought? Is it by letting himself be overcome by a partial, superficial, and inadequate interpretation of his thinking? In my opinion, this would ap-pear to be the case when in the final published section of *Being and Time* Heidegger wanted to push the theme of community in a direction that didn't belong to his thinking, one that he himself had excluded, which is to say, that of community's destinal occurrence: "But if fateful Da-sein essentially exists as being-in-the-world in being with others, its occurrence is an occurrence-with and is determined as *destiny*. With this term, we designate the occurrence of the community, of a people. Destiny is not composed of individual fates, nor can being-with-one-another be conceived of as the mutual occurrence of several subjects."[42] We know the unforeseen and indeed utterly ruinous consequences that Heidegger will suffer some years later, when that destined community will take on the national traits of a "true German community" (*echte deutsche Gemeinschaft*). Certainly, we need to be on guard against any kind of forced homology between languages that have always maintained an undeniable margin of heterogeneity; Heidegger never identified his own position with the crude biology of blood and earth. But rather than reject it at its core, he limited himself to providing that biology with a spiritualist meaning that objectively wound up augmenting the ideological short-circuit between the cosmopolitanism of the spirit and the particularism of a national community.[43] I've expanded elsewhere on the mytho-poetic character of such a sequence—the political implementation of the philosophy founded in the aesthetic modeling of the political as well as its deep genealogy that dates to a specific reception of Fichte's *Discourses on the German Nation*.[44]

All of this is well known, so there's no need to return to it here. More of interest, however, is the identifying of the intermediate conceptual steps through which the most discerning thinking of community could slip into its most devastating negation. What *might* have taken place is a fact, but *how* it could have taken place remains a problem. The first response, in a way "philological," to the question refers to the belatedness with which the theme of community was introduced into the analytic of existence. We saw how Heidegger interpreted existence in a way that was originally communitarian; when, that is, *Dasein* is always already *Mitsein*. There remains, nevertheless, the fact that the convergence between the two concepts was constructed a posteriori; that the theme of *Mitsein* appears only in the twenty-fifth paragraph of *Being and Time*, after Heidegger had already discussed *Dasein* independently of it. The question doesn't belong to the formal order of analysis but rather to that of substance: if *Mitsein* presupposes *Dasein*, this means that *Mitsein*, insofar as it is said to be originary, is always derived from and a supplement to *Dasein*, which it also ought to constitute. Yet not even *Mitsein* can be assumed to be prior to *Dasein*, which is the other road that Heidegger is led to travel, superimposing it in point of fact over the first.

From this point a second and more fundamental response to the opening question appears with regard to the translation-betrayal [*traduzione-tradimento*] read in a historical-political key of communitarian semantics, now addressed to the question of the origin and, more precisely, to its alleged authenticity. We have already seen how Heidegger considered the truly authentic dimension, or better, the proper, of being-there not in opposition to that of the improper. The improper is not to be thought of as a degenerate form of something preceding it that was then corrupted—which therefore required returning to its primigenial condition—but instead as its very same content. Improper in this case isn't other than proper but is *Dasein* itself understood in its most proper impropriety. Not only, therefore, is *Dasein* revealed as improper at its very origin but in fact the very same origin is improper, as it is one with our communitarian condition. There we do *not* need to rediscover it, repeat it, or chase after it because it is always with us: we ourselves are within the singular plurality of our existence. Here too, nonetheless, Heidegger doesn't remain faithful to this perspective. It is as if he didn't bear up or that he wavered when faced with the conceptual radicality of the perfect correspondence between proper and improper. Finally, the pressure became too great, and it is then that he numbly inserts a subtle ethical difference between the two terms that produces that dialectic of loss and discovery, of alienation and its removal, of having lost and then reappropriating that will make some speak of a "jargon of authenticity."[45] Here, therefore, we have the vertical reference to the absolute singularity of a death that is always more than proper and what that implies: the unjustified identification of everyday life with undifferentiated leveling; the juxtaposition of an authentic and unqualified [*piena*] word, with all of the rhetoric of courage and will, of foundation and self-affirmation, and of institution and decision. If the origin was lost, it needs to be recouped based on the dialectical entanglement of presupposition and destination that Heidegger himself deconstructed. The community, once presupposed as something that precedes our condition, is thus now seen as a part of our destiny and, for that reason, is redesigned and reconstructed according to its originary essence, its originary "to have been." Here is the terrible syllogism that captures Heidegger within his own discourse and that imperceptibly changes the most drastic thought of community considered in its most traditional philosophical-political mythologeme. It is one that transforms the "in common" of all in *a* particular community that masters its own future by rediscovering its own purest origin. This and nothing else was Heidegger's Nazism: the attempt to address directly the proper, to separate it from what is improper, and to make the improper speak affirmatively the primigenial voice; to confer upon it a subject, a soil, and a history, as well as a genealogy and a teleology. A teleology through *its* genealogy.

We already know what that might be, where Heidegger might find such a destinal origin. It is there where that long-standing "reappropriative" tradition, which from Hegel on (though already in Johann Gottfried Herder) arrives at Husserl, had already been searched for. It concerns ancient Greece. Greece is the land of the Foundation because it possesses the power [*potenza*] of that Beginning, which is "greatest surpassing everything that comes afterward, even if this turns against the beginning, which it can do only because the beginning *is* and makes possible what succeeds it."[46] For that reason Germany needs to look to Greece as one looks to the beginning that destines Germany to what lies ahead, tearing it out of the hands of the new materialistic powers of Russia and America that press in upon it. Only by repeating that beginning [*inizio*] will the community with a destiny be up to the task that awaits it: "The beginning *is* still here. It isn't *behind us*, like an event that happened long ago, but lies *in front of us* . . . The beginning . . . calls us to reconquer once again its greatness."[47] What kind of destructive potential is carried within this ideology of the reproductive mimesis of an originary model will be made clear when the *völklichstaatliche Dasein* takes on the national meaning of the *deutsche Dasein* and its space will be localized in the land between Reno and Istro. Only then can being-for-death be transformed as well into work-of-death, and in this way can the flame of the *Geist* take on the colors of blood. Only then will the originary community need to be made "final," in the sinister sense of carrying to its conclusion all that does not belong to it, which finally includes itself.

Nonetheless, Greece itself had pointed to another possibility in Heidegger and sometimes even in the same texts from him: a way to see the origin in itself as subtracted from every historical-destinal unification because it is conscious of that fragmentation or dispersion (*Streuung*) that makes up our common existence: "our being-with," Heidegger could write, "is a fundamental metaphysical determination of dissemination (*Zerstreung*)."[48] Now this dissemination of the origin not only isn't juxtaposed but is made an integral part of the Greek beginning [*inizio*]. We already see it in *Introduction to Metaphysics*, when the origin is split in the difference between *anfänglicher Anfang* and *anfängliches Ende*, that is, between an "initial beginning" and a "final beginning"; between a beginning that founds as the most solid of grounds (*Grund*) and a beginning that withdraws itself as a bottomless abyss (*Abgrund*). After all, even the Greece that Heidegger points to as model for Germany isn't the same as the one imitated by Rome and then by all of the subsequent neoclassicisms. Rather, the object in question is an Ur-philosophical Greece that precedes the historical origin, as the origin of the origin (or rather as its unthought), which is the reason why Greece cannot be imitated because it is historically undefinable.[49] Here already in this revoking of historicity and of imitation (but of something that cannot be imitated), we perceive a refusal that is within the historical-operative incline [*precipitazione*] of the mimetic principle: the only way to be faithful to a commencing [*cominciamento*] is by *not* repeating it, by respecting its peculiarity and giving life to something that is completely new. If the origin precedes itself, that is, if it is prior to every "prior" that is historically recognizable, this means that the origin is *already* a part of its after, that it is perfectly contemporaneous with it, and that therefore it doesn't have to, indeed cannot, be repeated, reactualized, or completed beyond its simple "to be given."

Yet in the *Contributions to Philosophy (from Enowing)*, this process of a gift-giving [*donativa*] dehistoricization of the originary *cum* is further accelerated in a dismantling of the epochal principles that reveal the anarchic nature of being as a relation of gift giving [*donativo*].[50] This is how the proposition is to be interpreted according to which "fullness is preparedness for becoming a fruit and gifting. Herein holds sway what is the *last*, the *essential end*, *required* out of the beginning but not carried out in it."[51] The historical dimension doesn't disappear but is instead subjected to a continual excess that puts an end to the absoluteness of the beginning at the same instant in which it opens to the other that is announced within. For this reason "the *last* god is not an end but rather the beginning as it resonates unto and in-itself and thus the highest shape of not-granting, since the inception withdraws from all holding-fast and holds sway only in towering over all of that which as what is to come is already seized within the inceptual—and is delivered up to its [the inceptual's] determining power."[52] What does the "initial" withdraw from? Evidently from that movement of becoming an entity of the origin that is implicit in every form of the historicization of time and of the localization of space that tempted Heidegger during the same years in contradictory fashion. This is contrary, however, to the most rigorous direction of his own thought, which, in the theme of *Ereignis*, rediscovered the conflictual co-belonging of beginnings and of those that begin [*inizianti*], and therefore the impossibility of every return to an origin separated from its and our *cum*. Unlike the poet and his mad demand to rediscover the common origin, namely, the originary community, mortals know that they cannot experience directly and immediately the community, not because it is barred to them by law, as Kant would have it, but because community *resides* precisely in its own withdrawal, just as the unveiling preserves its own proper veiling and memory the forgetfulness of what has been cut out. This is why mortals look "timidly" on the hopeless attempts by the poet. This is why they pull back from the poet's re-search [*ricerca*], because in the climb toward the source, the poet risks forgetting that this is already confused with the sea and that our docking resides in our perpetual wandering [*errare*]. Yet in this fear something remains that calls on the same re-search of the poet and that in some fashion belongs to the re-search. They, the "others," despite everything (including the difference that separates them from the poet), remain his *friends* because they share finally the same destiny [*sorte*]. They remain friends of the poet because this kind of shared destiny is nothing other than that *common friendship* that was from the beginning the object of his gaze: "They are the friends, joined in a friendship that is founded upon their being destined for future poethood. The friends about whom the poet inquires, among whom he himself belongs, are the concealed (and still concealed even today) mariners who are remembered at the beginning of the poem."[53]

Excursus on Heidegger

But is it true that the poet "is near the source," that *unlike the mariners* who are busy headed in a direction without end and without possibility of return, the poet is "the one who stays behind in the homeland"?[54] That the word of the poet "establishes becoming-at-home in its own proper element"?[55] It seems to me that it is the poet to whom Heidegger refers that makes a positive response extremely problematic. Of course, we need to be careful when reading what Heidegger writes about Hölderlin (Hölderlin is the one alluded to previously) and to see it as having more than one meaning while keeping an open mind.[56] For our part, we need to avoid misunderstanding Heidegger's attempt to keep Hölderlin apart from the most serious of misinterpretations, namely, that of inscribing his poetry in a "fatherland" or a "people" from which it is as far removed as from a Christian sort of apologetics.[57] We should also eliminate any doubt about how Heidegger characterizes Hölderlin's *Heimat* as neither biologistic nor nationalistic, which means not only recalling his general point that "every nationalism is metaphysically an anthropologism, and as such subjectivism," but also his observation that the essence of the homeland, however, is also mentioned with the intention of thinking the homelessness (*Heimatlosigkeit*) of contemporary man from the essence of Being's history, so that when Hölderlin "is concerned that his 'countrymen' find their essence . . . [h]e does not at all seek that essence in an egoism of his nation. He sees it rather in the context of a belongingness to the destiny of the West."[58] And of the West, not thought "regionally as the Occident in contrast to the Orient, nor merely as Europe, but rather world-historically out of nearness to the source."[59]

Without losing sight of this objectively communitarian arrangement that Heidegger assigns to Hölderlin's poetic experience, let's keep our attention fixed on a not so irrelevant detail concerning the reasons for this definition: the assimilation, by Heidegger, of Hölderlin to Nietzsche, who had the same capacity for "homelessness" [*spaesante*]. More important, however, is the fact that Heidegger makes such a comparison in order to distance Hölderlin from the other philosopher responsible for founding, or at least for having set up [*sistemato*], the nationalist axis between Greece and Germany: "Each of the two friends Hegel and Hölderlin stands under the great and fruitful spell of Heraclitus in his own way, with the difference that Hegel looks backward and closes off, while Hölderlin gazes forward and opens up."[60] It is the modality with which the juxtaposition with Hegel is presented here, however, that brings us back to the initial doubt we noted vis-à-vis the appropriateness of Heidegger's interpretation of Hölderlin. For now let's say that Heidegger situates the two authors sequentially along the same line. They are juxtaposed, but more in relation to the temporal direction (from past to future rather than from future to past) rather than in relation to the merit or the method of their thought. Before getting to the matter at hand, let's make another lateral move. We know that Heidegger begins to be swayed by Hölderlin's poetics and Nietzsche's philosophy more or less in the phase in which he allows his interest in Kant to recede (though certainly he never abandons it), so much so that there appears to be a substitution between the two. But—and here is the question that Heidegger perhaps never asked himself—is it really possible to "substitute" Kant with Hölderlin, or isn't Kant precisely the philosopher who frees Hölderlin from every kind of subjugation with regard to Hegel?[61] The Moses who moving "in the free and solitary desert of speculation, bringing the implacable law of the sacred mountain" constitutes "the only possible philosophy of our time."[62] This recognition of Kant that we find more than once in Hölderlin is significant because it places at the heart of their relation the question of community that Heidegger also raises in the theme of homelessness. But Heidegger reintroduces the question of community in its absolute removal from the Hegelian conciliation. Indeed, what else does that "desert" *of* the "law" refer to if not to a finiteness that escapes any kind of totalization or that straddles (with no intermediate terms) sensibility and reason, the human and the divine, existence and essence, which only Kant had the fearlessness to argue for; to a fracturing of the subject, divided and in conflict with itself, beginning with its own temporal constitution? Hölderlin himself seems to allude to this when he recalls that "time is always that when it is calculated in pain, because on the one hand, the soul follows the multiple change in time and understands the simple flow of hours, while on the other the intellect doesn't deduce the future from the present."[63] The fracturing between present and future marks the caesura that blocks any form of knowing beforehand or a repetition between what was and that which can no longer be. "Thus compare that time with ours: where will you find a community (*Gemeinschaft*)?" Hölderlin asks himself in a fragment attributed to him with the fervid title *Communismus der Geister*.[64] It also blocks the possibility of the dialectic as the mode of resolving opposites in a world defined by the originacy of the split. This is how the following proposition is to be understood: "in this birth of extreme hostility seems to be realized the supreme reconciliation. Nevertheless, the singularity of this moment isn't anything other than a product of supreme conflict."[65] The "parts" are not related to each other in a synthesis but in an unending battle that keeps both of them on their feet. It's as if the co-presence of the principles of harmony and strife, of the cosmos and chaos, of the *peras* and the *apeiron* had always connoted a struggle that was bound to eternally feed on itself, since the conflict between struggle and non-struggle is itself a form of struggle. Hölderlin's antagonism can't be resolved dialectically, because there is no within that comes before the split. Rather, there is an originary splitting, an *Ur-Teilung* that is constituted by the co-presence of polarities that cross precisely at the point in which they diverge the most. "The representation of the tragic," he writes, "is founded principally on the fact that the portentous . . . becomes comprehensible because the unlimited becoming one is purified by the now unlimited having been divided."[66] Once the origin has been struck, the split is also reflected in the way in which it relates to the origin: it can no longer be the Hegelian relation of a resumption, of the rebirth and the return, since there is nothing from which to start again or to which to return. There is no dawn that rises again, nor is there a harbor in which to moor, but only a figure that withdraws and comes apart the more we try to reach it. This is what Hölderlin means when he emphasizes how "beginning and end never coincide in any way": the impossibility for modern Europe to seek and find its identity in what in turn is never identical to itself, namely, Greece.[67]

As we know, the crucial text in this regard is the letter of December 1801 that Hölderlin writes to his friend Ulrich Böhlendorff, in which he notes that "we cannot have anything that approaches them [the Greeks]."[68] And the reason is that every people tends to excel not in what is innate— for the Greeks nature, for the moderns art—but exactly in the contrary. Thus, imitating the Greeks isn't possible because of both their perfection and their lack of propriety. Not because they are too far removed from us, but because we are too much like them and because they too experienced our disasters and they too share our destiny of infidelity. They too are "outside themselves" in the sense that they were able to appropriate only what was extraneous to them, unless—and here is the most important passage of the letter—we don't want to imitate in the Greeks exactly that principle of alienation [*estraneazione*], that which isn't Greek. Break every dialectical resolution between past and present. Definitively cut the bridges with our presumed origin. That origin isn't ours and isn't where we think it is. The origin is always elsewhere: a differential repetition of an origin that is already and forever irretrievable. This is why, more than the origin, Greece is the missing site of the origin's lack, of its deficiency or defect. Greece is a lacuna, a caesura, a vertigo, rather than a site, a fatherland, a rootedness. Land yes, but also a land that has been shaken, dug up, and cut apart by its own otherness. A foreign land that originates from that which is foreign [*estraneo*], Asia, and one directed to what is foreign. A land that is incapable of remaining at ease with itself. One not having been founded and for this reason incapable of creating any identity, least of all that of the continent evoked as its son, unless that continent can utilize that impossibility in the most radical of ways: identifying itself with its own proper, originary impropriety. How does one imitate what can't be imitated, if not by reproducing otherness within oneself or through a withdrawal from a land, a land that withdraws [*Terra-che-si-ritira*]? In the withdrawal it rediscovers something that isn't an essence, or a destiny, let alone a fulfillment. If anything, it is the sign of a twilight, a true *occasus* that finds again in the Orient its own unoriginal origin. Didn't Hölderlin want to "correct" Greek art through that "Oriental, mystical principle" overcoming the limits of Europe?[69] Doesn't the purest water originate in Oriental streams that carry it to the West? Isn't it *that* "source" that evokes such "fear"? "But wealth has its beginning in the sea."[70]

If there isn't any doubt that the Hölderlin that emerges here is a long way from the Hegelian dialectic, it is also true that we can't help seeing that such a reading is equally distant from the interpretation that Heidegger offers. It's true that in his reading, Heidegger accentuates the theme of extraneousness [*estraneo*] and the improper, which he ascribes to the poet of homelessness, except, however, by understanding homelessness as that which permits, precisely because of the "journeying in the foreign," the attainment of the proper.[71] The problem here, which concerns the relation between proper and improper, is one we have encountered frequently, as it's a problem that is identical with community. Certainly, Heidegger never considers the question of what is proper without including its contrary.

The improper isn't only the obstacle that the proper has to overcome to be realized but it is the proper's very own presupposition. Yet doesn't it wind up reproducing again another form of the dialectic? If the proper is not the improper, which is what Heidegger suggests in other texts; if the improper breaks off from the proper, even in the intrinsic form of a presupposition; if the improper is a or even the point of departure for a reappropriation—in that case doesn't the improper reproduce the moves of a dialectic synthesis? Doesn't it change the origin of community from its self-declared originacy in *cum* to a different necessity? Doesn't it make that *cum* the premise and the promise of a finality that is outside a common existence that we always already are?

The answer to these questions I want to seek out in the sea because the sea constitutes exactly that place of dispute. It is this dispute that puts Heidegger and Hölderlin in contact with each other, but at the same time distances them. Let's start with what they have in common. The sea is the site of the improper, that is, of that which isn't proper because it is the site of being far from home and of wandering. It is the moving and extreme form of that split that we are subjected to, the *element* of uprootedness and for that very reason the loss of control over our own destiny. That we are *mariners* has no other meaning than this: our condition is that of a voyage that takes us far away from ourselves. But, and here the break between the two perspectives becomes clear, does that journey fix its point of arrival beyond the voyage, or does the point of arrival coincide with the journey itself? Despite the oscillations and inversion of meanings, I would say that Heidegger opts for the former. And Heidegger also thinks that he has inferred it precisely from Hölderlin, who at least beginning with the failure of *Empedocle*, chooses the second: "In the sea's wide-open spaces there is prepared the final decision of the turn from the foreign to what is properly one's own."[72] Here is how Heidegger reads the line from *Andenken*, "But it is the sea / That takes and gives memory": "When its openness is passed through, it leads to the foreign shore, which induces a reflection on what is foreign, what is to be learned, so that, with the return home, the appropriation of what is one's own can be accomplished."[73] Reading this way doesn't do anything but attribute to the sea the same dialectical role that Hegel had assigned to it in his genealogy of Europe. Hegel also considered the sea as the origin of "commingling," "heterogeneity," and "extraneousness":

"the country now under consideration is a section of territory spreading itself in various forms through the sea."[74] And this land (Europe) is inextricably united to peoples—Cari, Frigi, Lycii—all struck by the same seas. Still, if we are to mark the true direction of Hegel's discourse—from East to West, which is to say from the improper to the proper—the clarification arrives soon after that "the free and beautiful Greek spirit . . . cannot be caused by anything other than the overcoming of that heterogeneity" since "the Greeks . . . gave new form and independence to these foreign elements, through the spirit that belonged to them."[75] How such an overcoming might take place is explained soon after, when Hegel recognizes the mission of that people in the expansion and the conquest that the sea makes possible and in some sense demands: "the sea invites man to conquest, and to piratical plunder, but also to honest gain and to commerce."[76] Hegel here is responding from the perspective of the mainland to a line of thinking called "thalassic-oceanic," which from Athens to the Atlantic powers is understood perfectly as the *vis aggressiva*, war fever and a desire to pillage, the demon submerged in those seas, which shows itself to be the most powerful vehicle of the "unleashed technology," as Carl Schmitt described it.[77] Contrary to every ingenuous apologia for unimpeded navigation, this voracious potential for acquisition, this violently appropriating potential for taking by violence, is carried along by the same seas. How could a sea that is incapable of defending itself or offending anything hold out against the powers of land? How could it, indeed, be victorious in the name of the scepter of absolute sovereignty, as we already see occurring in Hobbes's *Leviathan*, if the "whale" of the sea wasn't just as strong as and even more ferocious than the "bear" of the land?[78]

This isn't Hölderlin's sea. It isn't the pushing against of the waves that crash against the land. And it isn't the *hybris* that raises the tide. The tide is raised but only until that point is reached when the tide begins to recede, as Simone Weil remarked on the occasion of the Nazi invasion of Europe: "In the sea, a wave mounts higher and higher; but at a certain point, where there is nevertheless only space, it is arrested and forced to descend. In the same way, the German flood was arrested, without anybody knowing why, on the shores of the Channel."[79] So too for Hölderlin. The sea withdraws, and in this withdrawal it is actualized not in two distinct passages but within one movement: it withdraws giving itself as a gift to others, and it gives itself as a gift as it withdraws. The sea's withdrawal leaves the land to be. Isn't this the very same figure of community, its originary *munus*, by which I mean what gives us a "common name" only through the lack of "our own name"? In this instance, the sea doesn't refer any longer to the limitless but rather to the finitude of our existence. More than a victory, it decrees a shipwreck, not in the sense of an unforeseen accident but as the very same condition of our being in the world, perfectly symbolized in Blaise Pascal's "you are embarked."[80] Jacob Burckhardt would have responded: "We should like to know on which wave in the ocean we are drifting, but we ourselves are the wave."[81] Yet Hölderlin had already asked what we are in the community *of the* sea in the second version of "Mnemosyne":

We are a sign without meaning.
Without pain we are and have nearly
Lost our language in foreign lands,
For when the heavens quarrel
Over humans and moons proceed
In force, the sea
Speaks out and rivers must find
Their way . . .[82]

Hölderlin's verses constitute the exact reversal of that heroic epic of the sea that Hegel philosophically "sang" under the mark of the infinite expansion of Europe. Contrary to this vision, Hölderlin's sea reminds us of our shared inability to be appropriated; pure crossing [*traversata*] without "forward" or "back," as Hölderlin makes clear in the third version of the lyric. An absolute present withdrawn as much from the sirens of utopia as from the calls of nostalgia—Theodor Adorno will also remark upon this in his polemic with Heidegger.[83] The present is the time of the loss of the origin. It is that which divides the commencing [*cominciamento*] of the possibility from its representation. The metaphor empty of the sea refers to such an impossibility. That it doesn't have an end, nor a direction, nor a logic means that the origin itself has been cast so deeply into the abyss that it cannot be shown except in the movement with which it withdraws.[84] This is the sea: the eternal coming and going of waves: withdrawing as a countermovement of the stroke; the undertow that leaves something on the earth, and vice versa, because the sea in question isn't to be understood in opposition to land but rather as its secret meaning; the oscillating, precarious, and troubling dimension that constitutes the hidden undercurrent of land, that which land is incapable of seeing by itself, its blind spot. This is why Hölderlin recalls that his land was at other times called by men "the Concealed,"[85] the same "mother earth" to whom the silent song of the community is directed: "Instead of open community, song I sing."[86] In this regard, it's useful to remember that Heidegger, in one of his characteristic "expropriating" thrusts, juxtaposed to the founding dimension of the World another one of the Earth portrayed as "self-secluding."[87]

Yet the only heir of this tragic and anti-dialectic Hölderlin was and remains Nietzsche. He is the only one to venture out onto the "open" sea, precisely toward the *periculum* [danger] that experiencing the sea would have on those who "attempted" it: "At long last our ships may venture out again, venture out to face any danger; all the daring of the lover of knowledge is permitted again; the sea, *our* sea, lies open again; perhaps there has never yet been such an 'open sea.'"[88] There has never yet been such an open sea because never before have seafarers known that there is no return voyage for them, that the *bateau ivre* doesn't have an anchor or a rudder: "We have left the land and have embarked. We have burned our bridges behind us—indeed, we have gone farther and destroyed the land behind us."[89] In addition, a land "traversed" by its own otherness is the only one that still accepts those who are "homeless," those "children of the future," who "feel disfavor for all ideals that might lead one to feel at home even in this fragile, broken time of transition."[90] This is why Nietzsche, contrary to the philosophy that would enclose us in the figure of having the same origin and the same telos, notes that Europe doesn't have only one origin, that indeed it doesn't have an origin, given that "the Hellenic [is] very foreign to us."[91] This is why one cannot return home to Europe. Europe has no other future [*avvenire*] than its future coming [*avvenire*], without which no originary mask is able to guarantee it and protect it:

It is only the aggressive and gratuitous gift of oneself to the future, commented the most ingenious interpreter of Nietzsche *sans patrie*, in opposition to reactionary avarice, bound to the past that enables the figure of Zarathustra, who demanded to be disowned, to present such a strong image of Nietzsche, when the gaze of others was fixed on the land of their fathers, on their fatherland, Zarathustra saw the LAND OF HIS CHILDREN.[92]

It is the only way of recognizing that community, which land [*la terra*] still tries to conceal in the closing of its borders, to return to that great sea that borders and traverses community—as its fatal truth. "Be that ocean, linked to the *extreme limit*, at the same time makes of man a multitude, a desert. It is an expression which resumes and makes precise the sense of a community."[93]

5

Experience

That the chapter on Heidegger closed with a passage from Bataille isn't without importance. We might even say that Bataille lies *at the end* of Heidegger's philosophy: no longer within it, and not simply outside it either, but rather in that no-man's land that delimits a discourse, placing it within its own exteriority. That exteriority still always belongs to "it." This is even truer in the case of Heidegger's thought, which presents itself both as a philosophy of the end and the end of philosophy. Bataille is situated exactly on the margin that divides them: on the moving and jagged line in which a philosophy of the end opens to the end of philosophy. Bataille's word (he would surely have said its existence) acts like a wedge that separates these two perspectives; a blade that cuts Heidegger's philosophy, "making a decision" [*decidendola*] about itself; or more precisely, about that mythological block in which Heidegger's philosophy was joined to the search for the most proper possibility without noticing how in the process his philosophy was exposed to an extremely serious risk of misunderstanding. If we read the citations in sequence that Bataille dedicates to Heidegger, we can sense a tension that is neither pure extraneousness, as some who are preoccupied with "saving" Bataille from a politically embarrassing affinity with Heidegger would like, nor is it an intentional juxtaposition, as Maurice Blanchot once said when speaking about the metapolitical experiences of Bataille, of "the tacit and implicit answer to the Sur-philosophy that leads Heidegger (momentarily) to not refuse himself to National Socialism and to see in it the confirmation of the hope that Germany will know how to succeed Greece in its predominant philosophical destiny."[1] There is something true in such a formulation, since the discriminating line touches the figure of the origin. Yet how can we not emphasize the categorical, lexical, and stylistic abyss that divides these two authors, especially with respect to the overall tonality of their discourses?[2] How can we bring together Heidegger's cold ontology with Bataille's incandescent anthropology; the systematic form of a work written for posterity with the fragmentary nature of texts without a recipient and almost without an author; the anguished responsibility of *Dasein* compared to the game of defense of the sovereign excess? Yet all of these considerations, rather than suggesting an absence of relation or frontal juxtaposition, allow us to think perhaps of an inversion or a voiding of meaning brought about by a common *interest* that explains how Heidegger could have considered Bataille to be the greatest French philosopher of his time. Before we define that common interest with greater precision, it's worthwhile seeking proof of these theses in both the offering and withdrawing [*coinvolta e insieme ritratta*] modality, which is precisely "double," of the references Bataille makes to his German interlocutor: a "nervous attraction" (*un attrait énervé*)—as he once put it—that left him with "a violent silence."[3] Bataille returned many times to that "silence" and described it more fully. It isn't only a psychological reaction of surprise or refusal when reading Heidegger but rather the very same form of a relation constructed in the inverse of its obviousness; or if we prefer, of an indivisible divergence from its opposite, such as what passes between two parallels originating from the same point:

I don't want to be a disciple of Heidegger's . . . The little I know of *Sein und Zeit* seems to me sensible and despicable. My thought, if it's possible, in some point is born from his. On the other hand one could, I imagine, find a parallel between them. This notwithstanding I chose a completely different path and that which I come to say in the end, isn't found in Heidegger, except in a silence (he could not, I think, give to *Sein und Zeit* a second volume without which the work remains suspended). That said, this Heidegger is no longer in his place at my house than would be the painter with the same ladder with which he had earlier painted the walls.[4]

Bataille's words coincide, therefore, with the unsaid in Heidegger's philosophy. They are inscribed in the empty space of his figure just as the white remains after one tears the painting out from its frame. We saw that such a frame, shared by both authors, is constituted by the question of the end of philosophy, but it is with respect to the interpretation of the end that Heidegger and Bataille part ways. We know what the phrase meant for Heidegger: "The end of philosophy is the place, that place in which the whole of philosophy's history is gathered in its most extreme possibility. End as completion means this gathering."[5] We also know that in such a completion he finds that the new task of a thought is philosophy's unthought-of horizon. What else can this mean if not that this horizon still remains inscribed with the orbit of that philosophy; that philosophy "ends" by regenerating the end in its new beginning [*inizio*]? It's true that such a beginning leaves the traditions of philosophy behind, but it does so in order to restore its authentic origin to it, which as we know, coincides with the conceptual language of the Greeks. Certainly, Heidegger knows that such a language is enclosed in a silence that for us cannot be broken: we aren't able to speak it without at the same time betraying it. Indeed, Heidegger goes so far as to say that the gaze opened by the end of philosophy "is no longer, is never again, Greek." Nevertheless, he adds that it isn't only that it is still "its own way Greek," but also that "to enter into thinking this unthought . . . means to pursue more originally what the Greeks have thought, to see it in the source of its reality."[6]

What Bataille once and for all breaks with is this dialectic of origin and realization, of loss and rediscovery, of being diverted and then of returning. And Bataille does so largely inspired by the very same Nietzsche that Heidegger had placed within the confines of Western metaphysics. It is as if Bataille inverts the roles that had been established in Heidegger's grand design. It isn't Nietzsche, who marks a thought that cannot be reduced to Western metaphysics, but rather Heidegger himself who remains imprisoned within philosophical tradition. It is Heidegger's way of understanding the "end of philosophy," which is still "philosophical," that places him within that history that he thought he had surpassed, but which in fact Heidegger follows and reinforces by elaborating a further step. That step is truly "final," but only when seen from the perspective of the line that it ends. It isn't by chance that such an end remains dialectically associated with that Greek beginning [*inizio*] that it both surpasses and reactivates. It is its *beyond* rather than its *other*. It is this "subsequency" [*ulteriorità*] of the Heideggerean end that Bataille wants to put an end to; ending it both as the origin from which it is generated and to which it responds like some faithful echo. He therefore wants to put an end to every recommencing, every repetition, every mimesis, however formulated and elaborated. The end of philosophy isn't the epochal task that opens a virginal space for new knowledge but precisely a "non-knowledge" (*non savoir*), which from the beginning destines thought to a chronic "unfulfillment" (*inachèvement*). This occurs, on the one hand, when "incompleteness is not restricted to the lacunae of thought; at every point, at each point, there is the impossibility of the final state."[7] On the other hand, if it were otherwise, which is to say if non-knowledge were simply the limit or the still untouched terrain that extends beyond knowledge—that zone of the real that knowledge hasn't still made its own, or if it were limited to only being the not known—even then we would still not have taken one step outside that philosophy, which beginning at least from Hegel's formulation, has always been self-represented as limited by an alterity that is outside itself and for this very reason is *identifiable* as such. What else is absolute knowledge if not that which recognizes what it *still* continues to lack and that *already* for this reason holds back from its inevitable capture? It is from this movement of progressive conquest that Bataillian *non-knowledge* withdraws itself, not as a provisional unknown but as an unrecognizable absolute, as what can never be grasped by knowledge because it constitutes its very shadow. Here is the meaning of non-knowledge. It isn't a form of thought that is future, subsequent, or superior to philosophy but its bare "non." It is the obscure hole [*foro*] in which knowledge, any kind of knowledge, dissipates without leaving any trace other than that of the loss of its own object. It's for this reason that every attempt to conceptualize it is bound to "fail insofar as unknowing, that is, insofar as NOTHING, taken as the supreme object of thought, which takes leave of itself, which quits itself and becomes the dissolution of every object, was not involved in the solution of the problem."[8] Now it is this self-canceling dimension that is missing in Heidegger's philosophy, which is put on the defensive to preserve itself, indebted to a knowledge that encompasses everything except the only thing that matters: how to move beyond itself [*uscire da stesso*]. "To leave itself behind" [*decollarsi*]. To sink into "the blind spot" that opens within and then vanishes.[9]

Nevertheless, we need to be on the lookout for any possible confusion. Non-knowledge for Bataille doesn't constitute a separate and autonomous space from that of knowledge. If it were otherwise, we would still be within the dialectic sketched previously between the known and the knowable. Non-knowledge, on the contrary, coincides with knowledge even if it is its negative modality: *non*-knowledge, precisely, or knowledge of nothing, the nothing-of-knowledge. But let's move forward a bit. If we wanted to name it positively, what name should we give it? Can we speak affirmatively of non-knowledge? Or alternatively, what is non-knowledge alone considered to be, and not in relation to the knowledge that it overturns? The term Bataille uses to express "the *affirmation* of this radical negation, a negation that has nothing more to negate," is an "inner experience."[10] It isn't an accident that the polemic with Heidegger is focused on this affirmation, on the fact that such a lack is missing in Heidegger. If the thought of the latter remains marked by the subordination of experience to knowledge, here what will be at issue is "moving from the vacillating approximations of the philosophies of existence to objective determinations furnished by experience."[11] Without discussing the legitimacy of ascribing Heidegger to the wing of philosophical existentialism, which is dubious at best, let's linger further on the point at hand. Heidegger lacks the concept of experience, and he lacks it precisely because he deploys in its place that knowledge that negates it in the form of an affirmation so absolute as to not affirm anything, to affirm nothing [*il nulla*].

The distance separating Bataille's understanding from all other possible philosophical definitions of "experience" is already clear enough in this first formulation.[12] What he thinks, indeed through the means with which he thinks it, is other; is the contrary of that *expérience* organized around the same self of Rousseau, because it is completely turned inside out. But it is also opposed to that experience [*Erlebnis*] of the phenomenological type, of any sort of lived, emotive, participative, or fusional sort. On the contrary, it refers to something that cannot be assimilated to the usual possibilities of life, so much so that it must be sought, according to Michel Foucault, in that point in life "that is as close as possible to the 'unlivable.'"[13] In that point where life withdraws or is interrupted like a syncope that traverses and decenters it in a "maximum of intensity and the maximum of impossibility at the same time."[14] It is as if experience, despite its declared "interiority," pushes life toward what is outside it, toward that edge of the abyss in which life itself faces its own negation, communicating with what breaks it, with what destroys it. This is the reason why inner experience has little to do with the Hegelian *Erfahrung*, which if anything might be considered to be its (voided) inverse: not intellectual grasping a perceived datum but rather the folding of the intellect on its unintelligible side. Certainly, such a notion contains within it the idea of something traversed, of a "voyage" (*Fahrt, fahren*) undertaken, but a voyage without destination and with no return, as only Nietzsche, even more than Hölderlin, had sensed. The event [*accadimento*] or the accident of experience leads to such a fall, the *periculum* of an *experiri* that is on the verge of slipping into an unlimited *perire*, shorn of every *peras*. The only experience that perhaps can approach Bataille's is the one that Walter Benjamin describes, not by chance one always "poorer," and indeed absent as such, since there isn't a "poverty" of experience, but only the experience *of* poverty and experience *as* poverty:[15] "the experience of non-experience" or of the impossibility of experience?[16] Why is experience impossible? Why can we not experience it except as impossibility? Why is experience always lacking something? Why is it nothing other than this lack? Bataille's response arrives quickly: because experience is what carries the subject outside itself and for which reason therefore there cannot be *a* subject of experience. The only subject is experience but it is the experience of the lack [*destituzione*] of every subjectivity. We read earlier in Heidegger: "To undergo an experience with something—be it a thing, a person, or a god—means that this something befalls us, strikes us, comes over us, overwhelms and transforms us."[17] Bataille, however, pushes this experiment of desubjectivization further: "Call the subject into question," as Foucault explains, "meant that one would have to experience something leading to actual destruction, its decomposition, its explosion, its conversion into something else."[18] But into what precisely? What is it overturned into within experience? What is Bataille looking for in the dissolution of the subject? Here is the crucial point of Bataille's agreement and disagreement with Heidegger, one that Bataille will continue to see as the epicenter of non-knowledge, as what escapes knowledge because it is completely one with its exteriorization. It concerns community.

A sentence from *What Is Metaphysics?* struck me: "Our Dasein (*unseres Dasein*) says Heidegger, in our community of seekers, professors and students is determined by knowledge." No doubt in this way stumbles a philosophy whose meaning should be linked to a Dasein determined by inner experience . . . This less to indicate the limits of my interest in Heidegger than to introduce a principle: there cannot be knowledge without a community of seekers, nor inner experience without a community of those who live it . . . [C]ommunication is a phenomenon which is in no way added to Dasein, but constitutes it."[19]

In this text more than elsewhere is disclosed all of the tension of the relation between Bataille and Heidegger, a tension that results both from a fascination with and a challenge to Heidegger; a desire to identify with him as well as a rejection of him, but which also includes paradoxical equivocations and obvious misreadings, which resulted from the fatal transposition of *Dasein* into "*réalité humaine*" (thanks to Corbin's first translation of Heidegger), which Sartre later legitimized, until we come to the contentious claim of the originally constitutive character of community.[20] We know that it was Heidegger who first grasped and theorized the constitutive character of community in those chapters of *Being and Time* dedicated to *Mitsein*. Yet those chapters (as well as most of Heidegger's other work) were unknown to Bataille, despite having boasted that he was the first to introduce Heidegger to France, when he hadn't read more than the text he cited and then only in translation.[21] Does this mean that he is completely off base when he distances himself from the German philosopher? Things are more complicated than that. Bataille isn't wrong when he singles out the specific site of his difference with Heidegger in the theme of community, nor is he wrong in linking that difference to the mode in which that theme is related to philosophy. How, Bataille asks, can a philosophy that even declares itself to be "at an end" speak of community as *one* of its objects (which is exactly what Heidegger does when he limits the analysis of *Mitsein* in one of the sections of *Being and Time*)? Isn't the community properly that which deprives philosophy of meaning as discipline, outstripping philosophy's every ability to include it? Despite his scarce familiarity with Heidegger's work, on this point Bataille isn't wrong. The distance between any philosophical discipline and the *non savoir* resides exactly in the fact that while the first tends inevitably to exclude the community (or on the contrary to reduce it to one of its parts), the second coincides completely with community: so, while "it is difficult to imagine the life of a philosopher who would be continually or at least quite often, beside himself (*hors de soi*)," the experience of non-knowledge is "as such for others."[22] Or better: *of* others, since it is by definition incapacitated from knowing; that non-knowledge cannot be anything other than knowledge of the other, simultaneously in the objective and subjective sense of the term.[23] Non-knowledge isn't the production or the attribution of meaning but knowledge's being exposed to what denies and negates it. Whereas knowledge tends to stitch up every tear, non-knowledge consists in holding open the opening that we already are [*nel tenere aperta l'apertura che già siamo*]; of not blocking but rather of displaying the wound *in* and *of* our existence.

Bataille's thought diverges in other ways from Heidegger's. We have seen how experience for Bataille coincides with the community insofar as it is the unpresentability of the subject to itself. The subject cannot be present [*presentarsi*] to itself. It is missing from itself. This means, however, that the subject persists in some way as subject even if it is subject to a lack. This lack, in short, is inflected subjectively, albeit without taking on the characteristics of a metaphysical *subiectum*. Things are different for Heidegger, for whom what is lacking is the being of the entity and not the subject. Here we see the space separating Heideggerean existence from Bataille's *déchirement* [laceration]. In Heidegger there is no wounding simply because there is no individual subject to wound. It is true that in some texts Bataille also seems to associate the *blessure* [wound] with the very depths of things in a form that recalls the Heideggerean opening of being. Yet imperceptibly (or suddenly) he returns to it, making its subject that which exists [*esistente*], even if we are dealing with that which exists that only coincides in part and never completely with man (in line with the constitutively "lacerating" [*déchiré*] character of its anthropology). "In this sense, human existence is only embryonic within us—we are not entirely men."[24] We'll return to the question of Bataille's antihumanism later, but for now let's dwell on the lack that separates us from ourselves. It is the same lack that puts us in communication with what we are *not*: with our other and the other from us [*l'altro da noi*]. What is this other; with what do we enter into communication? Bataille's response is double or split depending upon the different grades or quality of communication. Above

all, our other is constituted by objects, by the object from which our subjectivity is revealed to then adopt its own proper identity, but in which the
subject is then led to be lost in a movement that winds up dragging the
object down with it in the same loss: "Experience attains in the end the
fusion of object and subject, being as subject non-knowledge, as object the
unknown."[25] It is as if Bataille, unlike Heidegger (need we say this again?),
setting out from an "idealistic" conception of the relation between subject
and object understood as two separate and juxtaposed entities, needed to
annul both to escape the assumption that he himself had initially made; as
if "that subject, object, are perspectives of being at the moment of inertia,
that the intended object is the projection of the subject *ipse* wanting to
become everything, that all representation of the object is phantasmagoria
resulting from this foolish and necessary will."[26]

Yet to the otherness of the object is added (and penetrated within
a crescendo of communal [*comuniale*] passion) that of the other subject.
There is no subject without an other, because when "separate existence
stops communicating, it withers. It wastes away (obscurely) feeling that
by itself it doesn't exist."[27] The passage sketches out well enough the con-
tours of Bataille's conception of community. It runs along the limit that
separates (but also joins) the level of the real with respect to that of desire.
Even though human beings in fact are isolated one from the other, they
[*gli uomini*] believe that their truth resides in the moment in which such
separation collapses in the continuum of community: "The truth isn't
to be found there where men are taken into consideration in isolation:
truth . . . has its place only *in the movement from one to the other.*"[28] Still,
what does it mean to say that community is the "truth" rather than the
"reality" of human existence? Does it mean that this truth, as was the
case for Heidegger, is held in common from the outset or that it becomes
so only in the instant in which the "passage" is verified from one to the
other? Bataille doesn't decisively choose one or the other but tends instead
to superimpose them "dynamically" by reconstructing them thus: man
comes into the world with his own proper identity, once again cut by
the continuity of non-being from which he originates. His life, in other
words, coincides with the limits that separate him from others, making
him that particular being that he is. It's for this reason that he is forced
to defend these limits in order to guarantee his own survival. Indeed,

identifying these limits with the circumstance of being and not with that of non-being, he is terrorized by the possibility that he could lose these limits.[29] This instinct for self-preservation, nevertheless, doesn't complete his experience, but in fact constitutes its weakest vector, because the instinct for self-preservation is purely biological and is intertwined with a drive so completely opposite to it that without nullifying the first, it is in conflict with it. This is how we arrive at the paradoxical situation in which the individual desires what he fears (precisely losing the limits that "make" him be), set in motion by an irresistible nostalgia for his previous and subsequent state of not being individual. Out of this arises the perennial contradiction between desire and life. In the final analysis, life is nothing other than desire (for community), but the desire (for community) is necessarily configured as the negation of life.

I only communicate outside of me by letting go or being pushed to this outside. Still outside of me, I don't exist. There's no doubt in my mind that to let go of existence inside and to look for it outside is to take a chance on ruining or annihilating precisely whatever it is without which the outer existence wouldn't have appeared in the first place—the self—which is the precondition for there being a "mine." With temptation, if I can put it this way, we're crushed by twin pincers of nothingness. By not communicating, we're annihilated into the emptiness of an isolated life. By communicating we likewise risk being destroyed.[30]

We're now in position to compare more forcefully the Bataillian community with Heidegger's. Where for the latter the community is the modality of our existence that cannot be transcended, for Bataille community is our existence's excessive and painful extension over the abyss of death. It is death and not life that holds us within the horizon of the common. Certainly, for Heidegger as well the ultimate sense of life for each of us is found in the reference to one's own death. Yet whereas for him that death is precisely *proper*, in the sense that man relates to it as the most authentic of his possibilities, in Bataille, death represents the nullification of every possibility in the expropriating and expropriated dimension of the impossible: death is our *common* impossibility of being what we endeavor to remain, namely, isolated individuals. This explains the surplus of excitement (and also violence) that shakes Bataille's text when placed next to the "stability" of the Heideggerean universe. If in Heidegger the *cum* is the originary shape that defines our condition from the beginning, for Bataille the *cum* constitutes the limit beyond which one cannot have an experience without losing oneself. For this reason one cannot "remain" in it, in the *cum* except for brief periods of time (laughter, sex, blood) in which our existence reaches both its apex and abyss, fleeing outside itself. It is this spasm that's missing in Heidegger, not because existence for him remains closed in and on itself but because existence is always already to be found within its outside. This accounts as well for the different way they both think exteriority: time. Time, which Heidegger sees as the very same dimension of existence, for Bataille becomes the bloody wound that passes through it, opening exigency to its immanent otherness.

This is the moment when the individual finds out that he or she has become time (and, to that extent, has been eaten away inside), and when, on account of repeated sufferings and desertions, the movement of time makes him or her a sieve for its flow—so that, opened to immanence, nothing remains in that person to differentiate him or her from the possible object.[31]

This opening is the absent site of community: our not-being-ourselves; our being-other-from-ourselves. Attention though. It is also our being-other-from-the-other. This is the point in which the entire discourse slips on its most antinomic conclusion, or its absolute indeterminacy. In order for there to be community, it isn't enough that the ego be lost in the other. If only this "alteration" were sufficient, the result would be a doubling of the other produced by the absorption of the ego. Instead, it's necessary that the escape of the ego be determined simultaneously as well in the other through a metonymical contagion that is spread [*si comunica*] to all the members of the community and to the community as a whole.

For this reason, according to Bataille, "the presence of another person . . . is fully disclosed only when the *other* similarly leans over the edge of nothingness or falls into it (dies). 'Communication' only takes place *between two people who risk themselves,* each lacerated and suspended, perched atop a common nothingness."[32] This is Bataille's final rupture with Heidegger. If the community cannot be identified in the experience of my life, it cannot be identified either in the experience of my death that, insofar as it is inevitable, remains "inaccessible" to me as the most impossible of all the possibilities open to me.[33] What places me outside myself, in common with others, is rather the death of the other, not because one can experience that more than one's own but exactly for the opposite reason:

because it isn't possible. In fact, it is this impossibility that we share as the extreme limit of our experience. The experience of what cannot be experienced:

Death teaches nothing because dying we lose the benefit of the teaching it offers us. We can, it is true, reflect on the death of the other. We bring this impression that the death of others offers us to bear on ourselves. We can often imagine ourselves in the situation of someone that sees death but rightly we are unable to carry it out since we are alive. Considerations on death are even more derisory because of the fact that to live means to always have one's attention fail, and we can try as much as we like, but if death is in play, speaking about it is the worst sort of mystification.[34]

It's true, therefore, that the death of the other returns us to our death, but not in the sense of an identification and even less of a reappropriation. The death of the other instead directs us again to the nature of *every* death as incapable of being made properly one's own [*inappropriabile*]: of my death *as* his since death is neither "mine" nor "his" because it is a taking away of what is properly one's own, expropriation itself. Here is what man sees in the wide-open eyes of the other who is dying: the solitude that cannot be lessened but only shared. The impenetrable secret that joins us [*ci accomuna*] together as our "last":

If this is clear, we see that there is a fundamental distinction between *feeble communication*, the basis of profane society . . . and *powerful communication* which abandons the consciousness that reflect each other, to the impenetrability which they "ultimately" are . . . We cannot do without the reappearance, however agonizing, of the instant when their impenetrability reveals itself to the consciousness which unites and penetrates each other unlimitedly.[35]

Such a characterization of community offers the occasion as well for an overall summation of the discourse that we have undertaken thus far with a view toward a possible, albeit provisional conclusion. Which one would that be, and why would it move through Bataille's thought? The reason is that in no one more than Bataille do we find that founding opposition between *communitas* and *immunitas* laid quite so bare; an opposition that has constituted the hermeneutic line of inquiry of the present work, beginning with the definition of the Hobbesian paradigm. The categorical alternative that follows from this could be pushed to the point of seeing in Bataille the most radical anti-Hobbesian.[36] From the outset we have shown Hobbes to be the consistent promoter of an immunization directed toward guaranteeing individual survival. We also noted that for such a goal to be reached, in the name of the fear of death, Hobbes doesn't hesitate in theorizing the destruction, not only of every existing community that doesn't coincide with the state but also of the very idea of human community. Bataille more than anyone else dramatically opposes such a perspective. He rejects Hobbes's obsession with a *conservatio vitae* extended to such a degree that it sacrifices every other good to its own realization. He sees the culmination of life in a surplus that continually exposes it to death. He opposes Hobbes's hyperrational construction that is intended to hoard all the available resources in favor of future security and proposes a non-knowing that is literally sucked down [*risucchiare*] in the vortex of the present. He opposes the preliminary rejection of any kind of contact with the other that could threaten the solidity of the individual and finds the community in a contagion caused by the breakdown of individual borders and the mutual infection of wounds:

I propose to admit, as a law, that human beings are only united with each other through rents or wounds; this notion has, in itself, a certain logical force. If elements are put together to form a whole, this can easily happen when each one loses, through a rip in its integrity, a part of its own being, which goes to benefit the communal being.[37]

Of course, there are two "metaphysics," equally divergent, that form the basis for such a paradigmatic juxtaposition. On the one hand, in Hobbes there is a conception of man as a being who is naturally wanting, causing man to compensate for this initial weakness with a prosthesis or form of artificial protection. On the other hand, in Bataille we have a theory of a superabundance of energy that is universal and specifically human, which is destined to be unproductively consumed and to be wasted without any limits whatsoever. Moreover, on one side, there is an order governed by the law of necessity and by the rule of fear; on the other side a disorder entrusted to the impulse of desire and the vertigo of risk. Yet what matters most for our discussion and its objectives is the perfectly bifurcated result that such a contrast in perspectives establishes in the realm of human relations. If those who are inspired by the Hobbesian model emerge as confined to the "restrictive economy" of the contract, Bataille refers to a "munificence" purged of any mercantile remnants. This is the reason that the gift par excellence, that which has no motivation or demands another gift in return, emerges in the Bataillian community as that of life, of the abandoning of every identity not to a common identity but to a common absence of identity. The Bataillian man "ought first of all to recognize abandonment, then desire it so as to become finally the will of being abandoned. How will he be able to see in abandonment the most open mode of communication?"[38] Only one thinker would have known how to respond to this question with the desired lucidness. I'm referring of course to the Nietzsche that Bataille literally identifies with his own thought of community: "My life with Nietzsche as a companion is this community. My book is this community."[39] Why Nietzsche, and in what sense did Nietzsche never doubt "that if the possibility he recommended was going to exist, it would require community?"[40]

In order to grasp the importance of this superimposition of Nietzsche with community that accompanied Bataille throughout the course of his entire work, we need to turn once again to the particular "anti-Heideggerean" reading that Bataille offers of Nietzsche: Nietzsche not as the philosopher of the will to power but as the philosopher of the eternal return that coincides with a *chance* that continually risks being reversed into *malchance*. Nietzsche, for Bataille, is the thinker, who fighting against the entire Hobbesian tradition, was the first to teach not to "wish himself to be everything" and not always to wish himself differently.[41] To decide above all by himself. To make oneself not-whole but a part, a partition [*partizione*] of, a *partage* with the other that surrounds us and traverses us; to give oneself utterly since "a bestowing virtue is the highest virtue."[42] Above all, if one gives oneself, if one gives "to life"—to death: "This is your thirst: to become sacrifices and gifts yourselves."[43] Here Nietzsche is addressing himself to those "who stand at the midpoint . . . and celebrate their way to evening as their highest hope."[44] To those who push the meridian of nihilism beyond itself, into the abyss in which, together with every foundation, collapses the absence of foundation as well. To him that holds nothing back in a "will of loss" that completely coincides with Bataille's non-knowledge: "I am talking about the discourse in which thought taken to the limit of thought requires the sacrifice, or death, of thought. To my mind, this is the meaning of the work and life of Nietzsche."[45]

Nevertheless, it is in these last passages that an aporia seems to emerge that isn't completely ascribable to the productive antinomical character of Bataille's writing, and indeed is potentially capable of leading it to a *solution* that is inadequate with respect to its constitutive incapacity of being resolved. I am speaking of the theme of sacrifice and in general of the "sacred," which is obsessively present in all of Bataille's work as its inherent false and doubled bottom.[46] Doubled because it is expressive both of its most innovative vector and its most debatable effects. Isn't it precisely sacrifice that in fact lies at the center of the Hobbesian immunitary paradigm against which the Bataillian "mole" [*talpa*] had worked? Didn't that paradigm already achieve the sacrificial destruction of the community through the compulsory sacrifice of its members? Why, then, put it forward again on behalf of the "anti-Hobbes" as "the final question" and the "key of human existence"?[47] Bataille responds that it is this repositioning that constitutes the only way to break free of the Hobbesian logic of sacrifice, not by negating it through a spiritualization that would reproduce unaltered its dynamics,[48] as first Christianity and idealism had done, but turning it inside out on its bare exteriority; taking it on, therefore, no longer as a painful means for the realization of an ultimate purpose [*fine*], namely, that of survival, but as *purpose* itself, stripped of every instrumentality and reduced for that reason to *an* end. The end of dialectical sacrifice or of the dialectic of sacrifice in a sacrifice of loss, which loses and is lost without gaining anything.[49] This explains why in opposition to the ascetic sacrifice "*in a part* of itself which one loses with an eye to saving the other," Bataille affirms that "it is in the act itself that value is concentrated."[50] It is this explicitly anti-dialectical explication, not so much the fact that "the one who sacrifices is himself affected by the blow which he strikes," which distances Bataille's sacrifice from that intention to reappropriate that seeks the guarantee of infinite survival.[51] It is distant from the ritual of compensation that, in order to save the community from originary or mimetic violence, shifts it onto a scapegoat.[52] Sacrifice for Bataille is the contrary of all of this: it isn't the necessary bridge that leads to material or spiritual development, to some sort of redemption, but the "joyous" condition of being in direct contact with death,[53] reaching its "height," as Hegel said, without, however, leading a proper form of reasoning to its extreme self-consuming effect: "not having seen that sacrifice by itself testified to *all* of the movement of death, to the final experience (. . .), he [Hegel] didn't know how right he was."⁵⁴ Hegel did not know that only death and death alone constitutes the truth of man, whose meaning is different from and in opposition to the Hobbesian sacrificial logic because it is founded not on that which divides men but on what they have in common: "What links existence with everything else that *remains* is death: whomever [*sic*] faces death ceases to belong to a room, or to those dear. One is entrusted to the whims of heaven."⁵⁵

Yet here lies the difficulty that Bataille didn't respond to (if not by becoming increasingly diffident with regard to how he first responded, to the point that he treats sacrifice as an indecent "comedy" without ever distancing himself from this perspective).⁵⁶ What do we have in common beneath the "heaven" of sacrifice if not sacrifice itself? What is a community built around the sacrifice of its members as happens at Numantia in front of the Roman legions?⁵⁷ What does it mean to assume finally "death as the fundamental object of the common activity of mankind"?⁵⁸ Bataille always excluded the transitive meaning from these passages of a work of death with respect to the other; indeed he expressly wrote that "to sacrifice is not to kill but to relinquish and to give."⁵⁹ Yet he also wrote that "sacrifice is warmth, where one finds the intimacy of those who together compose the system of common works."⁶⁰ This testifies to a contradiction that he couldn't work himself free of except through a response that was too close to the one from which he wanted to distance himself; as if, once the Hobbesian sacrificial paradigm has been reversed, he wound up somehow enmeshed in it; or as if the circumference of his "community of death" emerged in turn as circumscribed by a larger and more ancient circle such as that of sacrifice, in an ambiguous layering whose borders aren't easy to decipher. The reasons for such an undeniable connection have been analyzed time and again: a residue of interiority that remains stuck in the exteriorization of the "inner experience"; a remnant of subjectivity in the communal sharing; a fleeing from transcendence that falls to an excess of immanence, or an immanence of the void—and what else is shared death but blood and nothing [*polvere*]—that is substituted by a full immanence, since losing oneself can reconstitute a totality, that, namely, of Nothing [*niente*]. The fact is that Bataille isn't always aware (even if he was the one who was most aware of this) that the community cannot be responsible for the work of life, nor of death, nor of each member, nor of all. It's true that Bataille didn't seek out in sacrifice the immortality of existence but, on the contrary, the cruel proof of its finiteness. It is here, nevertheless, in the illumination of this extreme truth that lies the shadow that covers his clearest perspective on community, when he refused to see in existence exactly that which cannot be sacrificed. Indeed, it is the Unsacrificable [*Insacrificabile*] itself. "Finite existence," writes Jean-Luc Nancy in what remains the most meticulous reading of Bataille, "doesn't have to give rise to its meaning with a burst that destroys its finitude. It's not just that it *doesn't* have to do it but, in a sense, it simply *can't* do it; thought rigorously . . . 'finitude' means that existence can't be sacrificed."[61] It cannot because existence is originally already "offered," in an origin more originary than every sacrificial scene, but offered to nothing [*nulla*] and to no one and therefore not sacrificed, if not to that finitude that it is. This means that existence ends before anyone can "end it"; that it is mortal before anyone can put it to death. Only this principle will be able, perhaps, to carry us away from the "Hobbesian moment" that is still so deeply ingrained in us. What we might find in that "outside" or what it might be no one today is able to say. Indeed, we don't see either its place or its time, though the distance of the horizon has never been a good reason for looking away.

Excursus on Bataille

We have already mentioned Sartre's name with respect to the erroneous translation of the Heideggerean *Dasein* in "*réalité humaine.*" Yet in "the comedy of misreadings" brought on by the first dissemination of Heidegger's work in France, the role afforded Sartre's humanism is even larger.[62] It is made clear in the "three-man game" that Sartre will come to play with Bataille. Proof will be found in the decisive role that the reference to Heidegger will take on in the tremendously acidic *compte rendu* that Sartre dedicates to *Inner Experience.*[63] It is more at the center of a dispute than might appear at first glance, to the point that it produces the sensation that Sartre doesn't want to concede to Bataille a relation to the German philosopher that instead he claims for himself. It is in relation to that claim that Sartre constructs his own critical judgment of Bataille.[64]

Bataille's error, according to Sartre's opening observation, "lies in believing that contemporary philosophy has remained contemplative; evidently he hasn't understood Heidegger, of whom he speaks quite often and always inopportunely."[65] What precisely though is the misunderstanding responsible for setting Bataille on the road of philosophical perdition? Sartre finds it soon after in a sort of exteriorization of subjectivity that places Bataille in contradiction with his very same intention to narrate his own inner experience as subject. That experience wouldn't really be truly and sufficiently inner enough. That experience Sartre attributes to a scientist's vanity, which will push Bataille "to what is diametrically opposed to the *Erlebnis* of the subject," that is to a full reappropriation of one's own inner experience,[66] is where the relation with Heidegger comes into play, or better, where Sartre's interpretation of Heidegger comes into play. We'll soon have the chance to note how much of a role the personal plays there. Whereas Heidegger understood the term *Selbstheit* to be an "existential return towards oneself, beginning with the project itself," that is, a doubling of consciousness on itself, Bataille turns the *ipse* inside out and in so doing delivers it over to an alterity that the subject is unable to assimilate. It is true, Sartre will admit, that Bataille is reutilizing in some way the Heideggerean *Freiheit zum Tod*, but whereas for Heidegger this freedom for death is lived by the subject within itself, precisely as an inner experience, Bataille on the contrary "corrupts"—this is the term that better than any other renders Sartre's pedagogical tone of attack—that experience, having it rest on something outside that misses it.[67] From Bataille's error that coincides with his misunderstanding of Heidegger, Sartre derives that tragic strabismus that takes up two reciprocally contrasting perspectives on the same object, in this case the *ipse*, which ends up breaking it insofar as it is an *individuum*, and splitting it up into a thousand pieces, dissolving every identity within it.

Yet for Sartre the real point at which Bataille errs with respect to Heidegger will be found in how community is conceived. What relation will be found, Sartre asks, between the community and the existence of individuals? Is the community more the result of the meeting and the interrelation between individual subjects who were previously isolated or what originally constitutes them in their "common" reality? Is community the subsequent product or the anticipatory deconstruction of subjectivity?

Sartre, who will rightly inscribe Bataille in the second of these options, can't help likening the Bataillian idea of communication with Heidegger's *Mitsein*, though he will quickly insert an essential difference between the two. Once again it is situated in the contrast between interiority and exteriority, immanence and transcendence, identity and alterity. On the one hand, Bataille, who is always influenced by a scientific outlook, looks at the community from a perspective outside the self, a position that for Sartre only God could have, and therefore Bataille understands community as an ensemble of things rather than as a subjective entity. On the other hand, Heidegger remains faithful to an internal gaze according to the parameters of an existentialist humanism that Sartre will continue to attribute to him. It's only from this point of view, evidently, that Sartre can declare that community for Bataille is closer to the "aggregates" that contemporary French sociology speaks about, whose circles Bataille frequented in that "strange and famous *Collège de Sociologie*," as Sartre expressed it with ironic distance, and not with Heideggerean *Mitsein*.[68]

For Heidegger—again always according to Sartre's reconstruction (though appropriation would be closer to the truth)—*Mitsein* is nevertheless a community of autonomous individuals [*uomini*] who, precisely because finite, are free to decide their own destiny based on their own specific designs [*progetti*]. Bataille instead places himself at the limit, on the limit between inside and outside, immanence and transcendence, humanity and nonhumanity. His subject is both autonomous and dependent, one and many, self and other from self. It is therefore no longer a true subject inasmuch as it is subjected to forces, instincts, passions that traverse it. Wanting to be everything, the subject is at the mercy of a nothing not produced by him but to which he submits; at the mercy of a nonknowledge that embarrasses and makes ridiculous his knowledge; at the mercy of a "pantheist" ecstasy that for Sartre is the reverse of an authentic inner experience. "The true inner experience," concludes the critic, "is in fact at the extreme opposite end of pantheism. Finding himself again through the *cogito*, man can no longer get lost; the abyss and the night are no longer nothing, he is everything to himself . . . Man is immanent to the human."[69] Thus, the result of Sartre's analysis, or his investigation, conforms exactly with what he presumes from the outset. What he wanted to demonstrate is demonstrated perfectly: Sartre's checkmate over Bataille coincides with and derives from the wrong-headed interpretation of the philosopher, here Heidegger, whom Sartre himself still believes to be the best interpreter.

It would be enough to wait patiently for Heidegger's *Letter on Humanism* in which every relation with Sartrian existentialism is sharply refuted in order to see that things weren't exactly as Sartre had argued.[70] Moreover, the appearance of an equivocation wasn't foreign to Heidegger himself when, perhaps to be free from the isolation in which he found himself after the war, he wrote to Sartre that *Being and Nothingness* constituted "an understanding so immediate of his own philosophy, which he had until then never encountered," even to the point of agreeing with Sartre's critique of "being-with" as well as Sartre's accent on "being-for-the-other."[71] In reality it is precisely the critique of *Mitsein*, of the "being-with" in favor of a conception of intersubjectivity centered completely on "being-for-the-other" contained in *L'être et le néant* that marks a clear line of demarcation between the two philosophers, despite and within the Sartrian equivocation vis-à-vis Heidegger's existentialism. But not only this. What matters more in this context is the fact that in contradiction to what is argued in *Un nouveau mystique* [*A New Mystic*], this line of demarcation coincides in large measure with the distance taken up with respect to Bataille, even if the latter is never deigned worthy of an explicit reference. In other words, if in *Un nouveau mystique*, Sartre attacks Bataille in the name of Heidegger, in *Being and Nothingness* he puts forward a series of protests against Heidegger that aren't any different from those addressed to Bataille.

But let's dig deeper into the question. In the section titled "The Immediate Structures of the For-Itself," Sartre already challenges Heidegger with having introduced the theme of *Dasein*, without first touching on the *cogito*, which is to say that Heidegger projected the *cogito* onto an "outside" that can no longer be referred to the interiority of consciousness.[72] As we saw, this is a criticism that resembles another one addressed to Bataille in the name of the same Heidegger. Certainly, Sartre agrees in understanding the *réalité humaine* as self-transcendence, as self-overcoming and non-coincidence, and indeed as the annihilation of one's own being. Yet we are dealing with a negation whose purpose is precisely, even if it is infinite and never finished, of "disalienating" the subject, of "reconverting him" back to his own proper identity, to what is his most authentic self. Now it is precisely this return, this reentry into the self that is outside the non-dialectic modality that Heidegger attributes to the idea of *Sorge*, to "cure" as (the expression here is from Sartre) "the escape from selfness" of *Dasein*.[73] Once the subject is outside itself, it can no longer return properly within because the escape outside deconstructs the same notion of subject-consciousness and opens it to an alterity that breaks through in an unthinkable dimension in the post-Cartesian semantics of the *cogito* that Sartre defends.

This dimension is that of the community, of the *Mitsein*, of the being-with. It is no accident that exactly here Sartre concentrates his polemic in the third section of *Being and Nothingness*. Sartre's attack moves in true circular logic. He begins by recognizing the originality of Heidegger's approach only to negate its formal and substantive legitimacy soon after. Heidegger goes beyond both Husserl's psychological model of Hegel's historicist one to the degree in which *Mitsein* isn't the product of bringing two or more individuals closer together, but rather is the originary presupposition within which the notion of individuality is irreversibly modified. It is exactly this modification of subjectivity that Sartre rejects. The motivation behind such a refusal is strictly logical. Heidegger's error, Sartre says, resides chiefly in an exchange of levels between the ontic and the ontological levels that logically isn't allowed; between the sphere of factuality and that of universal law. On the one hand, Heidegger transforms a number of empirical elements of our existence into the ontological structure of being-in-common. On the other hand, he confuses the abstract with the concrete, the other in general with the other in particular. For Sartre, in other words, the "we" is unattainable, considering the individual subject that Sartre is unwilling to relinquish given the presuppositions of his own position concerning the subject's own consciousness. The other isn't recognizable except as "non-I," that which the I essentially negates; in the same way as the I is nothing other than the negation of the other, what the subjectivity of the other needs in turn to negate (to remain as such) so as not to be objectified by the I (and thus disappearing as other). The relation cannot be one except of reciprocal negation. Any experience of we (of we as subject and we as object) isn't conceivable except with respect to an exclusion: we are "we" because we are *not* others, just as the others are "other" because they are *not* we.[74] This is what Sartre intends when he juxtaposes *cogito* to *Mitsein*, intersubjectivity to the community, "for self" to "with self." At no point do individual experiences cross; nor are they superimposed or included one in the other. On the contrary, they face off in a mutual battle. This is the reason that Sartre can say that "I grasp the other . . . in a fear which *lives* all possibilities as ambivalent" and that "the Other is the hidden death of my possibilities."[75] Human reality, because it is immanent to itself, is imprisoned in a tragic choice: to transcend the other or to allow itself to be transcended by the other. Sartre's conclusion follows without delay: "The essence of the relations between conscious-ness is not the *Mitsein*; it is conflict."[76] In these words—just as in all of Sartrean theater—echoes the impossibility of community that the "com-munism" of the succeeding years will not be able to deny but indeed will confirm and contradict.[77]

Without entering into the merits of the great communitarian failure of *The Critique of Dialectical Reason*, let's dwell a little while longer on the point that interests us most: what Sartre rejects in Heidegger's thought is what the latter shares with Bataille. Heidegger and Bataille are united by what Sartre rejects in both. It isn't difficult to identify the object in their proclaimed antihumanism. The texts of both that make it obvious are too well known to be called upon again. What we need to underscore, however, is that we are not speaking of the *same* antihumanism; a further verification of that parallel convergence, of that dissonant harmony sepa-rating Bataille from Heidegger through the same line that at other times joins them. Here too it isn't possible to reconstruct in detail the entire line of divergence between the two critics of humanism. Still, one could sum-marize it in the following formula: whereas Heidegger's antihumanism moves beyond humanist anthropology that "does not set the *humanitas* of man high enough" (as Heidegger himself expresses it in his *Letter on Humanism*), Bataille reverses it in his inferior border.[78] This becomes most evident in the relation that both take up with respect to the animal; the tried-and-true test of all antihumanisms. If in the rigorously antibiologist perspective of Heidegger, the animal is what is most extraneous to man (more than the same divine essence),[79] for Bataille the animal is part of us; the most deeply repressed part of ourselves: "The animal opens before me a depth that attracts me and is familiar to me. In a sense I know this depth: it is my own."[80]

The correspondence by contrast between Heidegger and Bataille doesn't end here. We know that for Heidegger what defines the insuperable line of discontinuity between man and the living other "poor in world" is constituted by our capacity for semantic elaboration, this in addition to that of language, and of the hand that gives, points to, and prays, which are never possible for the animal's paw. The hand, therefore, appears as a kind of privileged vehicle for the *munus* that "joins" us.[81] Again, Bataille will reverse the argument. Against every originary *logos*, what the grottos of Lascaux reveal is the unbreakable interweaving of humanity and animality produced precisely by the civilizing hand of man. In the design in which the superiority of the human species takes form, "man ceases to be animal giving to the animal (and not to himself) a poetic image,"[82] and indeed depicting himself with an animal mask. What comes to light in this text is certainly another and extreme mode for breaking the identity of the subject through its violent rootedness in that animal that at one time men "loved and killed";[83] something as well in close proximity of friendship and death refers to that same *communitas* that constitutes us without belonging to us.

Appendix: Nihilism and Community

What is the relation between nihilism and community? The response of different philosophies of community as well as of a widely held interpretation of nihilism moves in the direction of a radical juxtaposition between them. The relation between nihilism and community isn't one simply of otherness but rather of direct contrast that disallows for any points of contact or overlap. Nihilism and community mutually exclude each other: where there is one (or when there is one), the another isn't, and vice versa. Whether the contrast is situated on the synchronic level or along a diachronic trajectory doesn't matter. What does matter is the distinct alternative presented between the two poles that appears to take on meaning because one cannot be reduced to the other. With respect to its most specific meanings of artificiality, anomie, and insensateness, nihilism is seen as what makes community impossible or even unthinkable, whereas the community is always interpreted as what resists, contains, and opposes such a nihilist drift. Essentially, this is the role conferred on community by communal, communitarian, and communicative conceptions that for more than a century have found community to be the only shelter from the devastating power of nothing that goes completely unchecked in modern society. What changes in this scenario is the order that now and again is attributed to the two terms; what doesn't change is the rigid dichotomy that characterizes the relation between nihilism and community. Whereas Ferdinand Tönnies situates community before society according to a genealogy that every philosophy of twilight, betrayal, and loss of the last century will follow (be it on the left or the right), contemporary neocommunitarians on the other side of the Atlantic reverse the times of the dichotomy without discussing its underlying organization. It is the community (or better, the particular communities that Tönnies's archetype is broken up into) that succeeds modern society, in a moment marked by the crises of the paradigm of the state and by the spread of multicultural conflict. In this case community is no longer understood as a residual phenomenon with respect to the sociocultural forms that modernity assumes, but rather as a response to the insufficiency of modernity's individualistic-universalistic model. It is this society of individuals, who were already a destructive force for the organic ancient community, that now generates new communitarian forms as a posthumous reaction to its own entropy. Here returns the reciprocal exclusion that community enjoys with nihilism. The community advances or retreats; it expands or it contracts according to the space that the other has not yet "colonized." When Habermas juxtaposes a communicative rationality with a strategic one, he remains within the same interpretive paradigm, with an accentuation that smacks of the defensive. The "limitless community of communication" constitutes both the point of resistance and the reserve of meaning with respect to the progressive intrusiveness of technology. That it is understood as a transcendental a priori and not as a factual one according to the neocommunitarian approach doesn't change the basic hermeneutic frame: in this case as well, the community, understood as possible if not real, is taken as the demarcating line and the defense against the advance of nihilism; something replete (it could be a substance, a promise, a value) that doesn't allow itself to be emptied out by the vortex of nullity. It is another configuration of that conflict between the "thing" and "no-thing" that is the presupposition of the entire tradition that we are examining here. It is against that explosion (or implosion) of nothing that the community holds on firmly to the reality of the thing. Indeed, community is the thing itself that is opposed to its own destruction.

Yet is this really an acceptable presupposition, or does this presupposition in fact prevent us from thinking community in a way that is able to meet the needs of our own time, a time characterized by a fully realized nihilism? If we say yes, we would then necessarily be forced to choose between two hypotheses that are otherwise inadmissible: either we negate the constitutively nihilistic character of the current epoch or we exclude the question of community from our purview. If we are to speak of community in terms that aren't simply nostalgic, there does remain the path of circumscribing nihilism within one feature or one particular moment of our experience, namely, to think of it as a phenomenon that "ends," that is destined to come apart at a certain point or at least to recede; or to understand it as a disease that has reached only a fixed set of organs in a body that is otherwise healthy. Yet reductive reasonings of this kind butt up against every piece of evidence, all of which taken together point to nihilism not as a parenthesis or a condition but rather as the underlying tendency of modern society, which has arrived at its outermost point of expansion. And so? The only way to resolve the question without forgoing any of the terms will be found in bringing together community and nihilism in a unitary thought, seeing in the realization of nihilism not an insurmountable obstacle to community but instead the occasion for a new way of thinking community. Obviously, this doesn't mean that community and nihilism emerge as the same or even as only symmetrical, or that they are to be situated on the same level or along the same trajectory. Rather, it means that they cross each other at a point that neither can do without because such a point emerges as constitutive of both nihilism and community. This point, which goes unnoticed (or is repressed or nullified by contemporary communitarian philosophies, but more generally by the political philosophical tradition), can be denoted as "no-thing" [*niente*]. No-thing is what community and nihilism have in common in a form that has up to now gone largely unexamined.

In what sense? Leaving aside for the moment the underlying question of the relation that nihilism enjoys with no-thing—a question whose answer is anything but simple—let's focus instead on community. We have seen how community has traditionally been contrasted with nihilism as our very own thing [*cosa*], and indeed how its definition is identical with such an opposition between thing and no-thing: the community isn't only different from and irreducible to no-thing but coincides with its most direct opposite, with an "everything" that is utterly replete with itself. This, I believe, is exactly the perspective that needs to be not only problematized but fundamentally reversed. The community isn't the site of the juxtaposition but that of the superimposition between thing and no-thing. I have tried to support this assumption through an etymological and philosophical analysis of the term *communitas*, starting with the term *munus* from which community is derived.[1] What emerges conclusively from my discussion is the categorical distance community enjoys vis-à-vis every conception of a property that is collectively owned by a totality of individuals or by their having a common identity. According to the originary valence of the concept of community, what the members of a community share, based upon the complex and profound meaning of *munus*, is rather an expropriation of their own essence, which isn't limited to their "having" but one that involves and affects their own "being subjects." Here the discourse follows a crease that moves from the more traditional terrain of anthropology or of political philosophy to that more radical terrain of ontology: that the community isn't joined to an addition but to a subtraction of subjectivity, by which I mean that its members are no longer identical with themselves but are constitutively exposed to a propensity that forces them to open their own individual boundaries in order to appear as what is "outside" themselves. From this point of view, the figure of the other returns to full view, breaking with every continuity between "common" and "proper," linking the "common" instead to the improper. If the subject of community is no longer the "same," it will by necessity be an "other"; not another subject but a chain of alterations that cannot ever be fixed in a new identity.

If the community always consists of others and never of itself, this suggests that its presence is constitutively inhabited by an absence of subjectivity, of identity, of property. It intimates that it is not a "thing" or that rather it is a thing defined precisely by its "non." A "non-thing." Now how are we to understand this "non," and how is it related to the thing in which it inheres? Certainly not in the sense of a pure negation. The no-thing-in-common isn't the opposite of an entity but something that corresponds to it and belongs even more intensely to it. It is precisely with respect to the sense of this correspondence or co-belonging that we need to be careful so as to avoid any confusion. The no-thing of *communitas* isn't to be interpreted as what community still cannot be, as the negative moment of a contradiction that is destined to resolve itself dialectically in the identity of opposites. Nor is it to be interpreted as the process of concealing in which the thing is withdrawn because it can no longer be unveiled in the fullness of a pure present. In each of these cases, in fact, the no-thing of *communitas* wouldn't remain the no-thing of the thing but would be transformed into something other that it would relate to either as teleology or as presupposition. It would either be its past or future, but not its simple present: what community is and not other from it.

In brief, no-thing isn't the condition or the result of community, namely, the presupposition that frees community from its one true possibility, but rather is community's only mode of being. In other words, community isn't incapacitated, obscured, or hidden by no-thing but instead is constituted by it. This means simply that community isn't an entity, nor is it a collective subject, nor a totality of subjects, but rather is the relation that makes them no longer individual subjects because it closes them off from their identity with a line, which traversing them, alters them: it is the "with," the "between," and the threshold where they meet in a point of contact that brings them into relation with others to the degree to which it separates them from themselves.

Referring to another term that has taken on a meaning opposed to its originary one, we could say that the community isn't the *inter* of *esse* but rather *esse* as *inter*, not a relation that shapes being [*essere*] but being itself as the relation. The distinction is important because it is one that restores in the most obvious fashion the superimposition of being and no-thing: the being of community is the interval of difference, the spacing that brings us into relation with others in a common non-belonging, in this loss of what is proper that never adds up to a common "good."

Common is only lack and not possession, property, or appropriation. The fact that the Romans understood by the term *munus* only the gift [*dono*] that was made and never the gift received (which was instead denoted in the word *donum*) signals that it is lacking in "remuneration," and that the breach of a subjective material that it determines remains as such, that is incapable of being made replete, made whole, or healed over; that its opening cannot be closed by any sort of compensation or reparation if it is to continue in fact to remain shared [*condivisa*]. The reason is that in the concept of "sharing with" [*condivisione*], the "with" [*con*] is associated with dividing up [*divisione*]. The limit that is alluded to here is the one that unites not through con-vergence, con-version, or con-fusion, but rather through di-vergence, di-version, and dif-fusion. The direction is always from within and never from without. The community is the exteriorization of what is within. For this to be the case (because it is opposed to the idea of interiorization or, for that matter, internment), the *inter* of community cannot be joined up except through a series of exteriors or "moving outside," through subjects open to what is properly outside of them. We see this decentering in the same idea of partition [*partizione*], which refers both to a "sharing with" and a "taking leave of" [*partenza*]: the community is never a point of arrival but always one of departure [*di partenza*]. Indeed, it is the departure itself toward that which doesn't belong to us and can never belong to us. For this reason *communitas* is utterly incapable of producing effects of commonality, of association [*accomunamento*], and of communion. It doesn't keep us warm, and it doesn't protect us; on the contrary, it exposes us to the most extreme of risks: that of losing, along with our individuality, the borders that guarantee its inviolability with respect to the other; of suddenly falling into the nothing of the thing [*niente della cosa*].

It is with reference to this no-thing that the question of nihilism is to be posed, but in a form that captures together with the connection also the distinction of levels on which it rests. Nihilism isn't the expression but the suppression of no-thing-in-common. Certainly nihilism has quite a lot to do with no-thing, but precisely with regard to its destruction. Nihilism isn't the no-thing of the thing but of its no-thing [*non è il niente della cosa, ma del suo niente*]. A nothing squared: nothing multiplied and simultaneously swallowed by nothing. This means that at least two meanings are given of nothing that are to be kept distinct despite (and because of) their apparent coincidence. As we have seen, whereas the first is that of the relation, the lacuna or the spacing that makes a common being a relation and not an entity, the second is that of its dissolution: the dissolution of the relation in the absoluteness of having no relation.

If we look at Hobbesian absolutism from this perspective, the steps toward such a "solution" take on an unmatched clarity. That Hobbes inaugurated modern political nihilism isn't to be understood simply in the current sense that he "dis-covered" the substantial nullity [*nulla*] of a world liberated from the metaphysical constraints with respect to every transcendental *veritas*, but rather in that he re-covers it with another, more powerful nothing that has the function of canceling the potentially disrupting effects of the first. Just so, the *pointe* of Hobbes's philosophy resides in the invention of a new origin that is directed to halting and reconverting through force the originary nothing, the absence of the origin, of *communitas*. Of course, this kind of contradictory strategy of neutralization, the emptying out a given emptiness through an artificial emptiness created ex nihilo, is born from a completely negative and indeed catastrophic interpretation of the principle of sharing with, of the initial sharing with of being. It is this negativity that is attributed to the originary community that justifies the sovereign order, the Leviathan state, which is capable of immunizing ahead of time against its unbearable *munus*. In order for the operation to succeed, that it be logical and rational (despite the high price of sacrifice and of renunciation that it requires), it's not only necessary that this common *munus* be deprived of its element of excessive gift giving in favor of what is defective [*difetto*] but also that this defect, in the neutral sense of the Latin *delinquere*, to lack, be understood as a true and proper "crime" [*delitto*], indeed as an unstoppable series of potential crimes.

It is this radical interpretive forcing—from a no-thing-in-common to the community of the crime—that establishes the erasure of *communitas* in favor of a political form founded on the voiding of every external relation in favor of the vertical one between individuals and sovereigns and therefore on their dissociation. Set in motion by the demand of protecting the thing from no-thing that seems to threaten it, Hobbes winds up destroying the thing itself with no-thing [*per annientare col niente, la cosa medesima*]; winds up sacrificing not only the *inter* of *esse* but also the *esse* of *inter* in favor of individual interest. All of the modern responses that have over time been offered in response to the "Hobbesian problem of order," be it in the form of decision, function, or system, risk remaining caught in a vicious circle. The only way to contain the dangers implicit in the originary deficiency of the animal-man appears to be the construction of an artificial prosthesis—the barrier of institutions—that is capable of protecting him from a potentially destructive encounter with those like him. Yet to assume a prosthesis, a non-organ or a missing organ, as a form of social mediation means confronting one void with another even more extreme because it is from the outset one that has been seized and produced by the absence for which it needs to compensate. The same principle of representation, conceived of as the formal mechanism directed toward conferring presence on the one absent, does nothing other than reproduce and strengthen that void to the degree in which it isn't able to conceptualize its originary (and not derived) character. It isn't able to understand that the no-thing that it ought to make up for isn't a loss, be it of substance, of foundation, of value, that all at once comes to break up the preceding order. Rather, it is the character itself of our being-in-common. Modern nihilism did not want or know how to excavate any deeper into the nothing of the relation, and so finds itself consigned to the no-thing of the absolute, of absolute nothing.

It is from this absolute nothing that the modern philosophy of community tries to flee via an option that is both identical and different, which, nevertheless, winds up falling back into the same nihilism that it wanted to counter. What is made absolute now is the thing rather than no-thing. Yet what does it mean to make the thing absolute, if not to annihilate (and so once again to strengthen) the very same no-thing? The strategy is no longer that of emptying out but, on the contrary, of occupying the void determined by, indeed constituted by the originary *munus*. Beginning with Rousseau and comprising contemporary communitarianism as well, what appears as an alternative is revealed, however, as the specular reverse of the Hobbesian scheme of immunization (with which it shares the subjectivist lexicon applied this time not to the individual but to the collective in its totality). In any case what stops functioning, crushed as it is by the superimposition of the individual and the collective, is the relation itself, understood as the singular and plural modality of existence, annulled in the first instance by the absoluteness that separates individuals and in the second by their fusion in a sole subject that is enclosed in an identity with itself. If we assume the Rousseauean community of Clarens as our model of such a self-identification, which has been reproduced innumerable times, all of the characteristic features of it are there in vitro: from the reciprocal incorporation of those that are a part of it to the perfect self-sufficiency of the totality to which they give way, to the inevitable juxtaposition that results with regard to everything that is outside. The outside as such is incompatible with a community so folded in on itself as to construct between its members a transparency without any opacity (as well as an immediacy without mediations) that continually reduces each one to another, an other that is no longer other because it is now identified beforehand with the former. That Rousseau didn't foresee and indeed explicitly denies the translatability of the similar community of the heart [*communauté de coeur*] into any form of political democracy doesn't detract from the power of mythological suggestion that it has exerted not only on the entire Romantic tradition but also in some ways on the ideal type of Tönnesian *Gemeinschaft*, it too founded on the generality of a will that is essentially subordinated to that of its individual exponents.

Still, there is something else that concerns the unconsciously nihilist relapse of this opposition of community into the nihilism of modern society, with respect to what is revealed not only as fully consistent but in fact strictly functional as its simple reverse. Every time that the excess of meaning of a community—occupied by its own collective essence—wanted to counter the vacuum of sense produced in the individualistic paradigm, the consequences were destructive: first with regard to external or internal enemies against which such a community is constructed, and second with regard to itself. As we know, this concerns in the first instance the totalitarian experiments that bloodied the first half of the last century, but in a manner different from and certainly less devastating than all the forms of "fatherland," "motherland," and "brotherhood" [*fratria*] that have grouped legions of believers, patriots, and brothers around a model that is inevitably *koino*-centric. The reason that such a tragic coercion repeats itself (and never gives any hint of exhausting itself), lies in the fact that when the thing is made replete with its own substance, it risks exploding or imploding under its own weight. This occurs when subjects reunited in the communal chain recognize that the access to their condition of possibility is found in the reappropriation of their own communal essence. This in turn appears to be configured as the fullness of a lost origin and for that very reason can be rediscovered in the interiorization of an existence that is momentarily made exterior. What is assumed as possible and necessary is the elision and reoccupation of that void of essence that constitutes precisely the *ex* of *exsistentia*: its characteristic that isn't proper because it is "common." It's only through the abolition of its nothing that the thing can finally be fulfilled. Yet the realization of the thing, which is necessarily phantasmic, is precisely the objective of totalitarianism. The absolute indifferentiation that winds up suppressing not only its own proper object but the subject itself that it puts into operation. The thing isn't capable of being appropriated except by being destroyed. It isn't to be rediscovered for the simple reason that it was never lost. What appears lost isn't anything other than the no-thing out of which the thing is constituted in its communal dimension.

Heidegger was the first to search for the community in the no-thing of the thing. Without retracing here the complex journey of the interrogation of the thing that unravels across his entire work, we need to linger in particular over the 1950 conference titled "The Thing" (*Das Ding*), not only because the journey seems to culminate there but, more to the point, because the "thing" that in other places is examined in its aesthetic, logical, and historical features is here referred back to its communal essence. The expression is to be understood in a dual sense: in the first instance when Heidegger calls upon the most modest, habitual things at hand (here the jug), but also in the sense that this modesty is the custodian of the empty point in which the thing discovers its least predictable meaning, as was already noted in "The Origin of the Work of Art": "The inconspicuous thing withdraws itself from thought in the most stubborn of ways. Or is it rather that this self-refusal of the mere thing . . . belongs precisely to the essential nature of thing?"[2] It is to such an essence, "the thingness of the thing," that his discourse in "The Thing" is dedicated. It doesn't consist in the objectivity with which we represent it, nor does it consist in the production out of which the thing produced seems to "originate." And so? It's here that the example of the jug can be of help, but also the other things that are referred to in the essays from the same years, such as the tree, the bridge, the door. What is the element they all share? We are concerned here essentially with the void [*vuoto*]. The void is the essence of these things as it is of all things. It's this way for the jug, which is constructed around a void and which it, in the final analysis, has formed: "When we fill the jug, the pouring that fills it flows into the empty jug. The emptiness, the void, is what does the vessel's holding. The empty space, this nothing of the jug [*Die Leere, dieses Nichts am Krug*], is what the jug is as the holding vessel."[3] The essence of the thing is therefore its nothingness [*nulla*] to the point that outside of the perspective that it provides, the thing loses what is most proper to it, until it disappears or, as Heidegger himself expresses it, until it is annihilated: there where its essence is forgotten "in truth, however, the thing as thing remains proscribed, nil, and in that sense annihilated" [*In Wahrheit bleibt jedoch das Ding als Ding verwehrt, nichtig und in solchem Sinne vernichtet*].[4]

All of this might seem quite paradoxical: the thing is annihilated if it doesn't profoundly catch hold of what is most essential. But as we just saw, this essential character doesn't reside anywhere except in its void. It is the forgetting of this nothingness, this void, that hands the thing over to a scientistic [*scientista*], productivistic, and nihilist point of view that annuls it. Here too we find ourselves having to construct a distinction between two types of "nothingness" [*nulla*]: the first that restores to us the thing in its profound reality and another, on the contrary, that removes it from us and, rather than nullifying the former, nullifies the very same thing on which it is constituted. Some lines further on, Heidegger furnishes the key to resolving the apparent paradox: the nothingness that saves the thing from the void, to the degree in which it constitutes it as thing, is the void of the *munus*; of the offering that reverses what is inside to the outside: "To pour from the jug is to give [*Schenken*]."[5] And we are speaking of a common *munus* insofar as it is given in the gathering together and as what is gathered: "The nature of the holding void is gathered in the giving."[6] Here Heidegger evokes the high German words *thing* and *dinc* precisely in their original meaning of "reunion." The giving expressed by the void of the jug is also and principally a reuniting. How so? What reunites, through an offering, the void of the thing? Heidegger here inserts the theme of the "single Fourfold," of the relation between earth and sky, mortals and gods. Yet our attention should be focused rather on the relation as such: the nothing [*niente*] that it places in common and the community of nothing as the essence of the thing. Isn't it precisely this, the pure relation, that up to now in Heidegger constitutes the common element of all things evoked: the tree that joins the earth to the sky, the bridge that joins two banks of a river, the door that links inside and out? Aren't we concerned fundamentally (as is the case with *communitas*) with a unity *in* distance and *of* distance; of a distance that unites and of a far-awayness [*lontananza*] brought near? What, finally, is nihilism if not an abolition of distance, of the nullity of the thing that makes impossible every bringing closer? "The failure of nearness to materialize in consequence of the abolition of all distances has brought the distanceless to dominance. In the default of nearness the thing remains annihilated as a thing in our sense."[7]

The only author to take up the question left open by Heidegger, namely, the relation between community and no-thing in the epoch of complete nihilism, is Georges Bataille: "Communication cannot proceed from one full and intact individual to another. It requires individuals whose separate existence in themselves is *risked*, placed at the limit of death and nothingness."[8] The passage refers to a short text titled "Nothingness, Transcendence, Immanence" in which nothingness [*nulla*] is defined as the "limit of an individual existence" beyond which it "no longer exists. For us, that non-being is filled with meaning: I know I can be reduced to nothing" [*Ce non-être est pour nous plein de sens: je sais qu'on peut m'anéantir*].[9] Why is the possibility of annihilating oneself so charged with meaning and indeed constitutes the only meaning that is feasible in the phase in which every meaning seems to have run aground? The question brings us both to the Bataillian interpretation of nihilism and the point in which it aporetically traverses the site uninhabited by community. For Bataille, nihilism isn't the flight of meaning or flight from meaning, but rather meaning's enclosure within a homogenous and complete conception of being. Nowhere more than here does nihilism not coincide with what threatens to void the thing. On the contrary, it is what occludes the thing in a fullness without fault lines. In other words, nihilism isn't to be sought in a lack but in a withdrawal. Nihilism is the lack of a lack, its repression or its reindemnification; what subtracts us from our otherness, sealing us off in ourselves, making of that "we" a series of complete individuals who are turned toward their own proper interior, utterly settled upon themselves: "[B]oredom then discloses the nothingness of self-enclosure. When separate existence stops communicating, it withers. It wastes away, (obscurely) feeling that *by itself it doesn't exist*. Unproductive and unattractive, such inner nothingness repels us. It brings about a fall into restless boredom, and boredom transfers the restlessness from inner nothingness to outer nothingness—or anguish."[10] Here is made clear the double register of the semantics of nothing [*nulla*] as well as the move that Bataille makes from the first to the second: from the no-thing of the individual, of the proper, of the within, to the nothing-in-common of the outside. The latter is also a nothing [*niente*], but it is that nothing that tears us away from absolute nothing, from the nothing of the absolute because it is the nothing of the relation. Man is structurally exposed to (though one could also say constituted by) this paradoxical condition of being able to flee annihilation by implosion, only to risk his destruction through explosion: "With temptation, if I can put it this way, we're crushed by twin pincers of nothingness. By not communicating, we're annihilated into the emptiness of an isolated life. By communicating we likewise risk being destroyed."[11]

That Bataille, here as elsewhere, is speaking of "being" when alluding to our existence, isn't to be read simply as some sort of terminological imprecision due to Bataille's lack of professional, philosophical credentials. Rather, it is to be understood as the desired effects of a superimposition between anthropology and ontology within the common figure of lack or, more exactly, of a tearing (*déchirure*). It is true, in fact, that we can look on being outside our limits but only by breaking them and indeed by identifying ourselves with such a break. We can do this thanks to the fact that being from the beginning is also lacking with regard to itself, since the foundation of things isn't constituted by a substance but rather by an originary opening. We gain access to it, to this void, in the limit experiences that distance us from ourselves, that distance us from being the masters of our own existence. Yet these experiences are nothing other than the anthropological effect (or the subjective dimension) of the void of being that gives rise to them; similar to a large hole that is made up of many holes that open by turns within it. It is with this sense in mind that we can say that man is the wound of a being that is alternately and always already wounded. This means that when we speak of being-in-common or "communal" [*comuniale*] as the continuum into which every existence that has broken through its own individual limits falls, we must not understand this continuum as a homogenous totality, which is exactly the nihilist perspective. Nor should it be understood properly as being or as the Other of being, but rather as that vortex, the common *munus*, in which the continuum is one with what is discontinuous, as is being with non-being. This is why the "greatest" communication doesn't have the features of an addition or a multiplication but rather of a subtraction. It doesn't move between one and the other but between the other of the one and the other of the other.

The beyond of my being is first of all nothingness. This is the absence I discern in laceration and in painful feelings of lack: It reveals the presence of another person. Such a presence, however, is fully disclosed only when the *other* similarly leans over the edge of nothingness and falls into it (dies). "Communication" only takes place *between two people who risk themselves*, each lacerated and suspended, perched atop a common nothingness.[12]

We can certainly say that with Heidegger and Bataille twentieth-century thought on community reaches both its greatest point of intensity and its extreme limit. The reason is not that such a thought breaks off in their philosophies and moves in a mythic and regressive direction, nor that further elaborations, developments, and intuitions are missing in work done around them as well as after them that refer to the question of the *cum* (albeit under different names and elaborations, as the writings and the lives of Simone Weil, Dietrich Bonhoeffer, Jan Patočka, Robert Antelme, Osip Mandel'stam, and Paul Celan amply demonstrate). Rather, the reason is that these figures weren't able to think community except by commencing with the problem posed and left unresolved by Heidegger and Bataille. It's the same reason that all that separates us from them, namely, philosophy, sociology, and political science in the second half of the century, remains forgotten in the question of community, or worse, contributes to its deformation, reducing and impoverishing it to the defense of new particular entities. With regard to such a drift in meaning, one both felt in and produced by all of the debates currently under way concerning individualism and communitarianism, only recently has an attempt been made, particularly in France and Italy, to open again a new philosophical reflection about community at exactly the point in which the preceding one was interrupted in the middle of the last century.[13] The necessary reference to Heidegger and Bataille that such a reflection brings with it is accompanied, nevertheless, by the clear knowledge that their lexicon has inevitably been exhausted and is therefore to be subject to a condition, both material and spiritual, whose depths they could not truly know.

I am alluding once again to nihilism and more exactly to the further acceleration over the final decades of the last century that has taken place. This quickening probably allows (but also forces) us to reorient our thinking of community in a direction that Heidegger and Bataille were only able to intuit but not to thematize. What direction would that be? Without presuming to furnish an exhaustive answer to what constitutes the question of our time, we turn our gaze again unavoidably to the figure of "no-thing." "The question is, rather" writes the contemporary author who more than anyone else has the merit of clearing a way forward in the closed thought of community—how to understand the "nothing itself. Either it is the void of truth or it is nothing other than the world itself, and the sense of being-toward-the-world."[14] How are we to make sense of this alternative, and are we really dealing with an alternative? One might observe that from a certain point of view it is the absence of community (and even more the desert of community) that indicates the demand for community as that which we lack and indeed as our very same state of lacking; as a void that never asks to be filled with new or ancient myths but rather is to be reinterpreted in the light of its own "non." Yet Nancy's phrase just cited tells us something else that we might summarize this way. The result of the extreme realization of nihilism (its absolute uprooting, its extensive technology, its complete mondialization [*mondializzazione*]) has two aspects that are to be not only distinguished from each other but also made to interact. We could say that community is nothing other than the limit that separates and joins them. On the one hand, its meaning emerges as split, torn, and voided; and this is the destructive aspect that we know so well, namely, the end of every generalization of sense, the loss of mastery with regard to the complex meaning of experience. On the other hand, this disactivation or devastation of overall meaning opens up a space of simultaneity with respect to the emergence of a singular meaning that coincides with the absence of meaning, and that at the same time transforms it into its opposite. It is when every meaning that is already given, arranged in a frame of meaningful reference, goes missing that the meaning of the world as such is made visible, turned inside out, without enjoying a reference to any transcendental meaning. The community isn't anything else except the border and the point of transit between this immense devastation of meaning and the necessity that every singularity, every event, every fragment of existence make sense in itself. Community refers to the singular and plural characteristic of an existence free from every meaning that is presumed, imposed, or postponed; of a world reduced to itself that is capable of simply being what it is: a planetary world without direction, without any cardinal points. In other words, a nothing-other-than-world. It is this nothing held in common that is the world that joins us [*accomunarci*] in the condition of exposure to the most unyielding absence of meaning and simultaneously to that opening to a meaning that still remains unthought.

Notes

INTRODUCTION

1. On this point and others, see the crucial essay by Jean-Luc Nancy, *The Inoperative Community*, trans. Peter Connor et al. (Minneapolis: University of Minnesota Press, 1991), a text to which I owe an unpayable debt, as is the case for every *munus* given us in the form of the most unexpected gift.

2. On the ambiguous "return" of community, see more generally *Renaissance der Gemeinschaft? Stabile Theorie und neue Theoreme*, ed. Carsten Schülter (Berlin: Duncker & Humblot, 1990); and *Gemeinschaft und Gerechtigkeit*, ed. Micha Brumlik and Hauke Brunkhors (Frankfurt: Fischer Taschenbuch Verlag, 1993).

3. See in this regard the entry for "political" in Roberto Esposito, *Nove pensieri sulla politica* (Bologna: Il Mulino, 1993), 15–38.

4. As Michael J. Sandel expresses it in *Liberalism and the Limits of Justice* (Cambridge: Cambridge University Press, 1998), 143. The second expression comes from Philip Selznick, "Foundations of Communitarian Liberalism," in *The Essential Communitarian Reader*, ed. Amitai Etzioni (Lanham, MD: Rowman & Littlefield, 1998), 6.

5. See Émile Benveniste, *Indo-European Language and Society*, trans. Elizabeth Palmer (Coral Gables, FL: University of Miami Press, 1973), even if Benveniste explains that *totus* doesn't appear to be derived from *teuta* but rather from *tomentum*. Yet given that this term signifies "filling" [*imbottitura*], "compactness," and "fullness," the semantic framework doesn't change.

6. Max Weber, *Basic Concepts in Sociology*, trans. H. P. Secher (New York: Philosophical Library, 1962), 91 [emphasis in original]. Compare on this point Furio Ferraresi's "La comunità politica in Max Weber," *Filosofia politica* 2 (1997): 181–210, as well as Gregor Fitzi, "Un problema linguistico-concettuale nelle traduzioni di Weber: 'comunità,'" *Filosofia politica* 2 (1994): 257–268.

7. Ferdinand Tönnies as well in *Community and Civil Society*, ed. Jose Harris, trans. Jose Harris and Margaret Hollis (Cambridge: Cambridge University Press, 2001) thought the earth was the first thing that was properly possessed by the humanity community. On this point, see Sandro Chignola, "*Quidquid est in territorio est de territorio*. Nota sul rapporto tra comunità etnica e Stato-nazione," *Filo-

sofia politica 1 (1993): 49–51. More generally, see Étienne Balibar and Immanuel Wallerstein, *Race, Nation, Class: Ambiguous Identities*, trans. Chris Turner (New York: Routledge, 1991).

8. This is Carl Schmitt's well-known thesis. See especially *The Nomos of the Earth in the International Law of the Jus Publicum Europeaum*, trans. G. L. Ulmen (New York: Telos Press, 2003), 67–79. Let's not forget though that it was precisely Schmitt who attempted in his own way to distance the concept of "community" from the "tyranny of values." See *Le categorie del politico* (Bologna: Il Mulino, 1972), especially note 59, where Schmitt refers to his previous text on community, "Der Gegensatz von Gemeinschaft und Gesellschaft als Beispiel einer zweigliedrigen Unterscheidung," in *Estudios Juridico-Sociales. Homenaje al Profesor Luis Legaz y Lacambra* (Saragossa, Spain: Universidad de Santiago de Compostela, 1960), 160.

9. "That, again, which is common to anything else, will not be peculiar to the thing defined." *Quintillian's Institutes of Oratory: Education of an Orator*, trans. Rev. John Selby Watson (London: Henry G. Bohn, 1856), 39.

10. See Alois Walde and Johann Baptist Hofmann, *Lateinisches etymologisches Wörterbuch* (Heidelberg: C. Winter, 1938–1956).

11. *Thesaurus linguae latinae*, vol. 8, 1662; Egidio Forcellini, *Lexicon totius latinitatis*, vol. 3 (Lipsiae: In Libraria hahniana, 1835), 313.

12. Julius Paulus, *Dig.* 50.16.18.

13. Domitius Ulpianus, *Dig.* 50.16.194.

14. Netta Zagagi, "A Note on *munus, munus fungi* in Early Latin," *Glotta* 60 (1982): 280.

15. Benveniste, *Indo-European Language and Society*, 53–104; and *Problems in General Linguistics*, trans. Mary Elizabeth Meek (Coral Gables, FL: University of Miami Press, 1971). For Marcel Mauss, see *The General Theory of Magic*, trans. Robert Brain (London: Routledge, 1972), 108–121.

16. P.F., 125.18.

17. "A gift is properly an unreturnable giving . . . a thing which is not given with the intention of a return" (*Summa Theologica*, Ia, q.38, a.2, c). On the doubled semantics of the term *Gift*, see also Mauss, *Gift-Gift*, in *Mélanges offerts à Charles Andler par ses amis et élèves* (Strasbourg: Publications de la Faculté des lettres de l'Université de Strasbourg, 1924); and Jean Starobinski, *Largesse* (Chicago: University of Chicago Press, 1997).

18. Alfred Ernout and Antoine Meillet, *Dictionnaire étymologique de la langue latine* (Paris: C. Klincksieck, 1967).

19. Plautus, *Mercator*, 105.

20. Charlton T. Lewis and Charles Short, *A Latin Dictionary Founded on Andrews' Edition of Freund's Latin Dictionary: Revised, Enlarged, and in Great Part Rewritten* (Oxford: Clarendon Press, 1969). Manfred Riedel observes as much in

the entry for *Gesellschaft, Gemeinschaft* in *Geschichtliche Grundbegriffe. Historisches Lexicon zur politisch-sozialen Sprache in Deutschland,* vol. 2 (Stuttgart: Klett-Cotta, 1972), 804–805.

21. P.F., 127.7. See the entry for *munus* in *Realencyclopädie der Classischen Altertumswissenschaft,* ed. August Pauly and Georg Wissowa, vol. 31 (Stuttgart: J. B. Metzler, 1894), 650.

22. In this regard note the first meaning of *communitas* that, for example, the *Oxford Latin Dictionary* supplies: "Joint possession or use, participation, partnership, sharing," even if concluding with "Obligingness" (Oxford: Oxford University Press, 1982), 370.

23. J. L. Marion now suggests "gifted" [*adonné*] in *Being Given: Toward a Phenomenology of Givenness,* trans. Jeffrey L. Kosky (Stanford: Stanford University Press, 2002), 248–319. Always see, on the "impossible" semantics of the gift, Jacques Derrida, *Given Time. I, Counterfeit Money,* trans. Peggy Kamuf (Chicago: University of Chicago Press, 1992), though perhaps more relevant, *L'Ethique du don: Jacques Derrida et la pensée du don* (Paris: Métailié-Transition: Diffusion Seuil, 1992). I have already discussed this "deconstructive" line of the gift in relation to that "constructive" one elaborated for some time now by those authors grouped around the journal *M.A.U.S.S.* and, in particular, Alain Caillé and Serge Latouche in Roberto Esposito, "Donner la technique," *La revue du M.A.U.S.S.,* no. 6 (1999), 190–206.

24. Of course I am speaking of Paul Celan. Martine Broda shows the stronger coherence of the French title, *La Rose de personne,* with respect to the original German title, *Die Niemandsrose,* in his fine essay on Celan titled *Dans la main de personne* (Paris: Éd. du Cerf, 1986), 31.

25. "Though Greeks bring offerings, I fear them still." Virgil, *Aeneid,* trans. Charles James Billson (New York: Courier Dover Publications, 1995), 21.

26. Massimo Cacciari takes his cue from this for his *L'arcipelago* (Milan: Adelphi, 1997), which together with the preceding *Geofilosofia dell'Europa* (Milan: Adelphi, 2003), constitutes an irreplaceable framework for understanding the idea of community.

27. I refer the reader to Bernard Baas's important essay "Le corps du délit," in *Politique et modernité* (Paris: Collège International de Philosophie, 1992), to which I will have occasion to return later.

28. On the complex relation between *koinonia* and community, see the entry for *Gemeinschaft* in *Reallexikon für Antike und Christentum, Sachwörterbuch zur Auseinandersetzung des Christentums mit der antiken Welt,* ed. Theodor Klauser, vol. 9 (Stuttgart: K. W. & A. Hiersemann, 1996), 1202. For an understanding of the broad and differentiated literature on *koinonia,* Pier Cesare Bori's *Koinonia* (Brescia: Paideia, 1972) is still quite useful.

29. See in this regard P. Michaud-Quantin's *Universitas. Expression du mouvement communautaire dans le Moyen-Age latin* (Paris: J. Vrin, 1970), 147–166, pages dedicated to the terms *communitas, commune, communio, communia,* and *communa.*

30. See especially W. Elert, *Koinonia* (Berlin: Lutherisches Verlagshaus, 1957). Still helpful and moving in the same direction is the earlier text by Heinrich Seesemann, *Der Begriff "Koinonia" im N.T.* (Glessen: A. Töpelmann, 1933).

31. John 3:16; 7:37–38.

32. See Augustine's Confessions X, 6: "sharers in my mortality" (*consortium mortalitatis meae*). St. Augustine, *The Confessions of St. Augustine,* trans. Maria Boulding (London: Hodder & Stoughton, 1997), 240.

33. *De Trinitate,* XIII, 2, 5.

34. "The whole world is guilty because of Adam." Augustine, "Answer to Julian," in *The Works of Saint Augustine: A Translation for the 21st Century,* vol. 2 (New York: New City Press, 2001), 479.

35. "But the vessel unto dishonour was made first, and afterwards came the vessel unto honour." Augustine, *The City of God Against the Pagans,* trans. R. W. Dyson (Cambridge: Cambridge University Press, 1998), 635.

36. "It is written, then, that Cain founded a city, whereas Abel, a pilgrim, did not found one." Ibid.

37. Ibid., 639–640.

38. This reading of the "community of guilt" in Saint Augustine is put forward with particular force in Hannah Arendt's *Love and Saint Augustine,* ed. Joanna Vecchiarelli Scott and Judith Chelius Stark (Chicago: University of Chicago Press, 1996), 98–112 (the phrase can be found on page 103). Compare as well Alessandro Dal Lago's Italian translation of Arendt's *The Life of the Mind* [*La vita della mente*] (Bologna: Il Mulino, 1987), 29–33.

39. This is the title of Dietrich Bonhoeffer's *Sanctorum Communio. Eine dogmatische Untersuchung zur Soziologie der Kirche* (Munich: Chr. Kaiser, 1960), as well as that of Paul Althaus, *Communio Sanctorum. Die Gemeinde im lutherischen Kirchengedanken* (Munich: Kaiser, 1929).

40. Augustine, *Commentary on Epistle to the Galatians,* 56.

41. Augustine, *Confessions,* 217.

42. Bruno Accarino has helpfully called attention to this category, especially in relation to the bipolarity of *Belastung/Entlastung* in *La ragione insufficiente* (Rome: Manifestolibri, 1986), though he did so earlier in *Mercanti ed eroi. La crisi del contrattualismo tra Weber e Luhmann* (Naples: Liquori, 1986). Nevertheless, it is important to observe that where Accarino sheds light on the "aggressivity" of the gift, which is to say the restriction of individual liberty implicit in the premodern *compensatio,* it is as if he doesn't see the potentially sacrificial character of modern immunization, which is contained in the semantic of the *dispensatio.* It is on

that point that Pietro Barcellona lingers instead in his *L'individualismo proprietario* (Turin: Bollati Boringhieri, 1987).

43. Georg Simmel previously posed the question in his exemplary excursus on gratitude, which is included in his *Sociology*, trans. Kurt H. Wolff (New York: Free Press of Glencoe, 1964).

44. "Absolute" in the sense that Roman Schnur uses it in his *Individualismus und Absolutismus: zur politischen Theorie vor Thomas Hobbes, 1600–1640* (Berlin: Duncker & Humblot, 1963).

45. How can one forget the pages on the "fear of being touched" that open with a tragic and incomparable *coup de théâtre?* Elias Canetti's magnificent *Crowds and Power*, trans. Carol Stewart (New York: Farrar, Straus & Giroux, 1960). Eligio Resta refers helpfully to the same theme in *Le stelle e le masserizie* (Rome: Laterza, 1997), 67–70.

46. For an attentive and radical thematization of the relation between origin and politics, see Carlo Galli, *Geneaologia della politica* (Bologna: Il Mulino, 1996), as well as my own *L'origine della politica. Simone Weil o Hannah Arendt* (Rome: Donzelli, 1997).

47. On the Hobbesian moment seen from the perspective of its ending, compare the rich and productive analysis of Giacomo Marramao, *Dopo il Leviatano. Individuo e comunità nella filosofia politica* (Turin: Bollati Boringhieri, 1995), even if one might express some doubt about the effective end of the sacrificial paradigm.

48. This is the title of Peter L. Berger's essay, *The Pyramids of Sacrifice: Political Ethics and Social Change* (New York: Basic Books, 1974). On the persistence of the sacrificial paradigm, see as well Francesco Fistetti, *Democrazia e diritti degli altri* (Bari: Palomar di Alternative, 1992).

49. Compare also on this point Giorgio Agamben, *The Coming Community*, trans. Michael Hardt (Minneapolis: University of Minnesota Press, 1993).

50. Umberto Galimberti has drawn attention to these themes in various articles. See in particular "Nostro padre il buon selvaggio," *Repubblica* (August 13, 1997), as well as "Sapere tutto dell'amore e non saper nulla dell'altro," *Repubblica* (November 18, 1997).

51. The Bataillian formula, which Maurice Blanchot takes up in *The Unavowable Community*, trans. Pierre Joris (Barrytown, NY: Station Hill Press, 1988), is the center of the chapter "La comunità della morte" in my *Categorie dell'impolitico* (Bologna: Il Mulino, 1988), 245–322.

52. This is *the* question that Jean Luc Nancy asks us in his illuminating essay on the unsacrificable, which is included in *A Finite Thinking* (Stanford: Stanford University Press, 2003), 51–77.

CHAPTER I

1. Elias Canetti, *The Human Province*, trans. Joachim Neugroschel (New York: Farrar, Straus & Giroux, 1978), 115–116.

2. Ibid., 116.

3. Ibid., 131.

4. Thomas Hobbes, *Man and Citizen*, ed. Bernard Gert (Indianapolis: Hackett Publishing, 1998), 115.

5. Leo Strauss, *The Political Philosophy of Hobbes: Its Basis and Genesis* (Chicago: University of Chicago Press, 1936), 16.

6. Hobbes, *Man and Citizen*, 56. Compare with regard to Spinoza Remo Bodei's *Geometria delle passioni* (Milan: Feltrinelli, 1992), 72–93.

7. "As for Fear or Terror, I cannot see that it can ever be praiseworthy or useful; consequently it is not a particular Passion." René Descartes, *The Passions of the Soul*, trans. Stephen Voss (Indianapolis: Hackett Publishing, 1989), 116. Benedict De Spinoza, *Theological-Political Treatise*, trans. Michael Silverthorne and Jonathan Israel (Cambridge: Cambridge University Press, 2007), 195–207.

8. "As virtue is necessary in a republic, and in a monarchy honour, so fear is necessary in a despotic government: with regard to virtue, there is no occasion for it, and honour would be extremely dangerous." Charles de Secondat, *The Spirit of Laws* (Kitchener, Ontario, Canada: Batoche Books, 2001), 43.

9. In addition to the two miscellaneous volumes edited by Dino Pasini, *La paura e la città* (Rome: Astra, 1983), compare Giuseppe Sorgi, *Potere tra paura e legittimità* (Milan: Giuffrè, 1983), and Sorgi's other work, the excellent *Quale Hobbes? Dalla paura alla rappresentanza* (Milan: Franco Angeli, 1996), which I have kept particularly in mind over the course of the following pages.

10. [Esposito will, like many writing on community and power, distinguish between *potere*, which resembles power in English, and *potenza*, by which he intends to signal a more constructive and creative power of potentiality.—Trans.]

11. "I comprehend in this word *fear*, a certain foresight of future evil; neither do I conceive flight the sole property of fear, but to distrust, suspect, take heed, provide so that they may not fear, is also incident to the fearful." Hobbes, *Man and Citizen*, 113.

12. Carl Schmitt, *The Leviathan in the State Theory of Thomas Hobbes: Meaning and Failure of a Political Symbol*, trans. George Schwab and Erna Hifstein (New York: Greenwood Press, 1996), 31.

13. Elias Canetti, *The Human Province*, trans. Joachim Neugroschel (New York: Seabury Press, 1978), 218.

14. Friedrich Nietzsche, *Thus Spoke Zarathustra*, ed. Robert Pippin (West Nyack, NY: Cambridge University Press, 2002), 246.

15. Friedrich Nietzsche, *Beyond Good and Evil*, ed. Peter Horstmann (West Nyack, NY: Cambridge University Press, 2001), 88.

16. Guglielmo Ferrero, *The Principles of Power: The Great Political Crises of History*, trans. Theodore R. Jaeckel (New York: G. P. Putnam's Sons, 1942), 30.

17. Ibid., 32.

18. Hobbes, *Man and Citizen*, 113.

19. Franz Neumann, *The Democratic and the Authoritarian State: Essays in Political and Legal Theory* (Glencoe, IL: Free Press, 1957), in particular pt. I, chap. 5.

20. See as well Carlo Galli, "Ordine e contingenza. Linee di lettura del *Leviathan*," in *Percorsi di libertà* (Bologna: Il Mulino, 1996), 81–106.

21. Hobbes, *De Cive*, 113–114.

22. Thomas Hobbes, *The Elements of Law, Natural and Politic* (London: Oxford University Press, 1999), 78.

23. Thomas Hobbes, *Leviathan*, ed. J. C. A. Gaskin (Oxford: Oxford University Press, 1998), 85.

24. Hobbes, *Elements of Law*, 60.

25. Hobbes, *Man and Citizen*, 51.

26. Hobbes, *Elements of Law*, 58.

27. Thomas Hobbes, *Leviathan*, ed. Edwin Curley (Indianapolis/Cambridge: Hackett Publishing, 1994), 58.

28. Elias Canetti, *Macht und Überleben: drei Essays* (Berlin: Literarisches Colloquium, 1972), 7, 16.

29. Hobbes, *Elements of Law*, 79.

30. Hobbes, *Leviathan*, 76.

31. Hobbes, *Man and Citizen*, 49.

32. Schmitt, *Leviathan*, 33.

33. Hobbes, *Elements of Law*, 167.

34. See Alessandro Biral, "Hobbes: la società senza governo," in *Il contratto sociale nella filosofia politica moderna*, ed. Giuseppe Duso (Milan: Franco Angeli, 1993), 81–83.

35. Hobbes, *Elements of Law*, 109.

36. Arnold Gehlen, *Man, His Nature and Place in the World*, trans. Clare McMillan and Karl Pillemer (New York: Columbia University Press, 1988), 347.

37. See in this regard Helmuth Plessner, "Grenzen der Gemeinschaft. Eine Kritik des sozialen Radikalismus," in *Gesammelte Schriften*, vol. 5 (Frankfurt: Suhrkamp Verlag, 1980–1985), 102.

38. Marshall Sahlins, *Stone Age Economics* (Chicago: Aldine-Atherton, 1972), 169.

39. Hobbes, *Elements of Law*, 84.

40. Hobbes, *Leviathan*, 59.

41. See in this regard Yves Charles Zarka, *La décision métaphysique de Hobbes: Conditions de la politique* (Paris: J. Vrin, 1987).

42. Hobbes, *Leviathan*, 112.

43. Ibid., 143.

44. Ibid., 139.

45. Hobbes, *Elements of Law*, 132.

46. Hobbes, *Leviathan*, 127.

47. Ibid., 131.

48. Ibid., 208.

49. René Girard, *Violence and the Sacred*, trans. Patrick Gregory (Baltimore: Johns Hopkins University Press, 1977), 8.

50. Hobbes, *Elements of Law*, 106.

51. Ibid., 102.

52. Hobbes, *Man and Citizen*, 170.

53. Hobbes, *Leviathan*, 106.

54. The connection between Hobbes and Freud has already been examined in Giulio Maria Chiodi's "La paura e il simbolico. Spunti di piscoteoretica politica," in *La paura e la città*, ed. Dino Pasini, vol. 2 (Rome: Astra, 1984), 249–257; Francesco De Sanctis, "L'autorità della figura paterna," in *Società moderna e democrazia* (Padua: CEDAM, 1988), 255–276; and especially, in the most complete and elaborate form, Giacomo Marramao, "L'ossessione della sovranità: per una metacritica del concetto di potere in Michel Foucault," in *Dopo il Leviatano* (Turin: Bollati Boringhieri, 1995), 317–332.

55. Sigmund Freud, *Civilization and Its Discontents*, trans. James Strachey (New York: W. W. Norton, 1961), 58; Sigmund Freud, *The Future of an Illusion*, trans. James Strachey (New York: W. W. Norton, 1961), 15.

56. Freud, *Civilization and Its Discontents*, 42.

57. Sigmund Freud, "Dostoevsky and Parricide," in *Dostoevsky: A Collection of Critical Essays*, ed. René Wellek (Englewood Cliffs, NJ: Prentice Hall, 1962), 103.

58. Sigmund Freud, *The Uncanny*, trans. David McLintock (New York: Penguin Books, 2003), 148.

59. Freud, *Civilization and Its Discontents*, 79.

60. Sigmund Freud, *A Phylogenetic Fantasy: Overview of the Transference Neuroses*, trans. Axel Hoffer and Peter T. Hoffer (Cambridge: Belknap Press, 1987), 17–18.

61. Sigmund Freud, *Moses and Monotheism*, trans. Katherine Jones (New York: Vintage Books, 1939), 103–104.

62. Freud, *Moses and Monotheism*, 104.

63. Nietzsche, *Thus Spoke Zarathustra*, 34; Freud, *Moses and Monotheism*, 104.

64. Schmitt, *Leviathan*, 94.

65. The expression comes from Hans Kelsen. See also his other essay on Freud titled "The Conception of the State and Social Psychology, with Special Reference to Freud's Group Theory," *International Journal of Psycho-Analysis* 5 (1924): 1–38.

66. Freud, *Moses and Monotheism*, 172.

67. Sigmund Freud, *Totem and Taboo*, in *The Basic Writings of Sigmund Freud* (New York: The Modern Library, 1938), 917.

68. Schmitt, *Leviathan*, 94.

69. Ibid., 100.

70. Ibid., 98.

71. Freud, *Totem and Taboo*, 915–916.

72. Ibid., 917.

73. See in this regard Mikkel Borch-Jacobsen, "Le sujet freudien, du politique à l'éthique," in *Après le sujet qui vient* (Paris: Aubier-Montaigne, 1989), 53–72.

74. Freud, "Dostoevsky," 103.

75. On the metaphor of the "body" in Hobbes, see the satisfying analysis that Adriana Cavarero offers in *Stately Bodies: Literature, Philosophy, and the Question of Gender*, trans. Robert De Lucca and Deanna Shemek (Ann Arbor: University of Michigan Press, 2002), 160–168.

76. Canetti, *Crowds and Power*, 357 [emphasis in original].

CHAPTER 2

1. On the relation between Hobbes and Rousseau, see especially Robert Derathé, *Jean-Jacques Rousseau et la science politique de son temps* (Paris: Presses Universitaires de France, 1950).

2. Jean-Jacques Rousseau, *Social Contract and the First and Second Discourses*, ed. Susan Dunn (New Haven, CT: Yale University Press, 2002), 249.

3. Jean-Jacques Rousseau, "Fragment on the State of War," *History of Political Thought* 8, no. 2 (Summer 1987), 234.

4. Jean-Jacques Rousseau, *Discourse on the Sciences and Arts (First Discourse)*, ed. Roger D. Masters and Christopher Kelly, trans. Judith R. Bush, Roger D. Masters, and Christopher Kelly (Hanover, NH: University Press of New England [for] Dartmouth College, 1992), 81.

5. Rousseau, "Fragment on the State of War," 233, 234.

6. [Here Esposito is punning on the two meanings of *colpa* in Italian: the misdeed or offense itself and the guilt one feels from having committed the offense.—Trans.]

7. Jean-Jacques Rousseau, "Geneva Manuscript," in *Social Contract, Discourse on the Virtue Most Necessary for a Hero, Political Fragments, and Geneva Manuscript*, ed. Roger D. Masters and Christopher Kelly, trans. Judith R. Bush, Rog-

er D. Masters, and Christopher Kelly (Hanover, NH: University Press of New England, 1992), 122.

8. Rousseau, *Discourse on the Sciences and Arts*, 20.

9. Rousseau, *Social Contract*, 157, 159.

10. Jean-Jacques Rousseau, *Discourse on the Origin of Inequality*, trans. Donald A. Cress (Indianapolis: Hackett Publishing, 1992), 77.

11. Of course, I'm alluding to Étienne de La Boétie, *Discours sur la servitude volontaire* (Paris: Éditions Bossard, 1922).

12. Rousseau, *Discourse on the Origin of Inequality*, 55, 56–57, 68.

13. Jean-Jacques Rousseau, *A Discourse on Political Economy*, in *The Social Contract and Discourses* (London: J. M. Dent and Sons, 1923), 265.

14. Jean-Jacques Rousseau, *Emile: or, on Education*, trans. Allan Bloom (New York: Basic Books, 1979), 236.

15. See in this regard Raymond Polin, *La politique de la solitude* (Paris: Sirey, 1971), 7.

16. Rousseau, *Discourse on the Origin of Inequality*, 36.

17. Ibid., 12.

18. The theme is finely elaborated by Bernard Stiegler in *Technics and Time*, trans. Richard Beardsworth and George Collins (Stanford: Stanford University Press, 1998). I have kept the volume especially in mind over the course of the pages that follow.

19. Rousseau, *Discourse on the Origin of Inequality*, 18–19.

20. André Leroi-Gourhan, *Gesture and Speech*, trans. Anna Bostock Berger (Cambridge, MA: MIT Press, 1993), 10.

21. Rousseau, *Discourse on the Origin of Inequality*, 45.

22. Jean-Jacques Rousseau, *Essay on the Origin of Languages and Writings Related to Music*, trans. John T. Scott (Hanover, NH: University Press of New England, 1998), 306–307.

23. The text of Derrida's to which I refer is, of course, *Of Grammatology*, trans. Gayatri Chakravorty Spivak (Baltimore: Johns Hopkins University Press, 1974).

24. Rousseau, *Social Contract*, 162.

25. [The two meanings Esposito has in mind are "to be lacking" and "to be at fault." See *OED*, "delinquent."—Trans.]

26. Jean-Jacques Rousseau, *Judge of Jean-Jacques*, ed. Roger D. Masters and Christopher Kelly, trans. Judith R. Bush, Christopher Kelly, and Roger D. Masters (Hanover, NH: University Press of New England, 1990), 118.

27. See in this regard Bronislaw Baczko, *Rousseau, solitude et communauté* (Paris: La Haye, 1974), 263.

28. Émile Durkheim, "Le Contrat social de Rousseau," *Revue de Méthaphysique et de Morale* (March–April 1918), 138–139.

29. Rousseau, *Emile*, 39.

30. Ibid., 293.

31. See Benjamin Constant, *The Political Writings of Benjamin Constant*, trans. Biancamaria Fontana (New York: Cambridge University Press, 1988); Jacob Leib Talmon, *The Origins of Totalitarian Democracy* (Boulder, CO: Westview Press, 1985).

32. It is the criticism that Hannah Arendt makes of Rousseau in *On Revolution* (New York: Viking Press, 1936), 70–76.

33. Rousseau, *Social Contract*, 163, 164.

34. Ibid., 181.

35. Jean Starobinski, *Jean-Jacques Rousseau: Transparency and Obstruction*, trans. Arthur Goldhammer (Chicago: University of Chicago Press, 1971), 109.

36. Rousseau, *Social Contract*, 201.

37. Rousseau, *Emile*, 222.

38. L. G. Crocker, *Rousseau's Social Contract: An Interpretative Essay* (Cleveland, OH: Press of Case Western Reserve University, 1968), 170.

39. Rousseau, *Emile*, 120.

40. See Charles Taylor, *Sources of Self: The Making of the Modern Identity* (Cambridge, MA: Harvard University Press, 1989), as well as *The Ethics of Authenticity* (Cambridge, MA: Harvard University Press, 1992), and *Multiculturalism and the "Politics of Recognition"* (Princeton: Princeton University Press, 1994).

41. Rousseau, *Emile*, 39.

42. Pierre Burgelin, *La philosophie de l'existence de Jean-Jacques Rousseau* (Paris: Presses Universitaires, 1952), especially 115–190.

43. Jean-Jacques Rousseau, *Profession of Faith of a Savoyard Vicar*, trans. Olive Schreiner (New York: Peter Eckler, 1889), 21, 63.

44. Rousseau, *Emile*, 42.

45. Rousseau, *Profession of Faith*, 58.

46. Rousseau, *Emile*, 55.

47. Rousseau, *Profession of Faith*, 37.

48. Rousseau, "Geneva Manuscript," 78.

49. Jean-Jacques Rousseau, "Letter to Mirabeau, 31 January 1767," in *Correspondance générale*, vol. 16 (Paris: Armand Colin, 1924–1934), 238.

50. Rousseau, *Emile*, 83.

51. Ibid., 159.

52. Ibid., 78.

53. Jean-Jacques Rousseau, *Julie; or, The New Heloise: Letters of Two Lovers Who Live in a Small Town at the Foot of the Alps*, trans. Philip Stewart and Jean Vaché (Hanover, NH: University Press of New England, 1997), 566.

54. See in this regard Henri Gouhier, *Les Méditations métaphysiques de J. J. Rousseau* (Paris: Vrin, 1970), 101.

55. Georges Poulet, *The Metamorphosis of the Circle*, trans. Carley Dawson and Elliott Coleman (Baltimore: Johns Hopkins University Press, 1967).

56. Jean-Jacques Rousseau, *The Reveries of the Solitary Walker*, trans. Charles E. Butterworth (New York: New York University Press, 1979), 95.

57. Ibid., 81.

58. Karl Barth, *Protestant Theology in the Nineteenth Century: Its Background and History* (Valley Forge, PA: Judson Press, 1973), 228.

59. Rousseau, *Reveries*, 92 [emphasis my own].

60. Rousseau, *Emile*, 235.

CHAPTER 3

1. Eric Weil, "Jean-Jacques Rousseau et sa politique," *Critique*, no. 56 (January 1952), 11.

2. Immanuel Kant, "Bemerkungen in den *Beobachtungen über das Gefuhl das Schönen und Erhabenen*," in *Kant-Forschungen*, vol. 3 (Hamburg: F. Meiner Verlag, 1991), 38.

3. Immanuel Kant, "What Is Orientation in Thinking?" in *Political Writings*, ed. Hans Reiss, trans. H. B. Nisbet (Cambridge: Cambridge University Press, 1991), 247.

4. Immanuel Kant, *Critique of Pure Reason*, trans. Wolfgang Schwarz (Darmstadt: Scientia Verlag Aalen, 1982), 254.

5. G. W. F. Hegel, *Elements of the Philosophy of Right*, trans. H. B. Nisbet (Cambridge: Cambridge University Press, 1991), 57. On Hegel's criticism of Kant, the collection of texts titled *Hegel interprete di Kant*, ed. Valerio Verra (Naples: Prismi, 1981) is useful. See in particular Remo Bodei's essay, "'Tenerezza per le cose del mondo': sublime, sproporzione e contraddizione in Kant e Hegel," 179–218.

6. Ernst Cassirer, *The Question of Jean-Jacques Rousseau*, trans. Peter Gay (New York: Columbia University Press, 1954), 96.

7. Rousseau, *Social Contract*, 167.

8. Jean-Jacques Rousseau, *A Dissertation on Political Economy: To Which Is Added a Treatise on the Social Compact; or, The Principles of Politic Law* (Albany, NY: Barber & Southwick, 1797), 20.

9. Ibid., 23.

10. On the entire relation with Rousseau, see Paolo Pasqualucci's *Rousseau e Kant* (Milan: Giuffrè, 1974), especially the first volume. See also Katia Tenenbaum, "Il pensiero politico di I. Kant e l'influsso di J.-J. Rousseau," *Giornale Critico della Filosofia Italiana* 52 (1972): 344–392.

11. On this reading of the law, see the important essay by Jacob Rogozinski, *Kanten* (Paris: Kime, 1996), 136.

12. Cassirer, *Question*, 75–76.

13. Immanuel Kant, "Conjectures on the Beginning of Human History," in *Political Writings*, 233.

14. Ibid., 227 [emphasis in original].

15. Immanuel Kant, *Religion Within the Limits of Reason Alone*, trans. Theodore M. Greene and Hoyt H. Hudson (New York: Harper & Row, 1934), 34–35 [emphasis in original].

16. Ibid., 17.

17. Ibid., 38.

18. See with regard to this contrast William David Ross's *Kant's Ethical Theory: A Commentary on the Grundlegung zur Metaphysik der Sitten* (Oxford: Clarendon Press, 1954), 86–88; as well as Terence Charles Williams, *The Concept of the Categorical Imperative: A Study of the Place of the Categorical Imperative in Kant's Ethical Theory* (Oxford: Clarendon Press, 1968), 100. A more complicated and contradictory perspective on Kant's essay is found in the by-now classic work by Herbert James Paton, *The Categorical Imperative: A Study in Kant's Moral Philosophy* (London: Hutchinson, 1965).

19. Sergio Landucci analyzes the question in detail in *Sull'etica di Kant* (Milan: Guerini e Associati, 1994), in particular on page 69, when he rightly takes issue with the anti-intuitionist thesis of L. W. Beck ("Das Faktum der Vernunft: Zur Rechtfertigungsproblematik in der Ethik," *Kant-Studien* 52 [1960–1961]: 279–281), as well as the decisively constructivist thesis of John Rawls ("Kantian Constructivism in Moral Theory," *Journal of Philosophy* 72 [1980]: 515).

20. Immanuel Kant, *Critique of Practical Reason*, trans. Thomas Kingsmill Abbott (Mineola, NY: Courier Dover Publications, 2004), 29 [emphasis in original].

21. Ibid., 34.

22. Immanuel Kant, *Groundwork of the Metaphysics of Morals*, trans. Mary J. Gregor (New York: Cambridge University Press, 1998), 55.

23. Immanuel Kant, "Eternal Peace," in *The Philosophy of Kant: Immanuel Kant's Moral and Political Writings*, ed. Carl J. Friedrich (New York: The Modern Library, 1949), 458.

24. Kant, *Religion Within the Limits of Reason Alone*, 91.

25. Ibid., 86.

26. Jean-François Lyotard insists repeatedly on this impossibility in all his essays on Kant. See especially *The Differend: Phrases in Dispute*, trans. Georges Van Den Abbeele (Minneapolis: University of Minnesota Press, 1988).

27. Hannah Arendt, *Lectures on Kant's Political Philosophy* (Chicago: University of Chicago Press, 1982), 14–16.

28. Immanuel Kant, *Critique of Pure Reason*, trans. J. M. D. Meiklejohn (Boston: George Bell & Sons, 1878), 253.

29. For the association of Kant with Kafka, see Andrea Tagliapietra's introduction to Immanuel Kant and Benjamin Constant, *La verità e la menzogna. Dialogo sulla fondazione della morale e della politica* (Milan: Bruno Mondadori, 1996), 12–13.

30. In this regard, see Kant's *Lectures on Ethics*, trans. Louis Infield (Indianapolis: Hackett Publishing, 1980), 51–52.

31. For this interpretation I refer the reader to Bernard Baas, "Le corps du délit," in *Politique et modernité* (Paris: Osiris, 1992), 69–100.

32. Jean-Luc Nancy examines this theme in *L'impératif catégorique* (Paris: Flammarion, 1983).

33. Kant, *Religion Within the Limits of Reason Alone*, 66.

34. Friedrich Nietzsche, *The Anti-Christ* (London: NuVision Publications, 2007), 11.

35. Kant, *Critique of Practical Reason*, 79.

36. See in this regard Paul Ricouer's observations in *Finitude et culpabilité* (Paris: Aubier Montaigne, 1960).

37. Kant, *Critique of Practical Reason*, 80.

38. In addition to Alexis Philonenko's *Théorie et praxis dans la pensée morale et politique de Kant et de Fichte en 1973* (Paris: Vrin, 1968), I also have in mind, especially considering when it was written, Aldo Masullo's *La comunità come fondamento. Fichte, Husserl, Sartre* (Naples: Libreria scientifica editrice, 1965).

39. Lucien Goldmann, *La communauté humaine et l'univers chez Kant* (Zurich: Presses Universitaires, 1948); Karl-Otto Apel, *Towards a Transformation of Philosophy*, trans. Glyn Adey and David Frisby (Milwaukee, WI: Marquette University Press, 1998).

40. Jürgen Habermas, *Moral Consciousness and Communicative Action*, trans. Christian Lenhardt and Shierry Weber Nicholsen (Cambridge, MA: MIT Press, 1990), 77.

41. Hannah Arendt, *The Life of the Mind* (New York: Harcourt Brace Jovanovich, 1978).

42. Kant, *Lectures on Ethics*, 194.

43. Hannah Arendt, *The Human Condition* (Chicago: University of Chicago Press, 1958), 52.

44. For an exhausting and skillful critical reconstruction, I refer the reader to Simone Forti's *Vita della mente e tempo della polis. Hannah Arendt tra filosofia e politica* (Milan: Franco Angeli, 1994), 333–370.

45. Hannah Arendt, *Between Past and Future: Eight Exercises in Political Thought* (New York: Viking Press, 1954), 222.

46. Arendt, *The Human Condition*, 2. See as well on this point *Augusto Illuminati, Del comune. Cronache del general intellect* (Rome: Manifestolibri 2003). On Arendt's relation to community, which in my view seems more problematic than

might at first appear to other interpreters, see Laura Boella's postface, "Amore, comunità impossibile in Hannah Arendt," in Hannah Arendt, *Il concetto di amore in
Agostino* (Milan: SE, 1992), 151–165; as well as Adriana Cavarero's "Nascita, orgas-
mo, politica," in *Micromega, Almanacco di Filosofia* (1996): 541–549.

47. Arendt, *Between Past and Future*, 224. On the Viconian tradition, see
Hans-Georg Gadamer, *Truth and Method* (New York: Crossroad Publishing,
1985), 19–33.

48. Hannah Arendt, *Lectures on Kant's Political Philosophy* (Chicago: University of Chicago Press, 1983), 75. See as well Ronald Beiner's interpretive essay, "Hannah Arendt on Judging," in the same volume.

49. Jean-François Lyotard, *Lectures d'enfance* (Paris: Galilée, 1991).

50. Immanuel Kant, *Critique of Judgment*, trans. Werner S. Pluhar (Indianapolis: Hackett Publishing, 1987), 160.

51. See also Étienne Tassin, "Sens commun et communauté: la lecture arend-
tienne de Kant," *Les Cahiers de Philosophie*, no. 4 (1987): 81–113; as well as Laura
Bazzicalupo, *Hannah Arendt. La storia per la politica* (Naples: Edizioni scientifiche
italiane, 1996), 285–290.

52. Arendt, *Lectures on Kant's Philosophy*, 40.

53. Lyotard, *The Differend*, 168.

54. Jean-François Lyotard, "Sensus Communis," in *Judging Lyotard*, ed. An-
drew Benjamin, Warwick Studies in Philosophy & Literature Series (New York:
Routledge, 1992), 1–2.

55. Kant, *Critique of Judgment*, 128.

56. Jean-François Lyotard, *Postmodern Fables*, trans. Georges Van Den Abbeele
(Minneapolis: University of Minnesota Press, 1999), 141.

57. Kant, *Critique of Judgment*, 128.

58. [Esposito is here playing on the assonance and shared etymology between
veil and *reveal.*—Trans.]

59. See also Baas, *Le corps du délit*, 91.

60. See also Rogozinski, *Kanten*, 147–167.

61. G. W. F. Hegel, *Phenomenology of Spirit*, trans. A. V. Miller (Oxford: Oxford University Press, 1977), 359, 19. On Hegel's critique of Kant, see Franca Papa,
Tre studi su Kant (Rome: Lacaita, 1984), 17–58.

62. Lyotard, *Postmodern Fables*.

63. Jacques Lacan, *The Ethics of Psychoanalysis, 1959–1960*, trans. Dennis Porter
(New York: Norton, 1992).

64. Jacques Lacan, *Écrits: The First Complete Edition in English*, trans. Bruce
Fink (New York: W. W. Norton, 2006), 660.

CHAPTER 4

1. Martin Heidegger, *What Is a Thing?*, trans. W. B. Barton Jr. and Vera Deutsch (Chicago: H. Regnery, 1969), 59.

2. Ernst Cassirer, "Kant and the Problem of Metaphysics," in *Kant: Disputed Questions*, ed. Moltke S. Gram (Chicago: Quadrangle Books, 1967), 149.

3. Martin Heidegger, *Kant and the Problem of Metaphysics*, trans. Richard Taft (Bloomington: Indiana University Press, 1997), 141.

4. Ibid., 118, 141.

5. Ibid., 118.

6. Martin Heidegger, *The Metaphysical Foundations of Logic*, trans. Michael Heim (Bloomington: Indiana University Press, 1984), 182.

7. Martin Heidegger, "Letter on Humanism," in *Basic Writings* (San Francisco: HarperSanFrancisco, 1977), 205, 206.

8. See in this regard Henri Declève, *Heidegger et Kant* (The Hague: M. Nijhoff, 1970).

9. Martin Heidegger, *The Basic Problems of Phenomenology*, trans. Albert Hofstadter (Bloomington: Indiana University Press, 1982), 125.

10. Martin Heidegger, *The Essence of Human Freedom: An Introduction to Philosophy*, trans. Ted Sadler (New York: Continuum, 2002).

11. Heidegger, *Kant and the Problem of Metaphysics*, 151.

12. Martin Heidegger, *Introduction to Metaphysics*, trans. Gregory Fried and Richard Polt (New Haven, CT: Yale University Press, 2000), 212.

13. An excellent collection of materials on ethics in Heidegger can be found in *Con-tratto*, nos.1–2 (1993). See as well Franco Volpi, "L'etica rimossa di Heidegger," *Micromega*, no. 2 (1996): 139–163.

14. Martin Heidegger, "Davos Disputation Between Ernst Cassirer and Martin Heidegger," in *Kant and the Problem of Metaphysics*, 196.

15. Ibid.

16. See in this regard Jacob Rogozinski, *Kanten: Esquisses kantiennes* (Paris: Editions Kime, 1996), 40.

17. Heidegger, "Letter on Humanism," 235.

18. Heidegger, *Being and Time*, 254 [emphasis in original].

19. See more recently Emmanuel Levinas, "Mourir pour . . . ," in *Heidegger. Questions ouvertes*, ed. Eliane Escoubas (Paris: Osiris, 1988), 255–264. Levinas's essay is preceded by Miguel Abensour's helpful essay. See as well his important introduction to the republication of Levinas's "Quelques réflexions sur la philosophie de l'hitlérisme" (Paris: Payot & Rivages, 1997), 7–103. On death in Heidegger, I refer the reader to François Dastur, *La Mort, essai sur la finitude* (Paris: Hatier, 1994); and Claude Romano, "Mourir à autrui," *Critique*, no. 582 (November 1995), 803–

824. For Ricoeur, see Paul Ricoeur, *Oneself as Another*, trans. Kathleen Blamey (Chicago: University of Chicago Press, 1992), 349.

20. See Martin Heidegger, *Elucidations of Hölderlin's Poetry*, trans. Keith Hoeller (New York: Humanity Books, 2000), 56–59.

21. See in this regard Jean-François Courtine, "Donner/prendre: la main," in *Heidegger et la phénoménologie* (Paris: Librairie Philosophique J. Vrin, 1990), 283–303. The quote from Heidegger comes from *On the Way to Language*, trans. Peter D. Hertz (New York: Harper & Row, 1959), 82–83.

22. Martin Heidegger, "Building, Dwelling, Thinking," in *Poetry, Language, Thought*, trans. Albert Hofstadter (New York: Harper & Row, 1975), 149 [emphasis in original].

23. Ibid.

24. Ibid.

25. Heidegger, "Letter on Humanism," 238–239.

26. Martin Heidegger, *Off the Beaten Path*, trans. Julian Young and Kenneth Haynes (Cambridge: Cambridge University Press, 2002), 267–268.

27. Heidegger, *Introduction to Metaphysics*, 141.

28. Heidegger, *Elucidations of Hölderlin's Poetry*, 57.

29. Heidegger, *Being and Time*, 189.

30. Ibid., 190.

31. Ibid., 118–119.

32. See Jean-Luc Nancy, *Being Singular Plural*, trans. Robert D. Richardson and Anne E. O'Byrne (Stanford: Stanford University Press, 2000), and the entire analysis Nancy offers of community in Heidegger. Also useful in this regard is F. Raffoul's doctoral thesis, "Heidegger et la question du sujet," in particular, volume 2, 528–530, École des Hautes Études en Sciences Sociales.

33. Heidegger, *Being and Time*, 111, 113.

34. Martin Heidegger, *The Fundamental Concepts of Metaphysics: World, Finitude, Solitude*, trans. William McNeill and Nicholas Walker (Bloomington: Indiana University Press, 1995), 6 [emphasis in original].

35. Ibid., 206.

36. On the objection to Heidegger, see I. E. Schuck, "Il rapporto inter-umano in *Essere e tempo* di Martin Heidegger," *Fenomenologia e società*, no. 1 (1988): 72–138. For Karl Löwith, see his "Heidegger Denker in dürftiger Zeit," in *Sämtliche Schriften*, vol. 8 (Stuttgart: Metzler, 1981). For Karl Jaspers, see his *Notizen zur Heidegger* (Zurich: Piper, 1978). Finally, Arendt's critique is made explicit in "What Is Existenz Philosophy?" *Partisan Review*, no.1 (1946): 34–56. Her partial correction can be found in "Concern with Politics in Recent European Philosophical Thought," in *Essays in Understanding, 1930–1954: Formation, Exile, and Totalitarianism* (New York: Schocken, 2005).

37. I am referring to Karl Löwith's "Das Individuum in der Rolle des Mitmenschen. Ein Beitrag zur anthropologischen Grundlegung der ethischen Probleme," in *Sämtliche Schriften*, vol. 1, 9–197.

38. Heidegger, *On the Way to Language*, 134 [emphasis in original].

39. See, for example, Carl Friedrich Gethmann, *Verstehen und Auslegung. Das Methoden-problem in der Philosphie Martin Heidegger* (Bonn: Bouvier, 1974).

40. Heidegger, *Being and Time*, 115.

41. Ibid., 298.

42. Ibid., 352 [emphasis in original].

43. See in this regard Eugenio Mazzarella's introduction to the Italian translation of the anthology *Antwort. Martin Heidegger im Gespräch* as *Risposta a colloquio con Martin Heidegger* (Naples: Guida, 1992), 27; as well as—with a different interpretive framework—Domenico Losurdo, *Heidegger and the Ideology of War: Community, Death, and the West*, trans. Marella and Jon Morris (Amherst, NY: Humanity Books, 2001).

44. See my *Nove pensieri sulla politica* (Bologna: Il Mulino, 1993), 122ff., as well as the bibliography contained there. For a different reading of community in Fichte, I refer the reader to Carla Amadio, *Morale e politica nella Sittenlehre di J. G. Fichte* (Milan: Giuffré, 1991), 253; as well as her *Fichte e la dimensione estetica della politica* (Milan: Guerini, 1994), 85.

45. Of course, I'm referring to Theodor Adorno, *The Jargon of Authenticity*, trans. Knut Tarnowski and Frederic Will (London: Routledge, 2002).

46. Heidegger, *Fundamental Questions of Philosophy*, 100 [emphasis in original].

47. Martin Heidegger, *Selbstbehauptung der deutschen Universität* (Frankfurt: Klostermann, 1983), 12–13.

48. Martin Heidegger, *Metaphysische Angangsgründe der Logik im Ausgang von Leibniz* (Frankfurt: V. Klostermann, 1978), 175.

49. See Marlène Zarader, *Heidegger et les paroles de l'origine* (Paris: J. Vrin, 1986), 257; as well as Werner Marx, *Heidegger und die Tradition. Eine problemgeschichtliche Einführung in die Grundbestimmungen des Seins* (Hamburg: W. Kohlhammer Verlag, 1980).

50. See Reiner Schürmann, *Heidegger on Being and Acting: From Principles to Anarchy* (Bloomington: Indiana University Press, 1986).

51. Martin Heidegger, *Contributions to Philosophy (from Enowing)*, trans. Parvis Emad and Kenneth Maly (Bloomington: Indiana University Press, 1999), 288.

52. Ibid., 293.

53. Heidegger, "Remembrance," in *Elucidations of Hölderlin's Poetry*, 151.

54. Ibid., 159, 150.

55. Ibid., 156.

56. See the wonderful book by Caterina Resta, *Il luogo e le vie. Geografia del pensiero in Martin Heidegger* (Milan: Franco Angeli, 1996) even if it remains well within a Heideggerean itinerary.

57. See in this regard Heidegger, *Basic Questions of Philosophy*, 110. See also *Elucidations of Hölderlin's Poetry* and *Hölderlin's Hymnen "Germanien und der Rhein"* (Frankfurt: Vittorio Klostermann, 1980), 220–221.

58. Heidegger, "Letter on Humanism," 221, 217, 218.

59. Ibid., 218.

60. Heidegger, *Introduction to Metaphysics*, 133. On the "double" genealogy of Europe, see my "Pensare l'Europa," *Micromega*, no. 5 (1999): 127–148, which I have drawn on in part here.

61. This is the thesis of Jean Beaufret. See his introduction to the French edition of Friedrich Hölderlin, *Remarques sur Œdipe et Antigone* (Paris: Christian Bourgois, 1965), which does tend, however, to underestimate the distance separating Heidegger from Kant.

62. Friedrich Hölderlin, "Briefe (an der Bruder)," in *Sämtliche Werke* 6, no. 1 (1954) (Stuttgart: J. G. Cottasche Buchhandlung Nachfolger, 1943–1985), 304.

63. Friedrich Hölderlin, "Note all'Antigone," in *Sul tragico*, ed. Remo Bodei (Milan: Feltrinelli, 1980), 77. On Hölderlin, see also Mario Pezzella, with an introduction by Remo Bodei, *La concezione tragica di Hölderlin* (Bologna: Il Mulino, 1993).

64. Friedrich Hölderlin, *Il communismo degli spiriti*, ed. D. Carosso (Rome: Donzelli, 1995), 73.

65. Friedrich Hölderlin, "Fondamento dell'Empedocle," in *Scritti di estetica*, ed. R. Ruschi (Milan: SE, 1987), 87.

66. Friedrich Hölderlin, "Anmerkungen zum Oedipus," in *Sul tragico*, 73.

67. Ibid., 74. I prefer to use the already-cited Ruschi translation, however. *Sul tragico*, trans. Riccardo Ruschi (Milan: Feltrinelli, 1996), 144.

68. Hölderlin, "An Böhhlendorff (December 4, 1801)," in "Briefe," 425–426.

69. Peter Szondi, *Poetik und Geschictsphilosophie*, vol. 2 (Frankfurt: Suhrkamp, 1974), 187; Walter Benjamin, "Two Poems by Friedrich Hölderlin—The Poet's Courage and Timidity," in *Selected Writings*, vol. 1 (1913–1926), ed. Michael W. Jennings (Cambridge, MA: Harvard University Press, 1996), 34.

70. Hölderlin, "Andenken," in *Le liriche*, ed. Enzo Mandruzzato (Milan: Adelphi, 1993), 563.

71. Martin Heidegger, *Hölderlin's Hymn: The Ister*, trans. William McNeill and Julia Davis (Bloomington: Indiana University Press, 1996), 240.

72. Heidegger, "Remembrance," 162.

73. Ibid., 163.

74. G. W. F. Hegel, *The Philosophy of History* (Kitchener, Ontario, Canada: Batoche Books, 2001), 245.

75. G. W. F. Hegel, *Lezioni sulla filosofia della storia*, vol. 3 (Florence: La Nuova Italia, 1941–1963), 12, 20.

76. Hegel, *Philosophy of History*, 108.

77. Carl Schmitt, *Land and Sea*, trans. Simona Draghici (Washington, DC: Plutarch Press, 1997).

78. See in this regard Massimo Cacciari, *Geo-filosofia dell'Europa* (Milan: Adelphi, 2003), 29. For another declination of the sea that links Hölderlin to Nietzsche, see also his *L'arcipelago* cited earlier; and in a different key, Franco Cassano *Partita doppia* (Bologna: Il Mulino, 1993), 137–146.

79. Simone Weil, *The Need for Roots: Prelude to a Declaration of Duties Towards Mankind*, trans. A. F. Wills (London: Routledge & Kegan Paul, 1952), 287. On the communitarian character of Weil's thought, life, and death, see Wanda Tommasi, *Simone Weil* (Naples: Liguori, 1977), and especially Angela Putino, *Vita biologica e vita soprannaturale. Comunità e politica in Simone Weil* (Rome: Città Nuova, 1998).

80. See Hans Blumenberg, *Shipwreck with Spectator: Paradigm of a Metaphor for Existence*, trans. Steven Rendall (Cambridge, MA: MIT Press, 1997), 18. On the same theme, compare Mariapaola Fimiani, *Paradossi dell'indifferenza* (Milan: F. Angeli, 1994), 142–154.

81. Jacob Burckhardt, *Judgment on History and Historians*, ed. Alberto R. Coll (Indianapolis: Liberty Fund, 1999), 269.

82. Friedrich Hölderlin, "Mnemosyne," in *Hymns and Fragments*, trans. Richard Sieburth (Princeton: Princeton University Press, 1984), 116.

83. Theodor W. Adorno, *Notes to Literature*, trans. Shierry Weber Nicholsen (New York: Columbia University Press, 1991–1992), 113–123.

84. For a non-dialectical reading of Hölderlin, see the important book by Georges Leyenberger, *Métaphores de la présence II. La philosophie de Hölderlin* (Paris: Osiris, 1994).

85. Hölderlin, "Germanien," in *Poems and Fragments*, 405.

86. Hölderlin, "Der Mutter Erde," in *Poems and Fragments*, 379.

87. Martin Heidegger, "The Origin of the Work of Art," in *Off the Beaten Track*, trans. Julian Young and Kenneth Hayne (Cambridge: Cambridge University Press, 2002), 25.

88. Friedrich Nietzsche, *The Gay Science: With a Prelude in Rhymes and an Appendix of Songs*, trans. Walter Kaufmann (New York: Vintage, 1974), 280.

89. Ibid., 180.

90. Ibid., 338.

91. Friedrich Nietzsche, *Daybreak: Thoughts on the Prejudices of Morality*, ed. Maudemarie Clark and Brian Leiter, trans. R. J. Hollingdale (Cambridge: Cambridge University Press, 1997), 103.

92. Georges Bataille, "Nietzsche and the Fascists," in *Visions of Excess: Selected Writings, 1927–1939* (Minneapolis: University of Minnesota Press, 1985), 193.
93. Georges Bataille, *Inner Experience*, trans. Leslie Anne Boldt (Albany: State University of New York Press, 1988), 27.

CHAPTER 5

1. Maurice Blanchot, *The Unavowable Community*, trans. Pierre Joris (Barrytown, NY: Station Hill Press, 1983), 13. For an example of saving Heidegger from political embarrassment, see J. P. Faye, "Bataille et Heidegger. Rapport au temps cruel," in *Georges Bataille et la pensée allemande* (Paris: Acte de Colloque, 1986), 47–54. On "political-impolitical" Bataille, see especially Francis Marmande, *Georges Bataille politique* (Lyon: Presses Universitaires de Lyon, 1985); my *Categorie dell'impolitico* (Bologna: Il Mulino, 1988), 245–312; Jean Michel Besnier, *La politique de l'impossible* (Paris: La Découverte, 1988); and the Italian introduction as well as notes by M. Galletti to Bataille's *Contre-attaques* (Rome: Edizione Associate, 1995).
2. On this score, see the important article by Rebecca Conway, "Gifts Without Presents: Economies of 'Experience' in Bataille and Heidegger," *Yale French Studies*, no. 78, "On Bataille" (1990): 66–89.
3. Georges Bataille, *Œuvres complètes*, vol. 4 (Paris: Gallimard, 1971), 365.
4. Ibid., vol. 5, 474.
5. Martin Heidegger, *On Time and Being*, trans. Joan Stambaugh (Chicago: University of Chicago Press, 2002), 57.
6. Martin Heidegger, *On the Way to Language*, trans. Peter D. Hertz (New York: Harper & Row, 1971), 39.
7. Georges Bataille, *Theory of Religion*, trans. Robert Hurley (New York: Zone Books, 1989), 11.
8. Georges Bataille, *The Accursed Share: An Essay on General Economy*, trans. Robert Hurley, vols. 2 and 3 (New York: Zone Books, 1991), 209.
9. Ibid., 111.
10. Maurice Blanchot, *The Infinite Conversation*, trans. Susan Hanson (Minneapolis: University of Minnesota Press, 1992), 205.
11. Bataille, *Œuvres complètes*, vol. 11, 304. On the subordination of experience to knowledge, see Bataille, *Inner Experience*, 7.
12. See in this regard Martin Jay, "The Limits of Limit Experience: Bataille and Foucault," in *Constellations* 2, no. 2 (April 1995): 155–174.
13. Michel Foucault, "Interview with Michel Foucault," in *Power*, ed. James D. Faubion, trans. Robert Hurley (New York: New Press, 1994), 241.
14. Ibid.

15. See Walter Benjamin, "Experience and Poverty," in *Walter Benjamin: Selected Writings*, ed. Michael W. Jennings (Cambridge, MA: Harvard University Press, 1999), 731–736.

16. Blanchot, *Infinite Conversation*, 210.

17. Heidegger, *On the Way to Language*, 57.

18. Foucault, "Interview with Foucault," 247.

19. Bataille, *Interior Experience*, 24.

20. See what Frederic de Towarnicki reports in *À la rencontre de Heidegger* (Paris: Gallimard, 1993), 73: "Heidegger had written him that the French translation of 'Dasein' couldn't be either 'réalité humaine' or 'être là' but if anything 'être-le-là' (de l'existence)."

21. Bataille, *Œuvres complètes*, vol. 4, 365.

22. Georges Bataille, *Eroticism*, trans. Mary Dalwood (London: John Calder, 1962), 260; Bataille, *Inner Experience*, 61.

23. Bataille, *Inner Experience*, 69.

24. Ibid., 91.

25. Ibid., 9.

26. Ibid., 54.

27. Georges Bataille, *On Nietzsche*, trans. Bruce Boone (New York: Paragon House, 1994), 23.

28. Georges Bataille, *Il colpevole*, trans. A. Biancoforte (Bari: Dedalo, 1989), 62.

29. See on this point Robert Sasso, *Le système du non-savoir* (Paris: Éditions de Minuit, 1978), 158; as well as Carlo Grassi, *Bataille sociologo della conoscenza* (Rome: Costa & Nolan, 1998).

30. Bataille, *On Nietzsche*, 24.

31. Ibid., 146.

32. Ibid., 20.

33. Bataille, *Inner Experience*, 71.

34. Georges Bataille, "L'enseignement de la mort," in *Œuvres complètes*, vol. 8, 199.

35. Georges Bataille, *Literature and Evil*, trans. Alastair Hamilton (London: Calder & Boyars, 1973), 171–172.

36. Elena Pulcini captures Bataille's counterposition with respect to the Hobbesian paradigm in her introduction to the Italian translation of Bataille's *Notion de dépense*. See *Il dispendio* (Rome: Armando, 1997), 25.

37. Georges Bataille, "The College of Sociology," in *Visions of Excess: Selected Writings, 1927–1939*, trans. Allan Stoekl (Minneapolis: University of Minnesota Press, 1985), 251.

38. Bataille, *Il colpevole*, 88.

39. Bataille, *On Nietzsche*, 8.

40. Ibid.

41. Bataille, *Inner Experience*, 26.

42. Nietzsche, *Thus Spoke Zarathustra*, 56.

43. Ibid.

44. Ibid., 59.

45. Bataille, *The Accursed Share*, vols. 2 and 3, 370.

46. On the theme of the "sacred" in Bataille, see the collected volume *Georges Bataille: il politico e il sacro*, ed. Jacqueline Risset (Naples: Liguori, 1987).

47. Georges Bataille, "La limite de l'utile," in *Œuvres complètes*, vol. 7, 263.

48. Decisive in this regard is the deconstruction of the dialectic of sacrifice enacted by Jean-Luc Nancy in *A Finite Thinking* (Stanford: Stanford University Press, 2003), 51–77.

49. See Roger Money-Kryle, *The Meaning of Sacrifice* (London: L. & V. Woolf and the Institute of Psycho-analysis, 1930); as well as Georges Gusdorf, *L'expérience humaine du sacrifice* (Paris: Presses Universitaires de France, 1948), 74–76.

50. Bataille, *Inner Experience*, 23, 137.

51. Ibid., 153.

52. This is according to René Girard's well-known thesis elaborated first in *Violence and the Sacred*, trans. Patrick Gregory (Baltimore: Johns Hopkins University Press, 1977).

53. Georges Bataille, "La practica della gioia dinanzi la morte," in *La congiura sacra* (Turin: Bollati Boringhieri, 2008), 117–119.

54. Georges Bataille, "Hegel, la morte e il sacrificio," in *Sulla fine della storia*, ed. M. Ciampa and F. Di Stefano (Naples: Liguori, 1985), 85–86.

55. Bataille, *Il colpevole*, 64 [emphasis in original].

56. Bataille, "Hegel, la morte e il sacrificio," 83.

57. Bataille, *La congiura sacra*, 83.

58. Ibid., 86.

59. Bataille, *Theory of Religion*, 49.

60. Georges Bataille, *La parte maledetta* (Turin: Bollati Boringhieri, 1992), 69.

61. Nancy, *A Finite Thinking*, 74 [emphasis in original].

62. See the reconstruction that François Fédier provides in "Heidegger vu de France," in *Regarder voir* (Paris: Les Belles Lettres / Archimbaud, 1995), which is almost completely dedicated to Jean Beaufret; see more generally, Jean Wahl, *Existence et transcendance* (Neuchâtel: Éditions de la Baconnière, 1944).

63. Jean-Paul Sartre, "Un nuovo mistico," in *Che cos'è la letteratura* (Milan: Il saggiatore, 1963).

64. See the role that Sartre assigns himself in the dissemination of Heidegger's thought in France in *Carnets de la drôle de guerre*, vol. 11 (Paris: Gallimard, 1995): 403–408.

65. Sartre, "Un nuovo mistico," 253.

66. Ibid., 254.

67. As Bataille makes clear to Sartre in his response, which is included as an appendix to *On Nietzsche*, as well as in the debate that he conducted with Hyppolite and Klossowski and others on the theme of sin, published in *Le Dieu Vivant*, no. 4 (1945).

68. Sartre, "Un nuovo mistico," 260.

69. Ibid., 275–276.

70. Or to wait for Beaufret's abrupt about-face, since it was he who had initially made the mistake of interpreting Sartrism as the French version of the analytic of *Dasein*. Note that although the letter of November 1946 to which Heidegger responded with his *Letter* was still written by Beaufret in a Sartrean language, in *De l'existentialisme à Heidegger* (Paris: Vrin, 1986), the very same Beaufret, with respect to Heidegger's thought, speaks of an "existentialism notwithstanding him" (34).

71. I'm citing from the letter that Heidegger wrote Sartre in October 1945, which was published by Frederic de Towarnicki in *À la rencontre de Heidegger*. See as well the timely comments of Franco Volpi in his introduction to *Lettera sull'umanismo* (Milan: Adelphi, 2006), in which the letter is included.

72. Jean-Paul Sartre, *Being and Nothingness: An Essay in Phenomenological Ontology*, trans. Hazel E. Barnes (New York: Citadel Press, 1956), 61.

73. Ibid., 276.

74. An incisive analysis of Sartre's dialectic of "nullity" can be found in Sergio Givone's *Storia del nulla* (Rome: Laterza, 1995), 170–179.

75. Sartre, *Being and Nothingness*, 240 [emphasis in original].

76. Ibid., 405.

77. This is also Aldo Masullo's thesis in *La comunità come fondamento: Fichte, Husserl, Sartre* (Naples: Libreria scientifica editrice, 1965), 345–466.

78. Heidegger, "Letter on Humanism," 210.

79. Ibid., 206.

80. Bataille, *Theory of Religion*, 22.

81. See Jacques Derrida, "Geschlect II: Heidegger's Hand," in *Deconstruction and Philosophy: The Texts of Jacques Derrida*, ed. John Sallis (Chicago: University of Chicago Press, 1987).

82. Georges Bataille, "Le passage de l'animal à l'homme et la naissance de l'art," in *Œuvres complétes*, vol. 12, 262.

83. Ibid., 272.

APPENDIX

1. See Chapter 1.

2. Heidegger, "Origin of the Work of Art," 12.

3. Martin Heidegger, "The Thing," in *Poetry, Language, Thought* (New York: Harper & Row, 1971), 169.

4. Ibid., 170–171.

5. Ibid., 172.

6. Ibid.

7. Ibid., 181.

8. Bataille, *On Nietzsche*, 19.

9. Ibid., 188.

10. Ibid., 23.

11. Ibid., 24.

12. Ibid., 20–21.

13. The books I am alluding to, in addition to my own, are: Jean-Luc Nancy, *The Inoperative Community*, trans. Peter Connor et al. (Minneapolis: University of Minnesota Press, 1991); Maurice Blanchot, *The Unavowable Community*, trans. Pierre Joris (Barrytown, NY: Station Hill Press, 1988); and Giorgio Agamben, *The Coming Community*, trans. Michael Hardt (Minneapolis: University of Minnesota Press, 1993).

14. Jean-Luc Nancy, *The Sense of the World*, trans. Jeffrey S. Librett (Minneapolis: University of Minnesota Press, 1997), 47.

Cultural Memory | *in the Present*

James Phillips, *Heidegger's Volk: Between National Socialism and Poetry*

Frank Ankersmit, *Sublime Historical Experience*

István Rév, *Retroactive Justice: Prehistory of Post-Communism*

Paola Marrati, *Genesis and Trace: Derrida Reading Husserl and Heidegger*

Krzysztof Ziarek, *The Force of Art*

Marie-José Mondzain, *Image, Icon, Economy: The Byzantine Origins of the Contemporary Imaginary*

Cecilia Sjöholm, *The Antigone Complex: Ethics and the Invention of Feminine Desire*

Jacques Derrida and Elisabeth Roudinesco, *For What Tomorrow . . . : A Dialogue*

Elisabeth Weber, *Questioning Judaism: Interviews by Elisabeth Weber*

Jacques Derrida and Catherine Malabou, *Counterpath: Traveling with Jacques Derrida*

Martin Seel, *Aesthetics of Appearing*

Nanette Salomon, *Shifting Priorities: Gender and Genre in Seventeenth-Century Dutch Painting*

Jacob Taubes, *The Political Theology of Paul*

Jean-Luc Marion, *The Crossing of the Visible*

Eric Michaud, *An Art for Eternity: The Cult of Art in Nazi Germany*

Anne Freadman, *The Machinery of Talk: Charles Peirce and the Sign Hypothesis*

Stanley Cavell, *Emerson's Transcendental Etudes*

Stuart McLean, *The Event and Its Terrors: Ireland, Famine, Modernity*

Beate Rössler, ed., *Privacies: Philosophical Evaluations*

Bernard Faure, *Double Exposure: Cutting Across Buddhist and Western Discourses*

Alessia Ricciardi, *The Ends of Mourning: Psychoanalysis, Literature, Film*

Alain Badiou, *Saint Paul: The Foundation of Universalism*

Gil Anidjar, *The Jew, The Arab: A History of the Enemy*

Jonathan Culler and Kevin Lamb, eds., *Just Being Difficult? Academic Writing in the Public Arena*

Jean-Luc Nancy, *A Finite Thinking*, edited by Simon Sparks

Theodor W. Adorno, *Can One Live after Auschwitz? A Philosophical Reader*, edited by Rolf Tiedemann

Patricia Pisters, *The Matrix of Visual Culture: Working with Deleuze in Film Theory*

Talal Asad, *Formations of the Secular: Christianity, Islam, Modernity*

Dorothea von Mücke, *The Rise of the Fantastic Tale*

Marc Redfield, *The Politics of Aesthetics: Nationalism, Gender, Romanticism*

Emmanuel Levinas, *On Escape*

Dan Zahavi, *Husserl's Phenomenology*

Rodolphe Gasché, *The Idea of Form: Rethinking Kant's Aesthetics*

Michael Naas, *Taking on the Tradition: Jacques Derrida and the Legacies of Deconstruction*

Herlinde Pauer-Studer, ed., *Constructions of Practical Reason: Interviews on Moral and Political Philosophy*

Jean-Luc Marion, *Being Given: Toward a Phenomenology of Givenness*

Theodor W. Adorno and Max Horkheimer, *Dialectic of Enlightenment*

Ian Balfour, *The Rhetoric of Romantic Prophecy*

Martin Stokhof, *World and Life as One: Ethics and Ontology in Wittgenstein's Early Thought*

Gianni Vattimo, *Nietzsche: An Introduction*

Jacques Derrida, *Negotiations: Interventions and Interviews, 1971–1998*, ed. Elizabeth Rottenberg

Brett Levinson, *The Ends of Literature: Post-transition and Neoliberalism in the Wake of the "Boom"*

Timothy J. Reiss, *Against Autonomy: Global Dialectics of Cultural Exchange*

Hent de Vries and Samuel Weber, eds., *Religion and Media*

Niklas Luhmann, *Theories of Distinction: Redescribing the Descriptions of Modernity*, ed. and introd. William Rasch

Johannes Fabian, *Anthropology with an Attitude: Critical Essays*

Michel Henry, *I Am the Truth: Toward a Philosophy of Christianity*

Gil Anidjar, *"Our Place in Al-Andalus": Kabbalah, Philosophy, Literature in Arab-Jewish Letters*

Hélène Cixous and Jacques Derrida, *Veils*

F. R. Ankersmit, *Historical Representation*

F. R. Ankersmit, *Political Representation*

Elissa Marder, *Dead Time: Temporal Disorders in the Wake of Modernity (Baudelaire and Flaubert)*

Reinhart Koselleck, *The Practice of Conceptual History: Timing History, Spacing Concepts*

Niklas Luhmann, *The Reality of the Mass Media*

Hubert Damisch, *A Childhood Memory by Piero della Francesca*

Hubert Damisch, *A Theory of /Cloud/: Toward a History of Painting*

Jean-Luc Nancy, *The Speculative Remark (One of Hegel's Bons Mots)*

Jean-François Lyotard, *Soundproof Room: Malraux's Anti-Aesthetics*